D1427084

C33~~~~~~00

The Well at the World's End

The WELL at the WORLD'S END

A.J. Mackinnon

Black Inc.

Published by Black Inc.,
an imprint of Schwartz Media Pty Ltd
37–39 Langridge Street
Collingwood VIC 3066 Australia
email: enquiries@blackincbooks.com
http://www.blackincbooks.com

The National Library of Australia Cataloguing-in-Publication entry:

Mackinnon, A. J. (Alexander James), 1963-

The well at the world's end / A. J. Mackinnon.

2nd ed.

ISBN: 9781863955430 (pbk.)

Mackinnon, A. J. (Alexander James), 1963---Travel.
Voyages and travels--21st century.

910

Illustrations and maps by A.J. Mackinnon
Book design by Thomas Deverall

Contents

*This book is dedicated to my father, whose map of life and love
has guided me from the very start ...
and to Chris, who is there on every adventure.*

Prologue

And whatten wull ye leave to your own bairns and wife,
Edouard, Edouard?
The Warlde's room! Let them beg through life!
Alas and wae is me, O!

—Scottish ballad

I am eight years old and have just been sent by my older brother
Richard to go and find as many rolls of toilet paper as I can. 'You're
the youngest,' he has explained, 'and can't get into as much trouble
as I can. Off you go.'

I wind my way through the white labyrinth of the ship's interior,
dodging passengers and a narrow-eyed ship's steward while I visit
every bathroom I can find. I return to the upper deck with ten rolls
of loo paper and find that it is almost too late. There is now a gap of
oily green water between the cliff of the liner's side and the Sydney
quay and there is a strong smell of diesel. Between us and the
crowds on the quay is a festoon of coloured streamers, red and green
and blue and yellow, thousands of them fluttering in the breeze and
stretching tighter and tighter across the widening gap until they
begin to break and curl up.

Richard, unwilling to fork out for the streamers from the ship's
shop but ever ingenious, now has what he needs. He grabs the loo
rolls from me and tells me to hold all the dangling ends of tissue
paper. Then he lobs each roll one by one in a true cricketer's throw
right across the gap in ten soaring arcs of fluttering paper. Three
rolls hit home among the crowd and I am almost sure that one elderly woman collapses from a blow to the head. I turn to grin nervously at Richard but he is not there. His figure can be seen ducking
away through the crowds along the railings. I wonder briefly why.
Two seconds later I turn the other way to find that the ship's steward
is bearing down on me, more narrow-eyed than ever. Richard is
usually right, but in one matter I now suspect he might be mistaken.

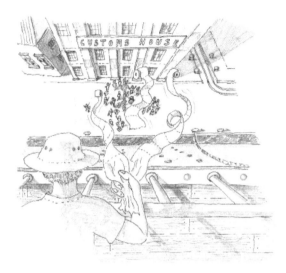

Sweet-faced and cherubic I might be, but, from the expression on the steward's face as he pushes his way along the crowded deck, I doubt that I am immune to the wrath of the authorities after all. Abandoning the loo rolls, I flee. I am not happy ...

*

I was pretty unhappy to be there in the first place, to tell the truth. A few months earlier our parents had broken the news: the whole family would be uprooted from our settled existence in Wollongong, New South Wales, and put on a ship bound for England. When first told the news, all four of us – Richard and my two sisters and I – had burst into tears and protestations at the unfairness of it all. We had cried for the two months leading up to the departure, we had howled in the back of the car as we drove to Sydney for the farewell, and we had stormed and sulked as we were pushed up the gangplank to the glacial bulk of the *Arcadia*.

But not long after hurling the illicit streamers, the protestations died on my lips. Even when I found Richard on one of the upper decks just as we were passing beneath the Sydney Harbour Bridge and he managed to convince me that the soaring funnels above us would be knocked off by the bridge's too-low-seeming span, thus killing us all, I didn't care as much as I ought to have. I had caught the romance, the danger, the fizzing uncertainty of being a traveller – it seemed a good way as any to die.

From that moment the magic of seafaring, of proper old-fashioned voyaging, has never left me. Tin trunks. Luggage labels. Ship's railings. Deck quoits. Crossing the line. Albatrosses. But the element that really soaked into my young mind was the slow turning of the great globe beneath our bow, day and night, mile by mile, week after week, latitude by latitude, port by port. Table Mountain. The Canary Islands. The fabulous bazaars of Casablanca, where I purchased with my pocket money the chief treasure of the whole trip, namely a plastic pen which, when tilted, sent a tiny camel gliding across a background of date palms and desert dunes. Back onboard there was a large map of the world on the wall of the purser's deck where our progress was marked daily by a little blue and white pin. Each day, Richard and my sisters and I would note our minute but steady progress.

The time spent in England was a child's dream: castles, oak trees, snow and duffel coats, squirrels in Regent's Park and pigeons in Trafalgar Square. And then, two years later, there was the return trip to Australia and the whole turtle-torn, sun-wheeling voyage in reverse.

In later years, I could barely bring myself to fly. It felt like cheating. I wasn't doing things properly. I was arriving at the other end having skimped on things along the way. This view of the world was crystallised when I came across an old Scottish ballad in which a young man is to be exiled for killing his father. When asked what he will leave to his own bairns and wife, he replies bitterly, 'The Warlde's Room! Let them beg through life!' The line is ironic, of course, but even so ... the Warlde's Room! As though there were indeed a whole wide world to inherit, a great round, windy ball of a place, deep and bright as a glass sphere, solid as a bowling ball.

The phrase suggested something else to me too, quite different. The Warlde's Room in my head looks like this. It is a spacious room in a quiet house with Sunday morning sunlight streaming in the bay windows and touching the writing desk. On the desk is a large atlas open at a particular page. This is mainly green and blue, criss-crossed by lines of latitude and longitude. It shows the whole world from pole to pole, from east to west. Tahiti is just across from Peru, and Peru is just down from Canada, a mere kayak trip away. And look! Here's a sprinkling of islands that I've never heard of, opal speckles on the blue. And here's a swathe of wrinkled mountains frosted with snow with scarcely a vowel in their names to soften the craggy spikes of consonants. And best of all, there are dotted lines everywhere, swooping in swallow-curves across oceans as shipping lanes, tracing minute red threads as roads or spidery millipede tracks as railways. It's that easy. It is quite small and manageable a place, after all, this world, and there's no need to resort to noisy aeroplanes and acres of grey tarmac. In fact, there's no room at all for such pragmatic ugliness, no room for anything more than the desk and the atlas in the still sunshine. This is the Warlde's Room.

PART I.

Chapter 1

That man is little to be envied, whose patriotism would not gain force upon the plain of Marathon, or whose piety would not grow warmer among the ruins of Iona!

—SAMUEL JOHNSON

The voyage recounted in these pages started in 1990 but really began some eight years earlier as I stood on the deck of a ferry on the first leg of a long journey to a remote speck of an island. I was just nineteen and on my way to the Well of Eternal Youth, on Iona, a tiny isle lying off the west coast of Mull, which in turn lies off the west coast of Scotland.

It was midwinter and the ferry was almost empty. Out on deck it was finger-numbingly cold, but on the horizon astern Oban looked like a brightly lit toy town, as clear and tiny as something seen through the wrong end of a telescope. Ahead, the mountains of Mull stood like cut-out purple shadows against a serene sky; they faded slowly to black as the west brightened to gold.

A gull was there, hanging like a child's mobile a few feet from the rail where I stood blowing into my cupped hands. It eyed me with a sardonic stare which seemed to suggest that it knew perfectly well I had contraband herrings concealed on my person and was prepared to wait all day if necessary. After a few minutes of uneasy silence, I broke down and explained that I didn't have any fish on my person but was on my way to Iona, if that was of any interest. The gull shot me a sceptical look and directed its attention to something behind me.

I turned to find a young woman wrapped in furs, the only other person onboard braving the chill of a Scottish midwinter evening. She was wrapped in a coat of such luxurious proportions that it looked rather as though she were being embraced by a Kodiak bear, but the face that emerged from the waves of fur was quite the most beautiful face I had seen in my short nineteen years. It was

heart-shaped. Her large brown eyes were like those of a fawn that has discovered a meadow full of butterflies. A stray wisp of auburn hair blew fetchingly across her wide, smooth brow. My heart thumped.

'Um … it's very pretty here, isn't it?' I faltered, turning to introduce myself. 'I'm Sandy.'

She turned and glanced at me dewily, and then spoke.

'Oh my *G-a-a-a-d!*' she exclaimed, and I nearly swallowed my tongue. 'Oh! My! GA-A-A-D! You are so *ri-i-i-ght! The* vibes here are so har-MO-nious!'

'Yes, harmonious,' I agreed and turned determinedly back to my own musings. But my new acquaintance was not one to let things drop so easily.

'Pixie,' she drawled. 'Pixie Peterson, nice to meet ya! Hey, whaddya say yer name was again?'

'Sandy.'

'Oh, that is so funny!' she said delightedly. 'Sandy? Oh, *you* are so funny! No, come on, what's yer real name, no kiddin'?'

'Sandy,' I insisted. 'Really.'

'Oh, you *are* a joker, I c'n see that, yes you are, yes you *are!*' She winked at me roguishly and punched me in the arm. I edged away a fraction along the rail.

'So where you headin' then, mystery man?' Pixie asked.

I told her that I was going to Iona – possibly. Possibly not, it depended.

Pixie almost swooned. 'Iona? Iona! Well, whaddya know, I'm headin' that way too. I'm on a pilgrimage, a pilgrimage to heal my soul! How 'bout you?'

I softened a little. If Pixie was on a pilgrimage to Iona, perhaps she had some redeeming features. After all, it was a place famed the world over for bringing to its holy shores people of humble faith and good will to find healing in the ruins of the old abbey or the sweet silence of its grassy hills and shores. The piety of St Columba still hung over the island, I had been told, and few people left its shores without being in some way touched by grace. As the ferry furled on, I got the full run-down from her.

Pixie was from California. She was a Pisces with a moon in Jupiter, and she had come to Iona on a mission. Her spiritual mentor back home in Berkeley, a man named Randy, had taught her all about her inner chakra and how to identify auras. His was pure gold, apparently – very rare. He was a babe, and he had moved in with her and taught her some other things I was possibly too young to understand. Randy's star sign was Qing-xin, the Dolphin. At my cautious look, Pixie explained to me with breathless awe that this was an ancient sign, which Randy had discovered unaided from ancient texts and which meant he was a reincarnation of an ancient Pharaoh. Anyway, Randy had been meditating on an astral plane recently and had accessed the arcane lore that Iona was still inhabited by druids and sat plumb on the intersection of no less than five ley-lines. He had sent Pixie as his most trusted acolyte to check the place out and report back, with a real live druid in tow if possible.

Would I care to join her?

Before I could reply, we arrived at Craignure on Mull, a bleak and cheerless ferry terminal on a windswept road that swept out of the moors, briefly touched the harbourside and wriggled its way back into the forbidding black hills as fast as it could go. On seeing the terminus, my heart sank. There was no inn or bed and breakfast at this time of the year and Iona was fifty miles and another ferry trip away beyond the darkening moor. Furthermore, the evening had turned damp and the bright azure-gold of the afternoon had been rapidly replaced by louring clouds and the first few spatters of icy rain. There was the ferry back to Oban, of course, but ...

Onto the desolate stretch of road, empty in the fading dusk, stepped Pixie Peterson in her voluminous furs and, with as much confidence of success as she might have displayed on Hollywood Boulevard, called out, 'Taxi? TAXI?!'

I was about to remark tersely that this was not exactly Fifth Avenue when to my astonishment a little man crawled out from under the jetty and informed Pixie in a soft Highland accent that he could take her across the island for a mere seventy pounds.

'Oh my G-a-a-a-d!' Pixie enthused. She shot me a ravishing look and asked very sweetly if I wouldn't mind sharing the ride. I hesitated. The fare was preposterous, my budget as a nineteen-year-old was tight, and I didn't think I could stand any more talk about druids. Then again, it was the only way out of there. I reckoned I could just about spare thirty-five pounds if I didn't eat for the next three days. Before I could say anything, Pixie had heaved my tatty rucksack into the waiting car, hustled me in beside her and, as we pulled out along the moorland road, was asking the driver if he knew any warlocks.

An hour later, we pulled into Fionnphort, the tiny village on the western coast of Mull and the departure point for the last short ferry-hop across to Iona. The driver and I had been treated to a running commentary on fairy lore, veganism, druidic practices and the true origins of the tarot, also discovered single-handedly by Randy of the golden aura. The driver shot me a look that implied that even seventy pounds was not going to compensate for the drive, when he could have been sitting at home by a peat-fire, boiling a haggis or sawing off his own foot with a whalebone knife.

On this side of Mull, a full North Atlantic gale was blowing and the rain was coming down like a shower of wet, slapping fish. Nevertheless the ferry was there and ready to depart, tossing among gouts of luminous spray in the darkness. As we struggled out into the storm, Pixie mouthed something about her purse being at the bottom of her luggage, so would I mind awfully fixing up the driver, be a darling, and she'd fix me up as soon as she could.

I peeled off seven ten-pound notes – almost my entire budget – and gave them to the driver, who lost no time in leaping into the car and disappearing at speed back up the road. I hurried after Pixie and came to where she stood surveying the access to the ferry. There was no gangplank, just the car-ramp, which every few seconds was deluged by the washing surge and fall of waves.

'Er,' I said, 'about the taxi fare ...'

But Pixie had other things on her mind. She eyed the waves, the big one coming in, the slow boiling retreat, the pause afterwards, and off she went, tottering on unsuitable heels up the ramp. She should have waited. An unexpected Atlantic wave came curling around the side of the ferry, caught her unawares and drenched her, furs and all, from neck to toe. She stood there open-mouthed and, for once, silent. I have never seen anyone wetter. With the lank fur plastered all over her like wet kelp, she looked like a Persian cat that had just swum the Channel.

Perhaps I would ask her about the fare later.

*

As soon as we touched down on Iona, the island's enchantment began to work its spell. Through the blustering rain came a young woman in a sou'wester who introduced herself as Judith and took us both up to the Argyll Hotel, the only guesthouse still open. There she went through the formalities while we dripped onto the tiled floor of the lobby.

'And will that be a double room?' she asked in her pleasant Western Isles lilt.

I flushed and stuttered a denial, but Pixie, clearly recovered from her drenching, punched me playfully in the arm and said, 'Hey, how 'bout it? Could be kinda fun.'

I went from a moderate tomato to deep beetroot. I gulped heavily and put my foot down. 'No, a single room for me, please,' I said hoarsely, looking straight ahead at an interesting lithograph of some ducks on a loch. I sensed a shrug out of the corner of my eye and caught a *sotto voce* 'Well, if ya wanna be snooty' from the depths of the damp fur. I also sensed an amused glance from Judith, but kept my eyes firmly on the ducks – eiders, I think, yes, definitely eiders – while I waited for Pixie to vanish upstairs and for the colour to recede from my face.

When Judith showed me up to my room, she must have noticed my relief at seeing a narrow and decidedly single bed. 'Aye,' she said, 'and the door locks too, just like this, see. You needn't be bothered about burglars in the night.'

My only problem now was how to recover my funds with my dignity intact.

*

That evening I went into the tiny sitting room and found myself in heaven. There were deep saggy armchairs in faded green chintz, a brightly crackling fire in the hearth and a bow window against which the Atlantic storm outside flung raindrops like handfuls of wet gravel. Best of all, there were shelves stacked two-deep with books: dog-eared paperbacks, Mary Stewart romances, old cloth-bound editions of Peter Scott wildfowl prints, bird and wildflower books, histories of Scottish architecture.

The first book that fell into my hand as I browsed was a little hardback of green cloth. It was all about Iona, and I was immediately entranced. Here was the Cave of the Pigeons and the Cave of the Otter. Here was the Bay of the Wounded Crane and the Spouting Cave, the Big Mound of the Angel and the Little Mound of the Visitors, and the Garden of Garath. Then there was the intriguingly named Bay of the Buried Coracle and the Hill with its Back to Ireland, both places associated with St Columba's determination not to return to his native Eire.

I read on, intrigued. I delighted over the name of the White Strand of the Monks, until I read with sorrow about the bloody massacre of the island's monks there in a Viking raid in 678 AD. I chuckled at the Island of the Cows and the Island of the Women and Columba's decree that 'Where there is a cow, there will be a woman, and where there is a woman, there will be mischief!' – hence his banishment of both these scourges from the main island to their appointed islets.

'Whaddya laughin' at, huh?'

It was Pixie, standing there in a pair of pyjama shorts and a cotton top, watching me with amusement. Unwrapped from the furs, she really was ... striking. *A fine figure of a woman*, I heard some inner voice say, and cursed it for sounding like an Edwardian great-uncle returned from the Subcontinent. I fumbled for an answer.

'Oh, just this thing about cows … and women … and cows, you know. On an island. Each—'

Pixie collapsed honking into an armchair. 'Oh, YOU. You are funny. Yes you are. Funny, funny, funny, that's what you are.'

I turned back to my book but she was not to be deflected. Inexorably she outlined her program for the morrow.

'First thing to do,' she said, 'is track down those druids, an' I guess that means lookin' for standin' stones an' stuff. Or oaks and mistletoe, I've heard, is a sure sign of druids. It's a matter of lookin' around. Then there's ley-lines. I've got a coupla' crystals in my bag, they're from Machu Picchu in Peru, and just the thing for stakin' out ley-lines, and where they cross, that's where the druid'll be, I guess. Mind if I smoke?'

As she lit a cigarette and blew acrid smoke into the little parlour, I pondered the likelihood of a druid standing waiting patiently at the intersection of two ley-lines. In fact, I pondered the likelihood of there being any druids, past or present, on Iona. As the book on my lap recounted, Iona was not that sort of place. Its fame was due to a quite different sort of magic: the magic of learning and enlightenment that Columba had brought to this part of the world some 1500 years before. Here this extraordinary man, part saint, part magician, had established a monastery that would survive for the next thousand years, a candle of Christian light untouched either by the heathen darkness all around or by the murky political turbulence of Rome.

True, there was an older magic here as well, and Columba seemed to have seamlessly bridged the gap between the old radiance and the new. Tales abounded of the saint talking with angels or fairy lords – who knew which?; of receiving messages from seabirds and seals and otters; of flying on invisible wings to find solitude and prayer in the lonelier corners of the tiny island. And that older magic, fairy magic, the whole Celtic miasma of raths and rides, of Tir nan Og and the Folk of the Shee, of selkies and urisks and tales of dazzling glamour hiding old bones and treacherous bogs, had here alone in the West been sanctified and cleansed of its darkness and made one with the new reason of Christianity. You see it, said the writer of the little book, in the fantastical weaving together of beasts and birds and Christian symbols in the Book of Kells, written, some say, by Columba himself on this very island.

In the meantime, Pixie had stubbed out one cigarette and started on another. 'And then there's fairy magic,' she was saying. 'It's very big in the States now, there're shops everywhere. I reckon we can get ourselves some genuine fairy rocks here. Where d'you think we might find some?' she asked wide-eyed, blowing out a long stream of blue smoke.

I stiffened in alarm as I realised that she was now consistently using the pronoun 'we'. It seemed I was to be included in the program.

'Y'know,' she continued, in a quieter voice, 'I've been lookin' for something really truly magical all my life. I reckon I might just find it here. Whaddya think?'

Now this made me really cross. It made me almost cross enough to do something quite dramatic like get up and poke the fire in a cross sort of way, or to close the book pointedly, or something firm like that. But I didn't, because I was only nineteen, and English at that, and it would have been appallingly rude, so I said, 'Hmm,' and thought furiously and quietly to myself about why I was so cross all of a sudden.

The fact was that Pixie had stolen my thunder. You see, like her, I too had always sought after magic. I too had always desperately wanted there to be something in the world that could not be explained away by income tax or bus timetables. Of course, I was infinitely more subtle, thoughtful and mature about it than this lunatic blowing smoke in my face, I was sure. I was able to reason with myself that there was true magic everywhere you looked if you had a mindset subtle and spiritual enough: magic in a budding flower, magic in a good book, magic in the intricacies of Pascal's triangle or in the poetry of Yeats – even in a bus timetable, if one could but see it.

But here was Pixie with her ridiculous notions of druids and crystals and vibrations, and she really believed too. Stupidly, naively, gauchely, she was going to ruin it. Her silly wishful thinking was forcing me to adopt the polar opposite of her views – to become the sensible, reasonable sceptic who looked down his nose at all these amusing fancies. That's why I was cross.

Taking advantage of the silence that had fallen after Pixie's wistful admission, I turned back to browse further through the book. Over the other side of the island, it said, was a white-sanded bay, the Bay at the Back of the Ocean. Here if anywhere, surely, was the World's End, the Uttermost West, the sea-lanes to the Blessed Isles. I sighed as my mind filled with cloudy images of golden apples and white sails filling and sweet music over the water. Except now all that sort of stuff was for the Pixie Petersons of the world. I turned the page.

Oh no. Another sweet blow. Here was a Well of the North Wind – I thought of George MacDonald's fairy stories – and here, even better, best of all – I could hardly believe it – the Well of Eternal Youth. Pixie forgotten, I read on.

On the very summit of Dun I, the highest hill of the island, a traveller may find at whiles the Well of Eternal Youth. Here, on the very brink of the hill, is a large triangular pool, bordered on two sides by walls of rock but on the third side by a fringe of green rushes. This is the famed Tobar na h-Aoise, beloved of the fairy folk and much sought after in the elder days by pilgrims from afar.

Any pilgrim who travels to this holy place, over land and over sea, who wishes for the fairies to grant their gift of eternal youth and beauty, must ...

I paused. The Well of Eternal Youth? The actual Well of Eternal Youth? Strangely poorly publicised, I thought, for the Fount of the Elixir of Life. I glanced at the front of the little book to see when it was published. No date. Old, then.

A picture of the Well floated before my mind, secret, reedy, high up on the hill's summit. A thousand old tales drifted in my head of magical rivers and pools: Achilles bathed in the Styx as a baby to be made invulnerable; Eustace in the Narnia books washing away his dragonish hide by moonlight with Aslan's help.

'Any pilgrim who travels to this holy place, over land and over sea, who wishes for the fairies to grant their gift of eternal youth and beauty, must ...' The words drew me in. But they didn't solve the problem of how I could avoid being dragged into tomorrow's spurious druid search. A waft of cigarette smoke brought me slowly back to the world to realise that Pixie was in full flow, something about contact lenses. 'Bang! Pow! I just went and popped the damn cornea, didn't I? Gee, there was fluid and stuff everywhere, hurt like hell, you bet!'

I could stand it no more. My own eyes weeping like popped grapes, I pushed the book from my lap and stumbled from the room, muttering my goodnights and my apologies. The only thing for it, I thought later as I climbed into bed, was to get up at the crack of dawn and set off to explore the island alone. Yes, that's what I would do, I thought sleepily to myself as waves of slumber engulfed me. A good night's sleep. An early start. Iona. All to myself. I snuggled deeper into the soft, warm bed.

Two minutes later, I got back out from under the covers, tiptoed across to the door, locked it firmly, shoved a chair under the door-handle and fell back into bed. Then I stared sleeplessly at the ceiling, thinking unaccountably of Bambi and meadows full of butterflies, before I finally drifted into sleep three hours later.

*

I slept in, of course. The sun was brightly streaming in the window when I awoke, and when I glanced out the window into the little lane between the hotel and the sea, people were already up and stir-ring in a mid-morningish sort of way. I dressed quickly, abandoned the idea of breakfast for fear of meeting Pixie in the dining room, crept downstairs and poked my head cautiously into the little sitting room. It was the book I was after, but it was no longer where I had left it. I made a cursory search, but footsteps outside the door had me cringing behind the armchair and I determined not to linger. Once the steps had faded down the corridor, I slipped from the room and out into the bright winter sunshine. The day was ahead of me, and as long as I looked sharpish about me and avoided an encounter with Pixie, the whole island was mine to explore.

It is a truly magical place, Iona. There is hardly a visitor to the island who does not comment on the air, clear and sparkling, heady as champagne but infused with a tranquillity that is found nowhere else in the world.

For the daytripper, there is an hour's worth of 'sites' to see: the ruins of the old nunnery, with daisies and speedwell starring the green turf between the quiet walls; the graveyard where stand the old stone crosses, intricately carved in flowing ribbons now lichened over in grey velvet. Here Macbeth is buried, and all the ancient kings of Scotland, but no-one knows exactly where they lie. Then there is the abbey itself, built in chunks of pinky-grey stone. Here I was especially interested to see the figure of Iohannes MacFingonus – John Mackinnon in the vulgar tongue – carved in polished black basalt and lying in effigy by the altar in the main nave. He was the last Abbot of Iona and there is a tale in my family concerning him

– who knows how true? It is said that when it came his time to die, instead of lying in state as a great lord and abbot should, he vanished into ignominy. The Reformation had swept through the whole kingdom in his lifetime and even here in this remote and holy place, the abbey had been smashed and its people scattered.

Some 150 years later, when the fortunes of the abbey had been restored and the bog below its bounds was drained, the villagers found the corpse of John Mackinnon, miraculously preserved by his great sanctity – or perhaps, more prosaically, by the tanning qualities of peaty bog-water. His body was brought up to the abbey for a proper burial and the local stonemason carved the great obsidian effigy that lies in pride of place today, his likeness captured a century and a half after his body was committed to the ground.

As interesting as these sites were, my feet were itching to wander further afield. I was tired of keeping a lookout for Pixie behind every cloister arch and gravestone and of jumping at every sound of approaching footsteps. Out on the open hills, I would have a better chance of seeing her coming and running like hell or plunging over a cliff into the sea in the time-honoured tradition of the stags around here. Besides, there were the caves and the bays, the big mounds and the little mounds … and the Well, of course. I would save the Well for last.

So I turned inland and uphill. Much of the island is covered in a fine green turf, the *machair*, sweet-smelling and nibbled short by sheep. I took off my shoes and socks and ran barefoot over the springy grass like some Arcadian shepherd-boy. The turf rolled and swelled in smooth green-gold hillocks; outcrops of pinkish granite broke through in places, warm in the sunshine. Little brooks ran in rivulets along the grassy hollows, peaty and brown as ale. The southern half of the island was wilder and lumpier, a rough terrain of bogs and hollows and heathery moorland – no more bare feet. If Pixie had only the one pair of clattering heels I saw last night, I would be safe enough here. For a blissful few hours, I scrambled my way around the rugged coastline. Later, with the aid of a map, I identified the places I had found: the Cave of the Otters, sadly devoid of otters; the Cave of the Pigeons, delightfully inhabited by one very elderly rock-pigeon and enough guano to fund a small Pacific nation. Then there was the tiny cove where I picked up a sharp flake of pure green stone, the famed Iona marble and a fairy stone if ever I saw one, and the Bay of the Coracle, where Columba buried his little boat so he wouldn't be tempted to paddle back home to Ireland if the solitude and the shellfish and the woman-cow politics all got too much.

Finally, I found my way to the Bay at the Back of the Ocean, a place that has haunted my sweetest dreams since. A wide sweep of white sand turns the shallow waters here as pale as bottle-glass, the palest of aquamarines. The gentlest of swells sets wavelets lisping upon the shore, and on the southern headland it is enough to set a benign sea monster snurgling to itself before shooting a plume of spray skywards from a deep crevice in the rocks – the Spouting Cave. But the western sky was growing cloudy and the sunlight was leaching away from the golden turf. It was time to turn northward once more to Dun I and my search for the Well of Eternal Youth.

Dun I is at the northernmost tip of Iona and is the highest hill on the island. By the time I was halfway up the hill, the brilliance of the day had turned to icy rain and freezing wind. When I reached the crown, the gale was of a ferocity I had never before encountered. I leant into the wind at a 45-degree angle, giggling maniacally. Play-fully I raised my arms like skinny wings and was instantly picked up and flung about twenty feet downwind like a pelican in a wind tun-nel. I landed with a squelch in a boggy patch of turf; another five feet and I would have been flung over the cliff behind me. I crawled back to my vantage point and stood up more tentatively. Where was the Well of Eternal Youth?

The summit of Dun I is no sharp peak but rather a flattish jumble of hummocks and hollows of turf, now rapidly becoming bogs. As I stood peering into the wind, a skein of flying cloud came racing up the hillside and swathed me in blinding fog. A few seconds later I could see no more than ten yards in any direction. If there really was a magical well up here, the elemental fairies were doing their damnedest to prevent me discovering it. Nevertheless, I would find it. Forget Pixie and her druids. Here was real magic and I was in the thick of it. I set off across the small plateau to find the Well.

An hour later, I gave up. I was numb, frozen in every limb and soaked through. The storm raged unabated and rain had given way to sleet, hail and a brief flurry of damp snow. I had explored the whole hilltop from north to south and east to west a dozen times to no avail. There were plenty of pools, yes, and I had floundered into most of them, but these were just puddles formed by the torrential icy rain. Nowhere was there a triangular pool bounded by rocks on two sides and reeds on the third. Of course there bloody well wasn't, I said to myself. This is a Well of Eternal Youth we're looking for here, not some bloody trig point on the Ordnance Survey map. These things don't exist, Sandy. They are myths. Please stop flapping around in this sub-zero gale searching for a mythical symbol and go home to a treble whisky and bed. That guidebook was clearly written centuries ago, probably by Pixie's great-grandmother as she accompanied Samuel Taylor Coleridge on his celebrated tour of the Highlands while both were off their faces on laudanum.

With these thoughts hammering in my head, I gave up and turned to find the path back down.

And there it was.

Right on the northern edge of the hill, nestled so close to the top of a sheer drop that its water was lapping over a lip of stone and falling away in a fine spray, was the Well of Eternal Youth. It was exactly as described in the book. There were the two vertical rocks; there were the green rushes, hissing and bending double in the furious wind. And between these three sides, a sheet of grey water, some twelve feet across and beaten like pewter.

Even as I watched, the wind dropped, the fairies defeated. I had found it and there was nothing they could do to stop me now. I knew what I had to do. There on that midwinter mountaintop, with the grey clouds clearing and all the isles of the world beginning to show on the sea's horizon around me, I stripped naked and gently, reverently, lowered myself into the pool.

There was a numbing shock of cold and my testicles took refuge somewhere high up under my ribs. Then, as I lowered myself further, there was a squidgy settling of my buttocks into the oozy mud of the pool's bottom, almost warm in comparison to the skin-biting ice of the water. Finally, my nipples blue and hard as slug-pellets, I knew what I had to do. Remembering Achilles and his mother's careless oversight, I lay back until I was submerged fully in the waters of the Well of Eternal Youth.

I had no idea how long you were meant to stay under on these sorts of occasions. I reckoned that a good thirty seconds of full holding-my-breath submersion would do the trick. I gave it as long as I could and then lurched upwards in a fountain of mud and water-weed and emerged pale-chested from the pool. I slithered out, danced onto a nearby mound of turf and paused to assess the effects.

It had clearly worked. I already felt a million dollars. I glowed with health and vitality. I punched the air and gave a whoop and even permitted myself to give an uncharacteristic hip-swivel at the sheer flood of joy thundering through my veins. I looked around for a lion to wrestle or a waterfall to swim up. If this was eternal youth, I was liking it very much. I spent the first glorious few minutes of my new immortality being towelled dry by the rough wind that had arisen once more. So ecstatic was I that I actually descended some way down the hill back to the village before I realised that I would be better off arriving back at the Argyll Hotel fully dressed. Almost reluctantly, I turned back, climbed into my horribly sodden clothes and headed down.

Later that afternoon, in the middle of a steaming hot and very deep bath of water the colour of tea, I was mugged by the first signs of the worst cold I have had in my life. Clearly being immortal did not prevent you getting sick. With streaming eyes and a nose that felt as though someone had been shovelling porridge up it, I draped my damp underwear over the radiator to dry, locked my door and fell into bed at five in the afternoon, waking only briefly an hour later to remove my now thoroughly singed underpants and stamp out the sparks on the bathroom floor. Then I returned to bed and didn't wake until eight the next morning.

The morning was grey and dullish and so was I, for today I would have to return to the mainland. Once I had settled the hotel bill, my money would have run out. Heading downstairs, I found Judith setting up breakfast for one in the rather austere dining room. She bade me sit down, took my order for the Full Scots breakfast with double helpings of everything and started towards the kitchen.

'Excuse me,' I called, 'sorry to bother you, but is the other person … the … um … the woman … Miss Peterson … up and about yet? I just wonder because …'

'Och, there's no danger for you there,' Judith replied. 'Miss Peterson was away out of here first thing yesterday morning. She up and left by the 6 a.m. ferry before any of us were awake to see her on her way.'

I gaped.

'Aye, and before we could trouble her with her bill, forbye,' she added grimly. 'We have a few every season, ye ken. The midnight flitters, we call them. Och well, good riddance,' she said, and turned to go back into the kitchen.

I stared at the packet of Puffa-Puffa Rice before me and fumed. Gone? I had spent the whole of yesterday skulking around the island for nothing? And she owed me thirty-five pounds! That would have paid for another night on Iona at least.

Another thought struck me. Purse at the bottom of her luggage, she had told me. But she hadn't had any luggage, just a small bag slung over one shoulder. She had been fooling me all along.

From the kitchen I could hear voices and laughter and caught a glimpse through the door of Judith and her husband sitting down to breakfast at a scrubbed kitchen table the size of a tennis court. Judith was juggling trays and oven mitts and the kitchen door to bring my breakfast out when I went over, helped her with a few things and tentatively asked if I might join them at the kitchen table if that would make things easier. 'Besides,' I added, 'it's a little bit chilly and posh out there and I'd love the company if you'll have me.'

They both smiled and agreed and soon I was wolfing down sizzling sausages and tomatoes and fried eggs elbow to elbow with Judith and her husband, Mark. As Judith got up to brew another pot of tea and make more toast, they both chatted about life on the island. Mark, in his navy-blue fisherman's jersey, was the island's postman and also operated a little wooden sailing boat called *Freya*; I had seen her down by the wharf on my walk yesterday, a beautiful slim vessel with a tan sail and a deep-blue hull. In the summer, he took people out to visit Fingal's Cave on nearby Staffa and to watch puffins and gannets nesting. In return, I told them about my experience with Pixie and my adventures of the day before. So at home did they make me feel that I even told them somewhat sheepishly about my bathing in the Well of Eternal Youth ... and about burning my underpants in the night. By the time another pot of tea had been made and drunk, it was high time for me to go – the ferry would be leaving in less than an hour.

As I was helping to wash up, I remembered something. 'Judith, I don't suppose you saw a little green book I was reading the first night I was here?' I asked.

'No, no, I don't think so. Mark might have picked it up but ... no. Was it important then?'

'Not really,' I said. I explained that I had been intrigued but had not had the chance to finish it ... but no, Judith explained, she hadn't seen it at all. Such a pity. And that was that. Then there was a flurry of packing, a hurried goodbye and an awkward hug and I was off to the ferry, running down the road under the grey sky. But just as the ferry was pulling in, Judith came running after me, something in her hand.

'Sandy!' she called. 'I've found that book you were wanting. It was in the other guest room, the one Miss Peterson had. I must've missed it yesterday, I was that cross to find her gone and all. Plain as a pikestaff it was, face down on her bedside table. She must've taken it to read after you went off to bed.'

'Yes, I suppose so. What a nuisance. Never mind, too late now,' I said, hitching up my rucksack. The small gaggle of foot-passengers was beginning to board.

'Found she had nothing else to do with her time, I suppose,' said Judith, giving me a meaningful look. I must have looked puzzled because she added, bluntly, 'She was expecting you to pay her bill, you realise. I feel sure she's not used to being turned down like that. And she hadn't the cash to settle her bill herself.'

'Oh!' I said. 'Ah.' The last few passengers were on the ramp.

'She should've shown more interest in fairy wells,' said Judith, her eyes twinkling. 'Then she'd have had you. Here, the ferry's off. Take the book with you. Remember us by it!' And before I could protest, she had pushed it into my hands, given me a last hug and trotted back up the road to the hotel.

I dashed across the ramp onto the ferry; by the time I had climbed the steps to the tiny saloon, we were fifty yards from shore and Iona could barely be seen through the thick salt-encrusted windows as it vanished astern. I sat and opened the book to pick up where I'd left off. Ah, here we are; the book fell open at the very page. The Well of Eternal Youth, Tobar na h-Aoise.

I started reading.

*

Do you know those old legends, the Celtic ones about Tir nan Og and the Land of Eternal Youth? The Apples of Idunn? The Tale of Oisin? They never end happily. Typically, here's what happens. The adventurer finds his way through many a peril to the Blessed Isle and there he eats of the apples and drinks of the waters of that land. He gains immortality, everlasting youth. But after a time of idle luxury, he wishes to return to his homeland, the mortal lands, just to see how his folks are getting on without him.

But no! He is warned by the king and queen of the new land that to return would be a folly, a disaster. For it is only here in the Land of Youth that you are forever young, they explain, and what seems like the passing of three days here is the passing of 300 in the mortal lands.

But no, Oisin, or Thomas the Rhymer or whoever he is insists on his way. He is given a fine white horse to ride and urged that on no account must he set foot on mortal soil. If he does, his immortality will fall from him in a twinkling.

'Yes, yes,' the hero says with the impatience of immortal youth, 'keep supper for me, will you?' and off he rides.

Well, sometimes it's a broken stirrup and sometimes it's a clod that flies up from a farmer's hoe but one way or another the young man's foot touches mortal soil and the spell is severed. Skin wrinkles, teeth decay, limbs wither, hair turns to dust and a thousand years overtake the fine fellow in an instant.

As the ferry ploughed across the strait to Mull, I read the passage again.

On the very summit of Dun I, the highest hill of the island, a traveller may find at whiles the Well of Eternal Youth. Here, on the very brink of the hill is a large triangular pool, bordered on two sides by walls of rock but on the third side by a fringe of green rushes.

That was it, that was the very place! As the ferry slowed and turned to pull into Fionnphort, the purple and green of Mull swung into sight through the saloon windows. Nearly there.

On I read, as I gathered up my rucksack and hoisted it absently onto my back.

From time out of mind, the waters of this well have been blessed with the power of giving eternal youth and beauty to those who seek it.

Over the speakers came the request for foot-passengers to disembark. Still reading, I shuffled down the steps and onto the car-deck.

Any pilgrim who travels to this holy place, over land and over sea, who wishes for the fairies to grant their gift of eternal youth and beauty, must …

And here the page turned.

Time to concentrate on dodging the waves as they slid and retreated across the car-ramp in fans of lacy white foam and jade green. Pause ... wait for it ... go!

Safely onto the landward side of the ramp beyond the waves, I turned the page and read on:

> ... must climb the height of Dun I as the sun is rising in the East and then, when the first rays of the sun quicken the waters of the Well, must drink deeply of the draught therein. Thus may Eternal Youth be won.

I was back on dry land. The solid tarmac of the Fionnphort carpark lay under my feet. And as I read the last few lines again, I laughed out loud.

Drink of the Well, Sandy, at sunrise. *Drink* the damned stuff. Not bathe in it. Nothing here about bathing, Sandy.

The old warnings were true, after all. In a trice, all my immortality, all my glee, all my feeling-forever-young-ness shrivelled, dropped away and was blown like corpse-dust on the gale of my laughter. I had striven to be a hero-traveller in a tale of my own making and had gloriously stuffed it up.

And with that, I hitched my rucksack on my back, stuck out my thumb and waited for a lift back across the mountains to a world that was still waiting to be conquered.

Chapter 2

Allons! The road is before us!
It is safe – I have tried it – my own feet have tried it well
    – be not detain'd!
Let the paper remain on the desk unwritten, and the book
    on the shelf unopen'd!
Let the tools remain in the workshop! Let the money remain
    unearn'd!
Let the school stand! Mind not the cry of the teacher!
                    —WALT WHITMAN, *Song of the Open Road*

Eight years later, I was in my fourth year of teaching English at an Adelaide school and knew beyond a doubt that eternal youth had evaded my grasp. The realisation hit me hard one day near the end of third term, a term characterised by unrelenting rain and an endlessly renewing pile of essays to be marked. I was taking a short break from the curriculum by reading *The Hobbit* to a class of twelve-year-olds, keeping a wary eye out for my Head of Department, who frowned on such needless excursions into fun.

I glanced around the class. Kevin Spottiswood was sabotaging the reading by shredding a piece of creative writing I had just returned to him. In response to the time-honoured topic 'What I Did on My Holidays,' he had written one sentence about throwing up on his sister in a plane and had then illustrated it in red biro with a picture of a jumbo jet crashing into a giant bloodshot eyeball. His opinion of me as a critic was now being made plain by his slow demolition of the essay in the back row. I was going to confiscate the paper but when he saw me approaching, he started eating the shredded mess. I let him, hoping he might soon pass out from a compacted bowel. I continued reading.

"'But Gandalf looked at the hobbit from under long bushy eyebrows that stuck out further than the brim of his shady hat …'"

Only that morning I had looked in my bathroom mirror and seen

Wat i Did in
my Hollidaye
by Kevin S.

a stranger looking out at me. Flabby-jowled, pouchy-eyed and with
skin the pallor of a lungfish, the face had stared back at me reproachfully. Where was the adventurer now? What had happened to the
merry-hearted youth and the mountains? This teaching lark was all
very well – my life's vocation, I rather thought – but that afternoon
I was in distinct agreement with D.H. Lawrence:

> What is the point of this teaching of mine, and of this
> Learning of theirs? It all goes down the same abyss.
> What does it matter to me if they can write
> A description of a dog, or if they can't?
> What is the point?
> … I shall sit and wait for the bell.

The bell, however, was still some way off and my Head of
Department had clear ideas about the importance of being able to
write on demand a passably accurate description of a dog. I read out
the next line of *The Hobbit*.

"'Then something Tookish woke up inside of him, and he wished
to go and see the great mountains, and hear the pine trees and the
waterfalls, and explore the caves, and wear a sword instead of a
walking stick.'"

At this point, Kevin Spottiswood fell off his chair with a clang
and the class became momentarily animated. While Kevin was sort-
ing himself out, I put the book down, wandered over to the window
and rested my forehead on the cool pane of glass. D.H. Lawrence
was right. This was the brink of the abyss. Way off in the distance, I
could see the grassy whaleback hills that border the city. Curtains of
rain were falling in soft showers, lit by the low sun. Suddenly,

through the green-silver dazzle, I caught a glimpse of the road that winds up over the hills to the world beyond. To those who know Adelaide, it is only the Mount Barker freeway – but the rain made the thin thread of tarmac shine like a silver clew leading to freedom. Wilderland beckoned! The Warlde's Room! Let me beg through life!

Five minutes after the bell went, I was downstairs in the headmaster's office, resigning my position, effective the end of the year. In a breathless patter of poetry, I explained to the Head my idea. I would fly to New Zealand for my Christmas holidays – a trip already planned – but I would cancel the return flight to Australia. Instead, I explained, gripping the edge of his mahogany desk and allowing a tremulous note to creep into my voice, my heart was filled with a deep longing to take off and see where the winds of adventure took me. I wanted to escape the predictability of time-tables, the confines of an ordered life. I was jaded. I was old before my time. I was twenty-seven, for crying out loud!

In fact, I said, struck by a sudden thought, there's a well I need to revisit.

'Do you know what a *peregrinatio* is, Mr Murray? Have you heard of St Brendan? That's what I want to do, you see? But ... and this is the main point, Mr Murray ... I'll do it the only proper way. No flying any of the way. I mean, you can't, can you? You can't just hop on a Boeing 747 with inflight video and reclining seats from Sydney to Glasgow if you're on a pilgrimage to the Well of Eternal Youth, can you? What do you think?'

I stopped, realising that I was banging the desk for emphasis. Mr Murray, to my youthful and impatient eyes, had all the skipping spontaneity of an arthritic Galapagos tortoise. He carefully re-arranged one or two dislodged items of stationery, leant back in his chair and there, in his hushed study and under his arid gaze, the idea suddenly – and not for the last time – seemed hopelessly absurd. I waited for his dry, considered comments on the whole foolish project. There was a long pause as he blinked slowly – it occurred to me that I had never seen him blink before – and just as I was on the point of retracting the idea and meekly asking for next year's time-table, he spoke.

'Good idea,' he creaked. 'Good luck, and do drop us a line when you have time.'

And at that he showed me courteously to the door, relieved perhaps to have rid his staffroom of a dangerous lunatic without recourse to the machinery of dismissal. For my part, it was all the blessing I needed.

*

That is not quite true. Although the next few months were ones of breezy preparation, I came to my final departure at Sydney airport with a certain trepidation about how my father viewed the idea. He had been very quiet over the last few months. Not that I could have – or would have – turned back at that point. My tatty fawn rucksack was packed; I had a tin-whistle, a change of clothes or two, a sleeping bag, some writing things and – prized above all these more practical items – a beautiful little brass and leather telescope given to me by my dearest friend Chris. Clearly he understood the Quixotic nature of what I was setting out to do. But what of my father?

And where exactly was my father? He had slipped away from our farewells at the airport terminus. This sort of lark was almost entirely against his way of doing things. Cautious, conservative, prudent and careful in all he does, he is a great believer in foresight, in booking ahead and in alternative plans worked out well in advance. The happy-go-lucky romanticism of his youngest son would surely be distressing him. Perhaps I should at least allow him to book me a hotel in Auckland, just to offer him a sop of comfort before I left.

Ah, but here he was, back with us, and some new purchase in his hand. He seemed not the least bit worried as he handed me a paper package as a final present. 'Something you might find useful in finding your way to wherever,' he said mildly.

I unwrapped it there and then. It was a map, a large world map showing the expanse of the globe from east to west. This was it, the Warlde's Room, blue and green and criss-crossed, and small enough to put in my pocket! Suddenly my idea seemed feasible after all.

An hour later, I was heading for New Zealand, my only remaining worry the chance of crashing into a giant bloodshot eyeball on the way.

Chapter 3

Sometimes you hear, fifth hand
As epitaph:
'He chucked up everything
And just cleared off,'
And always the voice will sound
Certain you approve
This audacious, purifying,
Elemental move ...
But I'd go today
Yes, swagger the nut-strewn roads,
Crouch in the fo'c'sle
Stubbly with goodness ...
       —PHILIP LARKIN, *Poetry of Departures*

Here's a tip, dear reader. If you are ever going off on a journey, planning to be a light-footed prince of the open road, swaggering the nut-strewn roads and living only on bread, cheese and honey, then make sure that the lid of the honey-jar is screwed on tight. And that the cheese is of a kind that can withstand the roadside temperatures of New Zealand in mid-January.

I failed to take either of these precautions, and as I opened my rucksack three days later to extract my wholesome lunch, there beneath the pines of a picnic reserve with an unpronounceable name, I found both cheese and honey melting oozily through my underwear in a sort of saccharine fondue. Undaunted, I did my best to make the most of the situation by combining lunch and laundry and spent a tentative half-hour licking the undergarments as clean as I could get them, feeling vaguely perverted as I did so, like some fetishist Paddington Bear.

I was hitchhiking at the time. I had tried the traditional thumb-out-and-look-wistful approach for a while, but the road was so empty and the day so warm and the smell of cheese so enticing that

I had abandoned it for the more Zen practice of lying on a bed of velvety pine needles under the trees and pretending that a lift to the next town was the last thing in the world I needed. Like every good hitchhiker since the world began, I accepted that somewhere – who knows where or how far away? – but somewhere, the car that was going to pick me up was on its way. That was a certainty. The only unknown factor was its precise time of arrival and I could live with that. In the meantime, I would lie under the pine trees and think.

It was only three days into the trip and already I was feeling trapped by the whole grubby touristic round. Rotorua was the chief cause of this. It is famous, of course, for its geysers, its mud pools, its thermal springs and the fact that dying of sulphur gas in the comfort of one's own home is commoner than in, say, Surrey or the Adelaide suburbs. Only the week before, a family had been found scalded to death by a rogue geyser that had erupted through their living-room floorboards one evening during the six o'clock TV news. Despite the frisson of excitement that this sort of thing might be supposed to lend to a stay in Rotorua, the presence of too many neon hotel signs, too many shopping malls, too many tacky toy kiwis and imitation jade tiki amulets had left me dispirited and full of doubts. Would it be like this all the way to Iona?

Late one evening in Rotorua I had been taken by a guide to a cultural treat, a restaurant where Maori dancers swung their poi-pois – fluffy luminescent pom-poms on strings – under UV lights to an electric organ accompaniment. As I sat coughing gobs of sulphur-coloured sputum into my napkin and watched the glowing balls gyrating in a disembodied dance, I wondered if I would look back on this night as the highlight of my travelling experiences. Perhaps, I thought glumly to myself, the whole damn world was now like this from pole to pole, a chain of tourist sites, each one engineered to process the tourists, fill them with pre-packaged culture and send them tidily on to the next site. In the meantime, the waiter was serving up a traditional Maori treat, which turned out to be pork and tinned pineapple with a complimentary Coca-Cola. Was there no escape?

Not a car had passed since I had started on these gloomy meditations, but the afternoon was growing dim and golden and the heavy fragrance of the pines threatened to cast me into a shady sleep. And perhaps it wasn't so bad after all, even if it was a little tame. Kevin Spottiswood, essay marking and the abyss were a long way away and surely there were some adventures still to be had. I repacked my rucksack, stuck out my thumb and set my mind to Zen mode once more. A mere four hours later, I was picked up by a saintly driver who must have wondered why his passenger smelt so redolently of pine needles and ripe cheese.

*

Two days later, the scenery of New Zealand stopped looking like Hampshire and started looking like Middle Earth. I commented on this to the driver of a silver Toyota who had picked me up some three hours before, a genial middle-aged businessman who had asked about my travel plans in a mildly interested way. Some 200 kilometres later, I was still telling him. It seemed to me that here was a sympathetic ear for my theories about what proper adventuring was all about. We'd already covered the Warlde's Room, with recitals of relevant excerpts of poetry, and had now moved on to my frustrations in realising my romantic ideal of travel.

'You see, it's like in *The Hobbit*, isn't it?' I burbled. 'I assume you've read *The Hobbit*, everyone's read *The Hobbit*, haven't they? You don't get Bilbo Baggins just flying off to the Lonely Mountain, do you? No, he has to walk every inch of the way, and that makes it proper travelling, do you see what I mean?'

'Um ... where did you want to be let off then?' asked the driver. Over the past hour, his comments had been getting more and more determinedly non-committal.

'You see, you don't exactly meet headhunters, do you, not in airports? Or encounter volcanoes?' I asked with some asperity. I was into my stride and not to be deflected by trivial enquiries. 'Mind you, I can't help feeling a little disappointed so far, I don't mind telling you,' I continued breathlessly. 'I mean, I've just spent a night in Rotorua. Have you been to Rotorua? Do you know how awful it is?'

'I live there, actually.'

'It's all souvenir stalls, air-conditioned restaurants, minibus tours, Coca-Cola ads, isn't it? And those plastic jade tikis—'

'I run a souvenir shop, as it happens.'

'Well, some of them are lovely, I'm sure. But take the whole Coca-Cola thing, you've heard of Odysseus, haven't you, everyone's heard of Odysseus, anyway, he went off with an oar over his shoulder, looking for a land where nobody would recognise it for what it was, so that he'd know he'd found a land where no-one had heard of the sea, can't remember why exactly, but that's not the point, right? Well, I'm thinking of wearing a Coca-Cola T-shirt, see, and travelling until I find a race of people that doesn't recognise the logo ... and then I'll know that I've come to a place really worth getting to, see? Not like bloody Rotorua, eh?'

The Toyota pulled up in the middle of a bleak stretch of moorland at the foot of a towering conical mountain that rose into the blue burning-glass of the sky.

'Here we are then,' said the driver, leaning over me and opening my door.

'Er ... where exactly?' I asked, looking about for any signs of habitation. There was not a building, not a person, not so much as a signpost in sight.

'The foot of Ngauruhoe,' the driver replied. 'A real live volcano for you to climb. You'll enjoy it.'

'And ... um ... the nearest hostel or café would be ... where exactly?'

'Twenty miles by road, I reckon, but much shorter if you go up over the volcano and down via the thermal pools over the other side. You'll be there by nightfall if you get a shuffle on. Nice adventure for you.'

'Um ...'

'And,' he added with an air of finality before closing the door on me, 'I can guarantee not a single jade tiki or Coca-Cola stall within fifty miles. Good luck, Odysseus.'

And off he drove down the moorland road. It is hard to tell in these cases, but I could almost swear there was a certain emphatic flourish in the plume of white dust that followed his spinning wheels as he sped away. I sighed. The volcano it would have to be then. Eyeing that soaring conical height balefully, and making a mental note to be more careful when it came to sharing my visions, I set off on the long ascent.

It was one hell of a climb, made especially heartbreaking by the fact that for every five strides upwards, there were three long slow slithers backwards in a minor avalanche of the shifting ash and gravel beneath my boots. When finally I reached the top, I found myself on solid rock at last: the rough red-black lip of a vast crater, looking down into a steaming pit. Actually, from too much reading of Willard Price's *Volcano Adventure*, I had expected to be looking straight down into a burning pit of fiery magma, and was a little disappointed to see that the crater resembled nothing so much as a gigantic ashtray, the only colour being the lurid splashes of sulphur yellow on the dusty cliff faces. When I dropped a hefty rock down, it was a full seven seconds – seven long seconds, in which I wondered belatedly if this might not trigger a fresh eruption – before I saw it strike the bottom and smash. Two seconds later, the boom and rattle came drifting up in a forlorn echo, and I felt momentarily giddy at the enormity of the drop.

The trek up had taken three hours. The descent down the other side took about twenty minutes, twenty hair-raising minutes of surfing on a shifting wave of gravel that tore my boots to shreds and filled my trousers with volcanic debris. When I reached the bottom of the cone, I stopped to calm my nerves, empty my undergarments of gravel and enjoy the feeling of being in control again in the quiet mountain air. Thirty seconds later I had to dive for cover as seven or eight big boulders, dislodged by the avalanche I had stirred up, went scampering by like a pack of black tapirs out for a romp. The driver of the Toyota had done me a favour after all. The near-death experiences that were to dog me for the rest of my voyage had started at last and I was happy once more.

I still had a long way to go, however, before I reached civilisation. I guessed that my best bet was to aim for the lip of the vast blue valley that lay over the shoulder of Tongariro in the distance. Besides, I could see far off the bright glint of what looked like a sprinkling of tiny green tarns. The day was blindingly hot and I was parched, so I turned that way with considerable eagerness. My route took me across a lunar landscape of bare twisted rock and finally to the tarns, which a sign declared were the Emerald Lakes. Any thoughts of a cooling dip or even a drink faded instantly. They were green in colour: a shiny, serpentine green, the sort of colour you associate with Listerine, or the stuff they spray people down with after nuclear accidents. I hurried on.

An hour later, I dropped out of that demonic landscape into deep woods that fulfilled all my dreams of what a New Zealand forest should be. Here was snarled moss, tree ferns, deep leaf litter, hanging lianas, sudden liquid birdsong from the high canopy and blessed coolness after the burning moonscape above. And here before my eyes, gurgling under the forest canopy, gushing in icy torrents, tumbling from pool to pool, was water of a most stunningly beautiful paraffin blue. I trusted it not one bit.

But then again, my tongue felt like a used Brillo pad. The sheer intensity of my thirst overrode my distrust. Convinced though I was that no water that colour could possibly be potable, I nevertheless plunged my head and neck under the first of these rushing cascades and drank as deeply as a horse, relieved to find myself gulping down perfectly good, clear, fresh water. As I sat back, I could feel my tongue unshrivelling and plumping like a raisin dropped into a glass of water. I dropped to my knees again and guzzled down another couple of gallons and then, swaying slightly and sloshing as I moved, I picked myself up again for the final descent. For another two hours I wobbled down the steep zig-zagging paths, my belly gurgling and galooping like a wineskin, down and ever deeper into the forested valley, a lost child among ancient benign giants. By the time the twinkling lights of the hostel in the valley below came into sight in the blue twilight, the Rotorua angst was rinsing away fast.

*

A few days later, I met my sister Maggie at Lake Te Anau, a great fjord slicing its way through wild mountains and our rendezvous point for the start of the Milford Track walk. I had not seen Maggie for a year or so but she was much the same as ever: sensible outdoor clothes, frizzy brown hair cut short and clear grey eyes in a thoughtful face.

Maggie is one year my senior. As children, we were inseparable: we played together, learnt together, made up long and complicated songs about dormice together, and she was always my staunchest protector. She protected me from the dangers of eating beetles, she protected me from Rodney Wall, the local red-haired bully, and she defended me against the chooks when we went into the coop to get eggs. But the thing she spent most of her energy protecting me from was myself. When we strolled to the corner shop to spend our weekly sixpence on sweets, for example, Maggie would dutifully try to curb my attempts to invent a new way of walking and explain to me patiently that my experimental ambulatory styles were precisely the reason why Rodney Wall kept knocking me down. If I admitted to a dislike of liquorice bullets, Maggie would instruct the shopkeeper to include at least a few liquorice bullets in my assortment. The theory was that if the bag were completely of my choosing, I would grow up to be self-indulgent and spoilt. The inclusion of a few medicinal bullets would inure me to the inevitable disappointments I would encounter later in life. Above all, I was to be weaned off all things frivolous. At six, Maggie had declared over the dinner table that clowns, ice-cream, pink icing and any creations of the Walt Disney company whatsoever were now on her list of things that would corrupt the soul. I knew that I too was expected to renounce such shallow fripperies.

In the light of all this, I had looked forward to this shared trek with mixed feelings – delight, yes, to be walking along singing the dormouse song together again, but I was also convinced that we would be on short rations. It was a joy to find, therefore, that the days of self-mortification were over and that we were both free to indulge in a little shameless gourmandery in the form of smoked mussels and brie. In fact, when the conditions were right and the rest of the group were either far behind or far ahead of me, I even permitted myself to take up a little private experimentation after a twenty-year lapse to see if I could perfect a new sort of walk after all.

The Milford Track is New Zealand at its most perfect. We walked for four days through wild valleys between soaring snowy peaks, and by rushing rivers that ran from jade-green pools to Harpic-blue torrents under the shadow of immense trees and jewelled ferns. I had not thought it possible to become heartily sick of waterfalls, but by the fourth day I had seen enough to last several lifetimes. Getting blasé, Maggie and I went for a stroll behind the 500-metre Sutherland Falls. It was possibly a mistake. We battled our way to a position behind the falling torrent of water, where we discovered to our consternation that it was impossible to see or hear or feel, or even to breathe properly. We were in a hail-storm shot through with prisms of colour, each one forming perfect rings of iridescence, dancing and hovering in the stinging spray all about us. It was like being mugged by a gang of rainbows.

Both Maggie and I were keen to see kiwis, those strange nocturnal birds that look like echidnas on stilts. Our guide kept taking us out along forest paths at night, there to sit in complete and utter blackness looking for kiwis. I didn't like to say so to the chap, but neither Maggie nor I could quite see the point. The night under the forest canopy was so utterly black, and we were forbidden the use of torches, so that as we sat in a huddled silence, a dozen kiwis could have been sitting snuggled up beside us and we would never have known it. Perhaps they too were peering into the inky darkness and wondering what it was we were all so patiently waiting to see. And after a while, perhaps, they would tiptoe away into the darkness, ever so quietly so as not to disturb our surveillance. Terribly polite birds, kiwis: we never saw one of them.

On our last night together, in a log-cabin hostel at the end of the fjord, Maggie and I sat up late over a couple of warming brandies and whiled away the evening reading and idly chatting in front of a fire. The rest of the residents had gone off to bed.

'Ah,' said I, swirling the brandy in the glass and watching it glint in the firelight. 'Just think. School starts tomorrow.'

'Mmmm,' replied Maggie absently, turning a page. Then she looked up. 'What did you say?'

'School starts tomorrow, I think. What's the date? Yep, definitely tomorrow.'

Maggie put down her book carefully. 'Sandy, if school is starting tomorrow, what are you doing here? Have you got an extra week off or something?'

'Surely I told you. Didn't I?'

'Told me what?'

'That I'd resigned? Didn't I? I must have mentioned it.'

'From Westminster? You've resigned from Westminster?'

'Yes … as of last December. I thought you knew. I'm going off to see the world, sort of thing. And get this, I'm not flying any of the way. Good, eh? Didn't Dad or Mum mention it?'

But no, it seemed that the news had not got through. While she digested this piece of information, Maggie went off to fetch another brandy. When she returned, she had a list of questions for me.

'When you say you're going to just wander aimlessly and see what happens, what do you mean exactly? I mean, does this mean you could still be in New Zealand in three years' time?'

'Well, no.'

'You see,' she went on. 'You've got to have *some* aims, even if they're not long-term ones. Be a free spirit if you must, Sandy, but you don't want to be a drifter.'

She said the word 'drifter' in the tone of voice people reserve for words like 'imbecile' or 'body odour.' Nobody in our family drifts.

'No, I suppose not.'

I didn't think I could explain about Iona to Maggie when she was in this sort of mood. Drinking from a magical Well of Eternal Youth, I suspected, would not count as a legitimate aim in her eyes. Not quite up there with, say, getting a job or finding a north-west passage or helping out in a leper colony in the Congo.

'Which brings us to the next point, Sandy, which is this. If you plan not to fly anywhere, but don't want to spend the next few decades here as a kiwi, how do you propose leaving the shores of New Zealand, hmm?'

'Um, that's sort of why I didn't want to plan too much because—'

'You do realise that New Zealand is an island, don't you? There's not actually a bridge to mainland Australia, you know?'

'Yes, I've got a map, you know. Dad gave it to me.' I rummaged in my bag and produced the folded map and the little brass telescope. 'And a telescope. Nice, isn't it?' I clapped it to my eye and adopted a Nelsonish pose. Maggie gave the telescope a withering glance and took the map firmly out of my hands.

'See,' she said, jabbing at the map. 'Lots of ocean all around. Too far to swim. Further than you think, Sandy.'

I winced a little but went on gamely. 'Yes, this has been worrying me a tad, I admit. I did wonder about freighters, you know, working my passage, peeling potatoes, that sort of thing.'

Maggie snorted. 'Sandy, I've seen you peel potatoes. If you're relying on your potato-peeling skills to secure you a passage, you'll be thrown overboard after the first bucketload. And anyway, freighters just don't take casual passengers nowadays. There are all sorts of union rules.'

'Well, I could build a raft. There was this raft built entirely of reeds, see, called the *Kon-Tiki*, and I'm sure that—'

'Sandy, you are not to build a raft. Is that clear?'

I nodded meekly. I knew better than to argue. Maggie sighed crossly and shook her head.

'You really haven't thought this through, have you?' She must have sensed I was crestfallen, because she added more kindly, 'Couldn't you fly just a little of the way? Just from here back to Australia? Or to Singapore or Cape Town and then travel overland from there?'

But no. I shook my head, tight-lipped. No flying, dammit. I'd made a promise to myself, and there were even clear instructions to that effect. I had looked them up in the little Iona guidebook before I left. '*Any pilgrim who travels to this holy place, over land and over sea ...*' There was no mention of international air-travel.

'Well, how then?' said Maggie, exasperated once more.

'Well, I did wonder about the bellies of whales. You know that story about Jonah? I've often wondered ...'

'No whales.'

'Well, no, but—'

'Sandy, no whales!'

'Right-o.'

We lapsed into silence while the fire hissed and crackled and threw leaping shadows around the log-cabin walls. The brandy winked and was still.

'You could try a yacht,' said a voice from the corner, deep in the shadows. There, seated in a cavernous armchair, a fellow traveller had emerged from behind an old *National Geographic* to contribute to our conversation. We hadn't noticed him there. He hadn't been on the Milford Track walk with us and for all I know, he could have been some resident oracle, emerging from the woodwork to offer timely advice. Whatever he was, his advice was welcome. It seemed that far, far to the north, in the northernmost region of New Zealand, there was a place called the Bay of Islands. Here, the man said, crewing jobs on yachts were to be had for the asking. From there, he went on, yachts sail away to the Solomons, to New Guinea, to Fiji, to Australia, to the Americas ...

The list went on and before I knew it, I was joining in, my own imagination leading the way down this suddenly hopeful avenue of wayward chance. I had grabbed the map and was scanning it. 'See, Maggie, hear what he says, yachts to Thursday Island, to Christmas Island, to Easter Island … to the Whitsundays, to Vanuatu, the New Hebrides, the Old Hebrides …' My mind drifted from the map and into a map of my own imagination: '… the Spice Islands, the Rice Islands, the Pretty-Jolly-Nice Islands, to Shangri-La, Xanadu and the Far Hesperides! Only make my way to this Bay of Islands,' I burbled, a glint of wild surmise in my eye, 'and I shall surely find myself on one of those yachts, this map tucked under my arm, saying to the salt-eyed skipper, "Er, where are we going exactly then?" What do you think?'

Maggie sat there, biting her lip and glaring a little at the stranger, who had retreated back behind his *National Geographic*.

'Well,' she said doubtfully. 'You could try, I suppose. And at least this gives you somewhere to aim at for now. So you don't just *drift*.' It was clearly a grudging acceptance and much against her own good judgment. Little brother was stretching his wings, and for a moment I felt a little sorry for her. I went to pour out a third brandy for both of us by way of a tiny compensation but I needn't have worried. It took just three seconds for Maggie to reassert the old order. 'But if you're really going to do it, Sandy, then you'll need an early night. You've got a long way to go tomorrow, and you certainly don't need another brandy.'

I stopped mid-pour, glanced at her face and decided not to argue. I carefully poured the brandy back into the bottle, corked it firmly and meekly went to bed.

*

The next morning, Maggie and I said our farewells. A big hug, lots of good-luck wishes and one final piece of sisterly advice.

'Sandy, you know that telescope, the one that Chris gave you?'
'Yes?'
'Well, it's very nice, Sandy, but when you need to use it …'
'Yes?'
'Please don't do it in public. You just look stupid.'

With this sensible counsel in mind, I waved goodbye and set off to walk out of town to the highway near Te Anau. This was it. This was really the beginning. School holidays had ended and all my friends and colleagues and students were starting a new year back home. But here was I, no longer just on a schoolmaster's holiday but a free agent, jobless, potentially penniless, and off on my world travels. I envisaged the vast bulk of the world looming to the north of me, curving in tawny golds and blues and sea-greens all the way round, and my location on it, a flea upon a flea upon a flea in size, clinging to the bottom, setting out to explore the miles under my own steam. It was a giddying thought.

Once I reached the main highway, I set my mental compass to the north, stuck my thumb out and thought northerly thoughts. I was wondering idly how long it would take to get to the Bay of Islands – five days? six days? – when my confidence in the rapidity and efficiency of New Zealand hitchhiking was given a welcome boost by the sudden appearance of a fellow hitchhiker hopping out of a battered station wagon just down the road from where I stood. He looked dazed and bewildered, but was otherwise smiling madly to himself. I asked casually where he had come from.

'Auckland,' he replied.

'Auckland?!' I squawked. Auckland was not only about a thousand miles north of here but also on a totally different landmass. It was as if he had casually mentioned that he had just hitched overnight from Edinburgh to Istanbul.

'Goodness,' said I. 'How many lifts did that take?'

'Just the one,' said he. 'Weird bugger he was. Picked me up in Auckland city, drove me all the way here, fourteen hours in one go, ferry and all. Had a dead lizard on the dashboard. Kittens, that sort of thing.' And with that, off he wandered, shaking his head.

'God bless New Zealand drivers, they even pick up LSD users,' I said happily to myself and settled down to wait, now rather expecting to be in Auckland by the next day. Sure enough, within minutes a white van had slowed down and stopped and I had given my instructions ('Auckland City Central Backpackers', please') to the cheerful red-haired young driver. I soon found myself tumbling into the back of the van and lying on a pile of old fertiliser sacks. I was cut off from any communication with the driver by a windowless panel, and so was unable to ask if the whitish powder coating my hands and beginning to itch was in any way detrimental to my health, but I was happy to be making good progress. I took my mind off the burning sensation in my hands by trying to remember how many miles translated into each degree of latitude and trying to guess how many degrees or minutes of the globe I was crossing off with each mile as I sped towards the equator.

I emerged a few hours later to find myself unaccountably in Invercargill, which, as I knew full well, happens to be even further south than Te Anau, right at the southernmost tip of New Zealand. In fact, Invercargill is about as far south as you can live in the world and not be a penguin. When I emerged from my nest among the fertiliser sacks and asked the driver to explain this merry re-routing, he replied with some considerable surprise, 'But you were on the wrong side of the road back there. I thought it was a bit odd, you wanting to head northwards. I thought you must be a bit confused. Still, Invercargill's nice, you'll enjoy it.' I would have stayed to argue the point, but the skin on my hands was beginning to bubble and I felt that the greater priority was to find a hostel and, if possible, a decontamination centre.

Despite the young man's optimism, I did not enjoy Invercargill one little bit. It is a town about which nothing at all interesting can be said except that it was a grey day, a grey town, bitterly cold and wind-bitten and just what you would expect from the most southerly town of this southerly land. I spent the night in a cheerless hostel, where I sat all alone in the freezing guest lounge in my sleeping bag and watched *Groundhog Day* on the telly. Oddly enough, it *was* Groundhog Day; that is, it was the second of February, the day Bill Murray gets stuck in a time-loop for the entire film. As I watched the movie, I hoped it wasn't an omen. This was meant to be the day on which I launched off into the unknown, not the day I got stuck in a rut.

The next day, making very sure I stood on the right side of the road, I started on my long flightless odyssey to Iona.

37

Chapter 4

You flagg'd walks of the cities! You strong curbs at the edges!
You ferries! You planks and posts of wharves! You timber-
    lined side! You distant ships! …
From the living and the dead you have peopled your impassive
    surfaces,
And the spirits thereof would be evident and amicable with me.
    —WALT WHITMAN, *Song of the Open Road*

Before setting out on my odyssey, I had done something rash. Two rather up-market friends of mine, Jonathan and Alicia, had hosted a farewell dinner party and invited along all those other friends of mine who were keen to see me on my way. It was a jolly occasion with free-flowing wine and lots of touching farewell speeches, mostly by me. There was an awful lot of stuff along the lines of 'Not for me the skippity-hopping of air-travel, the tinkly-tonkle of vodka chasers thirty-thousand feet up. No, my friends, my Romans, my countrymen! Phineas Fogg minus the balloon! Doctor Dolittle minus the duck! Tha's me!'

The wine was all the more potent for the fact that the actual meal was – to my philistine taste, at least – entirely inedible, consisting of things such as calf's tongue in aspic and shark's lips in a béchamel sauce. At the dinner party was one of my more eccentric friends, Newton, who was due to travel to England sometime later in the year, travelling through India and neighbouring places on the way. I was in a fanciful and sentimental mood and, to distract my attention from the candied sea-urchins I had just unwisely sampled, I made a sudden declaration of faith.

'Newton, old friend, old bean,' I slurred. 'Let us make a pact! I will meet you under the clocktower of the Kathmandu post office at midday on May the first! Come hurricane, head-hunters, hell or high water, I will be there!'

It was a grand gesture straight out of a book like *The Thirty-Nine*

Steps. Soon, however, I felt an urgent need to visit the bathroom, occasioned by the sea-urchins. Once in the coolness of the toilet cubicle and having said goodbye to the sea-urchins for ever, I thought better of such a rash undertaking and decided to tell Newton that it was a silly idea and not to bother about it. But then, when I returned to the table, I found he had already left. 'Oh well,' I thought, 'it's a sign.' Ever since then I had remained determined to stick to the agreement. This determination was now about to cause problems.

In Auckland, I started looking for boats heading for New Guinea, or east to the Pacific isles or anywhere really – so long as it was pretty soon, in time to have me in Nepal for our May Day rendezvous. Every yachty I spoke to – well, both of them – was adamant that I would be best off heading to the Bay of Islands, as our shadowy friend in the log-cabin hostel had recommended. This place, I was told, was a Mecca for the cruising world about three hours north, situated on the east coast just before the North Island starts tapering off to the wild needle headland of Cape Reinga and the Ninety-Mile Beach.

When I arrived one golden evening I found it to be stunningly beautiful, a sort of cross between deepest Devonshire and a sun-drenched Barrier Reef island. Here were rolling green hills, the rich green of dairy land, folding into winding forested river valleys where the tall Kauri trees grow. At the mouths of these valleys clustered little red-roofed villages, clinging to old wharves and jetties, bleached silver-grey in the sun: a white weatherboard church here on the green swell of a knoll, a hedge of hibiscus flowers all in bloom there, and everywhere a glimpse of the blue, blue sea, sprinkled with islands near and far, each with its own little village and quay.

But not for me the splendours of the archipelago. I was there on business, and I set about tuning my intuitive antennae to the certain foreknowledge that somewhere here was a yacht waiting to take me on the first major leg of my journey. So followed a seemingly timeless span of gentle searching, a sort of treasure hunt with a gleaming pearl of a yacht as the final prize. For a week, three weeks, I cannot remember, I wandered down blistering wooden jetties to faded boat clubs with noticeboards full of year-old bleached notices and dead blowflies. I hopped on inter-island ferries that ploughed white furrows from historic island to historic island. I spoke to grizzled seadogs sitting smoking on bollards, to smart American ladies

spring-cleaning their yachts, to old chuckling post mistresses in dark shops licking stamps – and everywhere received the same answer: no yachts would be leaving for New Guinea or the Pacific islands until well into May. They all had some piffling excuse about it being the hurricane season or some such nonsense – a very super-stitious lot, sailors. As someone who likes to have my good ideas put into action by others immediately, I found this sort of thing very irritating.

The one gleam of hope lay in the fact that I was constantly being directed to seek out a man by the name of George Bateman, reputed to be something of an oracle, who lived above the tiny harbour of Opua. One afternoon I wandered up to his whitewashed house on a hill above the wharf and knocked on the door. It was flung open by a handsome lady in a sari, her grey hair tied up in a bun with a pink hibiscus flower stuck in it, like a paper parasol in a tropical cocktail.

'Hello,' I began, 'I'm terribly sorry to bother you but—'

I got no further before the lady turned and called back into the house. 'George!' she called. 'George! Visitors!' She turned to face me once more, a welcoming smile on her face. 'Hello, do come in, how lovely to see you, I'm Dorothy, of course, and … GEORGE! … I'm so sorry, he's out the back, my goodness it's hot, isn't it, don't stand there, come through and meet the others, I expect you'd like a beer, now … GEORGE, ARE YOU THERE? … there you are, the beer's not terribly cold, I'm afraid, but … GEOR … oh, here's George, this is George, and this is Amy and Mike from the States, and this is my mother, and Bob and Dee over there off *Starchaser*, of course, you'll have seen her in the bay no doubt. Now, are you quite comfortable? An orange juice, perhaps? Now do tell us all about yourself and how we can help you … and my! We don't even know your name yet.'

That was how I met George and Dorothy Bateman and found that my informants had been quite right. There was not a yacht or captain in the whole of Northland who was not known to the Batemans: their itineraries, their crew requirements, their destinations, their rigging, their state of repair, their personality disorders. George, equipped with his own ship's radio, was in fact a sort of unofficial Harbour Master of Opua and surrounding ports. Most visiting yachties would come through that hibiscus-lined front door at some stage of their stay in New Zealand waters.

George was a short man with a sailor's rolling gait, a pair of rheumy eyes like an elderly spaniel, wispy white hair and a sunburnt face the pinky-orange colour and scaly texture of a large starfish. On both that first and subsequent visits, he would greet me in a hoarse whisper, which gave everything he said the air of a shared confidence, and would regale me with endless and fascinating tales of yachting life, which would leave me utterly bemused. The problem was that from the very start, George credited me with a rich knowledge of that life which I did not have. Consequently there were often times when he was asking me to share in the astonishing fact that a twenty-foot gaffer had managed to rig a side-warp on her lee side and so execute a perfect half nelson in the teeth of a roaring forty-fiver, can you believe that, Sandy, a side-warp?! On a gaffer?! … until Dorothy intervened with a welcome beer and a plate of the inevitable walnut slice.

On that first day when I explained my plans, both George and Dorothy shook their heads ruefully. The advice I had received was correct: no yachtsman who knew anything about anything would be venturing out into the Pacific, the Coral or the Tasman seas before mid-May. They were sorry; would I like to stay for dinner or at least another beer? But no. I was too despondent. Besides, I had another idea, and needed to get back to Auckland to start putting it into practice.

Since the idea of hitching on a yacht seemed out of the question, I decided that my next line of attack would be to get a passage on a friendly freighter. Travellers' tales that I had heard over the years abounded with such experiences, so much so that I wondered why my parents had ever paid full fare on a passenger liner all those years ago on our way to England. It seemed all one had to do was wander into a shipping office, have a chat with a passing captain and find oneself three days later steaming out into the Pacific, nestled down among sacks of potatoes or pig-iron in the hold somewhere. Presumably money might change hands at some stage, or better still, one could pay one's way with some deck-swabbing or by cutting up sauerkraut in the galley or even … here was an idea … by keeping the crew amused with the odd hornpipe on the tin-whistle. The world of international sea freight was about to unfold before me: shipping firms, cargo carriers, rusty tankers, tramp steamers, trawlers … and there was even the exciting possibility of stowing away!

An effortless hitch southward soon had me back in Auckland, and a more auspicious place than this for freighters it would be difficult to imagine. From here, cargo ships sail for every port in the world. Surely it would be possible to find a passage on one of these leviathans. A quick consultation of the Yellow Pages under 'Shipping' made me grin from ear to ear. I was right: Sofrana Lines, Columbus Cargoes, Unilines, Southern Star Shipping, NZ Maritime – the list went on for three whole pages and most of them seemed to be located within a few blocks of my hostel. I decided to eschew the impersonal approach of the telephone and just turn up. I felt excited, as though I were going for some sort of audition. As I set off into the Auckland sunshine, I considered my options. Papua New Guinea would be good. I could trek up through the highlands on my way to Nepal and perhaps discover a lost tribe or at least see some birds of paradise along the way. But I was quite happy to consider other options. One mustn't be fussy.

Sofrana Lines first, then, located, according to the Yellow Pages, on the tenth floor of the Union Building, West Auckland. Tramp, tramp, tramp, whistle, whistle …

Elevator, elevator. Whistle, whistle. New Guinea. Mmmmm …

Only they weren't there. A nice lady explained that they had moved just three months before to the East Plaza building across town, ten blocks away.

Never mind. Sun still shining. Tramp, tramp, whistle, whistle. East Whatsit building. Elevator to the thirteenth floor.

No sign of Sofrana Lines. Nice Lady No. 2 explains mirthfully that deary me, no, this isn't the East *Plaza* building, this is East *Place* Towers, quite different, you see, you passed the East Plaza building half an hour ago.

Sigh. Treat it as a sort of treasure hunt, Sandy, you like those, don't you? Tramp, tramp, tramp, not quite so much of the whistling this time, and I finally track down the East Plaza building, ascend the elevator and find Sofrana Lines.

Nice Lady No. 3 tells me that Sofrana cannot possibly help me as they have no ships going anywhere, anywhere at all, and I am tempted to ask how this can be so if they're a shipping line or perhaps they've changed their line of work to floristry, say ... but why don't I try Columbus Cargoes?

Okay. Where?

In the Union Building, former location of Sofrana, and my starting point three hours ago ... tramp, tramp, tramp ... and now, as I find out when I arrive there, also the former location of Columbus Cargoes. It seems that every shipping firm in Auckland has, in the three months since the printing of the telephone directory, decided that a change of scenery would be nice and shifted premises to an office block across the other side of town. Nice Lady No. 4 explains that Columbus Cargoes is now operating out of East Place Towers twelve blocks away, not to be confused with East Plaza, common mistake that, did I know my way, yes thank you, only too well.

By the time I had tracked them down three office blocks later and been told no chance, but try Unilines (*Where? The Regent Building. Oh, is it near here? No, Wellington actually*), my dream of birds of paradise – I was planning to make a hat from their plumes – was fading fast.

This whole process, so tedious in the telling but – I can assure you, dear reader – infinitely more tedious in the doing, went on for another five days, days in which the temperature in mid-city Auckland soared into the forties and my spirits plummeted, as did my expectations. It didn't help that every secretary I spoke to over those five days would finish our conversation on a faintly puzzled note, wondering if I had considered the possibility of catching a plane.

'Good God!' I'd cry. 'A plane! So simple, it's brilliant! Why did I never think of it? Air travel! That's certainly one use of the aviation industry I'd never even thought to consider. But now I see it all! How can I ever thank you?'

The only problem, of course, was that these outbursts were never directed at the kind ladies themselves but rather were muttered by me furiously as a form of mental and emotional sustenance as I strode through the baking streets to yet another futile encounter with the shipping firms of Auckland.

Over those five days, I learnt from a number of increasingly tetchy shipping-firm receptionists that times had changed. The unions had stepped in and new regulations had come into being, making the possibility of leapfrogging around the world as a casual part-time potato-peeler completely non-existent. It seemed that my romantic pretensions were being stymied at every turn. I couldn't possibly wait another two months for the yachting community to summon up the courage to set sail, and the freighter community had closed ranks. Auckland had lost its charm, the hostel was costing a bomb, and I longed to be on my way. It was time to do something naughty. This is what I did.

I knew from a shipping itinerary – I had sneaked a glance at a dossier while a kind lady was fetching me a glass of water – that Sofrana Lines *did* in fact have a ship leaving for Port Moresby in the next day or two, the *Quiros*. I had already been told firmly by the crew manager in the office that no, there was no possibility of taking a passenger, the insurance alone would be a nightmare if I cut my thumb on a rusty potato peeler, you understand, I'm sure. Getting nowhere, I wandered despondently away from the office block. However, half a block away, I thought to myself, 'Bugger this,' and rang the firm back. Putting on a fake Greek accent, with the idea that I might be taken for a member of the Onassis dynasty, I asked where the ship was docked and tramped off to find it. The jaunty whistling had resumed, a sure sign that my adrenaline was up and that I was bound for success.

At the entrance to the docks was a large security gate with two large guards. There were conspicuous notices saying *Trespassers Prosecuted* and *Entry Permits Required* and *Restricted Access*, the common theme being absolute non-entry for casual passers-by. So I took out a sheaf of papers, a manila folder and a pen, and, adopting a purposeful and slightly harried expression, strode up to one of the guards and muttered crossly, 'The *Quiros*? She's not where she's meant to be. It says here …'

The guard pointed out a large rusty-looking freighter lying at a nearby pier. I shook my head, gave an exasperated 'Tch' and put a large tick on my sheaf of papers. The guard gave me a rueful and commiserating shrug – *Bloody bureaucracy, eh?* – and I nodded a curt thanks and strode on towards the ship. A similar act took me past a second guard at the foot of the gangplank, past three sailors chipping paint on the way up the ramp, past two officers inspecting a hawser and finally found me directions to the bridge and into the presence of the captain himself.

My heart fell. This was no jolly son-of-the-sea, a fellow comrade-in-arms with a healthy contempt for the pettifogging rules of the unions. This was a surly Swede with black hair and warts, and despite all the winning charm I could throw at him, he was adamant. No. He couldn't take me, he wasn't allowed to. Union regulations forbade it. No, look, he really couldn't, there wasn't any room. No, I couldn't sleep on a sack of potatoes in the galley, no, nor onions, now please get off his ship. No, it really was impossible. Look, which part of the word 'No' was it that I didn't understand?

This is not how these things are meant to work out. Stories, and especially the story that I persist in regarding as my life, don't just fall flat like this. I burbled on. Sea-travel, I enthused. Palm trees. Foreign shores, Papua New Guinea and birds of paradise. Dolphins at the bow and typhoons on the starboard quarter. I'm not sure exactly what I said, but miraculously, after twenty minutes, I got him grudgingly to say the following: 'Look, look, shut up for a minute, would you? Here's what I say to you. If the bosses back at the office say I have to take you, then I will. I won't be happy about it but I'll have to, won't I? All right? Now please stop talking about headhunters and leave my ship.'

Yippee, I thought, the old Mackinnon determination paying dividends. I'll be on this ship, the good ship *Quiros*, when she sails at … when? Seven o'clock tonight! It was now 4.40. I had precisely twenty minutes to sprint the thirteen city blocks back to see the crew manager before the Sofrana offices closed.

Gangplank, docks and guards were a blur as I pelted back the way I had come. The rush-hour crowds of Auckland parted like the Red Sea before my torpedo-like haste. I arrived at Sofrana Lines melting into my boots with five minutes to spare and had to have a quick unscheduled lie-down on the grey carpet in front of the polished reception desk before I was able to speak coherently.

'Could I see the crew manager, please?'

I was told by the coolly disapproving secretary that the crew manager was in a meeting. I took a deep breath, pushed aside twenty-seven years of good breeding, imagined that I was from Texas, say, and insisted on seeing him at once. This was, after all, important. This was my one chance out of here before May. The crew manager emerged from his meeting looking less polite than previously. I told him in a glib rattle that I'd just popped down to see the captain of the *Quiros*, we'd had a good old chat, got on like a house on fire, he'd been rather taken by the idea of me coming along for the ride, getting up some entertainment for the crew perhaps, was an old friend of my Swedish godfather's in fact, funny thing, small world, and well, he'd just sent me along to clear it with the office so if he'd just dash off a quick note of approval, I'd be out of his hair in a jiffy. How about it then?

The answer was No.

No. No. No.

I was shown to the door and that was that. Short of forging a note from the crew manager – and I did consider it briefly – my plans to sail away from New Zealand by sea were scuppered. Something was wrong. The tide had turned. My luck had failed.

It would have to be a flight after all.

I went to the phone-box with a piece of paper in my hand. On it I had scribbled the number of New Zealand Airlines. Yes, I would swallow all my sarcasm and my pride and allow myself to be advised by the nice ladies of the Auckland Shipping Secretarial body. I would fly back to Australia on the first available flight out – that night, if there was one.

I tried the number and it was engaged.

In attempting to redial, I dropped the scrap of paper and it fluttered to the floor. It had another number on the back, one I had scribbled down earlier. But whose? Sofrana Lines? No. Something redolent of hibiscus and beer? Ah yes, of course, the Batemans' number up in Opua. I stopped mid-dial and hung up again. I had just enough money to give the Batemans a call, one last call before I ordered an air-ticket out of there. George answered the phone, and I recognised his friendly wheeze.

'Hello, who is it? Sandy? Yes, of course we remember you – Dorothy, it's Sandy! – yes, we were hoping you would ring. New Guinea you were after, wasn't it? Well, we've just had a letter from a skipper, nice fellow, Dutch I think, sailing in a week or so to Port Moresby. Yes, yes, looking for crew. Interested? Splendid. Well, here's his number, old boy. He's just half an hour outside Auckland, so you could probably see him tonight. Give him a ring.'

And I did. And later that night, I went to see him. He was a snowy-haired sea-captain with a face as brown as a nut, and a large cherrywood pipe that gave out quantities of fragrant blue smoke.

When I arrived, he poured out two large schnapps and explained that he had just two questions. I braced myself.

'Vat experience haf you had in ocean sailing?' he asked in a thick Dutch accent.

'Well,' I said casually, 'enough to know that if you want to execute a half-nelson in a roaring forty-fiver, the only thing is to rig a side-warp on her lee side, don't you agree?'

'Veery goot, *ja*. Now, veery important, zis next question, *ja*?'

'Yes?'

'Brahms or Haydn? Vich do you prefer?'

'Oh, definitely Haydn,' I replied.

There was a pause.

'Goot! Me too! Ve sail in a week.'

Yes, I would sail on a yacht with a lovely white-haired Dutchman who played Haydn as he sailed and who would be in Queensland by the end of March. I would then be well on my way to Nepal, where I expected Newton to be waiting in the shadow of the Kathmandu post office at midday on the first day of May. He'd jolly well better be there, that's all.

Chapter 5

There is nothing better than a change of air in this malady (melancholia) than to wander up and down, as those Tartari Zamolhenses that live in hordes, and take the opportunity of times, places, seasons.

—ROBERT BURTON, *The Anatomy of Melancholy*

On this particular trip, I must have written more than a thousand pages home in the form of letters to friends and family. Many of these were illuminated along the margins or the page-heads with amateur sketches done in a child's set of coloured pencils I bought somewhere along the way. They were a labour of love, a complete record of my every waking minute.

Of course, my good news about the Dutch skipper and my finding a yacht against all odds was one of the first things I had to share with my friends and family back home, and that very night five letters went to various parts of Australia telling them smugly of my good fortune, each one illustrated with a natty yacht sailing across the top of the front page, bearing a horn-pipe-dancing Dutchman and a grinning self-portrait joining in.

Three days later, I sent off five identically addressed letters telling them to forget it, the trip was off. These were free of illustrations, and in most of them the pen had gone right through the paper.

Having arranged to return in a fortnight and set sail, I spent a couple of days sitting in the front room of the hostel grinning from ear to ear at nobody in particular, waiting for strangers to ask what I was smiling at, and then telling them in no uncertain terms just how lucky and clever I was. When people started avoiding me, I had a thought. I would take up an offer I had received of staying at a nearby dairy farm, do a fortnight's work and earn some pocket money. A phone call to the farmer, Mr Lyle, confirmed that he was still happy to have me, so I hitched down and started work.

Up until that point, my agricultural experience had been limited to mowing the back lawn, so when I was woken in the pitchy dark that first morning and shown to the milking stalls, I was apprehensive. I had never milked a cow before. An hour later, I had milked 200 of them. It was a humbling experience, fondling the backside of a bovine and being painted with green cow-muck with every swish of a filthy tail. But udders were not the horrible saggy damp things I had thought them; they were warm and hairy and rather nice, actually. The cows, though a bit dopier than, say, hamsters on pethidine, were good-natured creatures and at least didn't keep pestering me as to whether the morning's classroom activities were going to be included in the assessment. And here's another thing: milk – not many people know this – when it first comes out of the cow is actually blue ... a very pale shade, admittedly, but quite definitely a washed-out winter-sky blue. Or perhaps that is only in New Zealand, and caused by the cows drinking all that Bombay Sapphire blue water.

Five o'clock in the morning had never been my favourite time for rising, but it was nice to know that after three hours' work in the dairy and a hot shower, the whole sunny day lay ahead of me, starting off with a farmhouse breakfast of porridge and brown sugar, pork sausages, fried eggs and tea served in a solid china pot, straight off the Aga stove. Then it was out to mend a gate, banging happily around with hammers and spanners in the open hedgerow, or to prune the young pine trees along a lonely field's margin, feeling like a character in a Robert Frost poem and smelling like Christmas. Yes, it was a good life, clean, hard, peaceful, slow-paced ...

All one and a half days of it.

On the second morning I went into the big barn, a cavernous place with hay and tractor oil and rain on the roof, and found Sooty the farm cat nursing a squirm of grey kittens in the straw. Lying in the middle of the floor was a dead goldfinch. A dead goldfinch! Now, this will mean nothing to you unless you have been secretly monitoring my inner life for the last thirty years, so let me explain why the sight struck a cold blow to my heart. I've always liked goldfinches. To be honest – and a little daft – I have always considered them to be my special bird, sacred not to Zeus or Apollo or Hermes, but to me, if that isn't too sacrilegious. And so in the odd, never serious, half-whimsical way people do such things, I have always been pleased to see a goldfinch because I've taken it as a cheering omen, a lucky sight, a nice-sort-of-bird-to-see.

So when I saw the drab bundle of feathers lying there, black and dull scarlet and faded gold, an ominous feeling came over me.

'My mind misgives some consequence, yet hanging in the stars, shall bitterly begin his fearful date with this sweet jester's death,' I misquoted to myself in a theatrical undertone before quickly dismissing the idea of an omen as foolish superstition. Indeed, I said to myself, what better proof could there be of the folly of such fond beliefs? Here was my supposedly lucky bird lying dead, and why! I was at the very pinnacle of my good fortune. I had a crewing position when all the world and his dog said I couldn't get one, I had two weeks to stay in this lovely farm, I was bang on schedule, how much luckier could I get?

Omens? Fiddle-faddle …

My musings were interrupted by Mr Lyle, who came out into the yard calling for me to come to the phone. Odd – I hadn't given anybody my phone number here, had I?

Yes, I had. One person. The Dutch skipper, so that he could ring me and tell me when he was ready to leave.

Or in this case, that he had taken the yacht – our yacht – *my* yacht – out for a trial run last night and smashed her straight onto a reef. The trip was off. Sorry, *Mynheer.*

Meanwhile, out in the barn, my goldfinch was being reduced to a scrunch of feathery splinters by Sooty and the kittens.

For the record, I was later told by a salty old seadog that he had witnessed my Dutchman's departure on his fatal last run. He had watched him sailing out of the harbour swigging from a large bottle of rum and muttering something like 'Reefs? Reefs? I'll show 'em bloody reefs, I vill!' so perhaps it was no bad thing that I did not find myself halfway across the Tasman Sea trying to restrain a sozzled Dutchman from taking on Lord Howe Island single-handedly. Nevertheless, I was back to square one. Despite my stubborn intuition about the almost magical significance of May the first as a meeting-date with Newton, I dashed off a letter to him, the gist of which was, 'Now look here. May the first?! You didn't think I was serious, did you? No, no, no, no, no, just a joke, laddie! Can't we make it July the first?'

I went on to explain that if I could wait another two months, I could have my pick of the yachts and entertain the very firm possibility of seeing some Pacific islands, of being attacked by Indonesian pirates, of marrying a Tahitian girl and having coconut oil rubbed into my deltoids, of getting shipwrecked, of becoming a Scarlet Pimpernel-like hero to the oppressed people of Malacca, of pearl-diving, of feeding stormy petrels by hand, of acquiring skin cancer, of learning to talk to dolphins, of discovering buried treasure on a desert island, of being keel-hauled by a rum-drunk captain, and of becoming the plaything and sole heir to some wealthy yachty widow, aged seventy-eight.

Plus (I added in a hastily invented postscript), May was apparently the mongoose season in Nepal, when torrential downpours and huge, savage, wet mongooses made travel impossible – so we'd just have to make it July the first instead.

I hoped to blazes that Newton hadn't already left.

*

My renewed search for yachts took me back to the Bay of Islands and up the hill to the hibiscus-bright verandah of the Batemans' house. There, over a cooling beer, I explained the outcome of the Dutchman's abortive trip and both George and Dorothy offered their condolences, supported with a slice of pecan pie and a long anecdote from George about Dutch rigging methods and their tendency to overblow in a fore-and-aft gale. Dorothy gently brought George back to the problem at hand, and after some teeth-sucking cogitation he hesitantly said, 'What about Les? There's always Les, I suppose.'

A flicker of alarm crossed Dorothy's kind face and I asked warily, 'Who's Les?'

The Batemans glanced at each other and then launched into a duet. 'Well, he's a marvellous fellow really ... salt of the earth ... not quite sure about … but safe as houses, you understand … difficult to pin down, perhaps … but worth a try … terribly experienced … a touch chaotic, perhaps … your best bet really for getting away this early, I suppose …' and so on.

It emerged that a local, an old salt called Les McLeod, had a small yacht called *Meilani* and that he was one of the very few yachtsmen who took little heed of the prevailing winds and would therefore be setting out soon enough – far sooner, at any rate, than the majority of sailors, who would not be leaving until May. He was an excellent sailor with vast experience and a gentle and amiable nature. As for wanting crew, he'd be bound to need somebody, being on his own. The only problem was that he was notoriously difficult to pin down. The only thing the Batemans could be fairly sure of was that he was somewhere along this stretch of the coast. It would take time and patience to winkle him out. He could be in any one of a number of coves or bays, estuaries or rivers, keeping quietly to himself as was his wont, waiting for the right time to set sail. Both George and Dorothy shook their heads at the enormity of the task and expressed their wish that they could be more helpful.

By the time I came to leave, I had decided that the quest was worth embarking on. I was a free agent, I had plenty of time and a good pair of walking legs and besides, there was nothing better left to do. I set out to find the reclusive Les McLeod.

I could not have had a more enchanting landscape in which to pursue my quarry. All my experience hitherto of the seashore had been bare and treeless – cliffs, sand dunes, mudflats or wide beaches. But here, the forest and the sea met and kissed. Burning blue convolvulus vines hung down the cliff-stone to trail along secluded sandy beaches; tree ferns stood with bleached driftwood about their shaggy boles; yellow leaves from tall kauri trees drifted in the seawater, calm and silky and warm as milk.

And out in the bays, filling every inlet and cove, every strait and passage, was another forest: a forest of masts, their halyards clanking like some strange frog-song, their pennants and flags hanging like strange bright blooms. But where among all these yachts was *Meilani*? Here my little telescope came into play. Often the yachts were riding at anchor out on the water, too far out to see their names properly. Ignoring Maggie's parting advice, I would whip out the telescope and scan the boats. One by one I would read their names: *Sea-Wanderer, Magic Dragon, Odyssey, Wave-Dancer, Argo, Happy-*

Part I

Go-Lucky, Sprite, Pegasus, Will-o-the-Wisp, Chieftain, Swashbuckler, Candyman, Western Star, Sunseeker ...
But no *Meilani*. Not on the first day, not on the second, and not even by the end of the first week. In the meantime, I was running out of funds. I was staying in a hostel in the regional centre of Paihia and, to pay my board and keep, started each day with two hours of cleaning: scrubbing bathrooms and toilets, changing pillowcases, sweeping and hoovering, cleaning up in the kitchen. I became briskly efficient, even inventing an ingenious new method to cope with the little curly hairs that congregate in baths and basins every-where. Each morning I spent a good half-hour chasing the springy little devils around with a sponge and still failed to remove them, until I hit upon the idea of using Blu-Tack. With a blob of this, I would go dab-dab-dab around the bath, picking up each bit of hair individually. By the end of the first week, I had collected enough short-and-curlies to stuff a small mattress. I thought I might present just such a mattress to Les as a contribution to the yacht-furnishings, if I ever managed to find him.

*

Finally, after days had turned into weeks, and weeks had turned into nearly a month, and all my following up of leads had come to nothing, I decided to take a new approach, eschewing the dull rigours of commonsense and following an older and wiser guide – Merlin. In particular, I had in mind the fifth-century Merlin drawn by Mary Stewart in *The Crystal Cave* and its sequels. In this retelling of the Arthurian legends, despite his fearsome reputation as an enchanter, the very human Merlin possesses in fact very little magic, but he does attune himself to the signs of wind and sky, of old way-marks and the residue of local legend. Small omens guide his way – a flooded ford, a broken stone cross, the flight of a falcon across his path – and it seems that good fortune or the gods are behind every hilltop shrine or cloud. I felt that in my quest for Les the Fisherman, I could do worse than try this approach. To that end, I bade farewell to Paihia and the Blu-Tack and headed north.

I travelled by omens. A goldfinch might flutter off down one laneway and I would turn my steps that way and waltz into some new adventure. A mangled crow lay at the roadside and I would shun that hitching spot and seek another, and so stumble onto some new and unforeseen delight. My travels took on the episodic nature of a treasure hunt or a quest in an old story, where the hero is directed onward only in short bursts of information. *You must find the tree in the forest whose berries are golden, and there you will be told what to do next,* says the old woman. *If you see a woodchopper along the way, you must offer him a piece of barley-bread,* sings the little bird. *He will help you further in your quest.*

Not that all such adventures were to the point. My first lift out of Paihia was provided by an earnest young couple who asked me where I was going and what I was doing. I explained that I was looking for a fellow called Les McLeod, a fisherman of sorts, and they immediately looked across at each other and said in unison, 'The fisherman! We know who you're looking for,' and gave each other big, crinkly-eyed grins across the car.

'Well, that was easy,' I thought, but they refused to elaborate. Instead, they took me to a sunny riverside meadow where stood an ancient and eccentric vehicle. It was an old-fashioned delivery van in dark green that had been converted into a sort of gypsy caravan, replete with white hens nesting on the dashboard, a pot-bellied stove, bunches of dried herbs overhead, red-and-white checked curtains, a net bag of brown onions, a tambourine, a very thin black cat with mad gold eyes, a crockpot stuffed with grubby dollar notes, an unhygienic-looking mattress covered in a faded burgundy quilt, and a dead rabbit strung up over the sink. There was also a large Bible and a stack of brightly coloured pamphlets.

'Does Les live here?' I asked tentatively.

'The fisherman?' my couple chorused. 'Yes, come and meet the fisherman. He is the only man you need to meet.'

A cup of tea was placed in my hands and there was a brief period of silent communion. 'Um …' I started, but before I could continue they whipped out a leaflet.

'Have you met Jesus Christ, the one true fisherman?'

I was sorely tempted to reply, 'No, does he have a yacht?' But I chickened out and mumbled, 'Er, I'm Anglican, if that helps,' instead.

'Praise the Lord!' they cried in unison. The cat scrabbled up the curtains in alarm.

'Yes, absolutely,' I replied, backing out of the caravan, knocking my head on the dead rabbit on the way out.

I hurried on along the road for a couple of miles; but as the day was hot, I sat down for a rest beneath a huge yew tree and played my

tin-whistle. A herd of six pigs came up behind me and oinked and squealed every time I stopped playing. Whenever I started up again, they'd scratch themselves against the wooden fence-posts and settle down to listen. This was all rather nice and pastoral. As I sat there in the sunshine, I noted with ridiculous pleasure that bees in New Zealand are real bumblebees, real honey-jumble dumbledores, fat and black and furry as mice. You could use them to stuff cushions with instead of curly shower-hairs. I was soon picked up by an old farmer in a battered old station wagon. Sitting on the dashboard was a collection of dusty items: a large rubber iguana; two wind-up toy birds with real feathers faded to drab white; three pin-ups of Betty Grable; a hideous china pussycat with a green bow and a plastic water-pistol. He asked where I was headed, but when I told him Manganui, a harbour village some eighty miles to the north, he muttered in a surly manner that he was just going a few kilometres up the road, bloody hitchhikers, thought they owned the place, pushy buggers, and then relapsed into a moody silence.

Twenty kilometres passed and I tentatively asked where he was headed. 'My brother's farm,' he said, 'just over the next hill. Don't push your luck, sonny.'

'No, no, absolutely, that'll be just fine, and thank you, thank you very much,' I burbled and sat back, relieved that I might soon be out of there.

Well, the next hill came and went ... and then another range of hills ... and a small town, and a river, and a long stretch of coastline, and again I ventured to comment, 'Look, don't go out of your way for me, will you, please,' to which he replied, 'Round the next bend and not a step further, chum, I'm not a taxi service you know,' and then launched out of his moody silence into a long and alarming story about what the Maoris used to do to strangers who desecrated their burial sites. We had just reached some of the gorier details when we drew up before a road sign saying Manganui. He swung the car violently off the road, down a little track to a bit of secluded beach, and stopped.

'Right, out you get, sonny. Photograph time.'

Oh God, I thought. *This is it. This is where I have to punch an old man in the face and run like blazes, seconds after he asks me to take all my clothes off and put them over there on top of his.*

I was just backing away when I remembered something. Something I had heard from that lucky hitchhiker way down in Te Anau … about a dead lizard and a photo and being taken the length of New Zealand just for the asking. Great Scott! This was the same man – the Angel of the North!

And so it turned out to be. The driver – his name was Jim – proceeded now to tell me his story. His manner had completely changed. No longer was I dealing with a surly dwarf. The transformed Jim danced around on the grass, rubbing his hands, clicking away with his camera and beaming from ear to ear while he told me his remarkable story. After the death of his wife a few years ago, he had retired from farming, intending to settle down to an idle old age after a lifetime of backbreaking work. However, as often happens with people who suddenly find their life devoid of purpose, Jim had become moody and depressed, a nuisance to his children and a miserable – and too frequent – presence in the local pub. During one particularly morose foray into the Slough of Despond, he had decided that the best thing would be to take his shotgun, drive out to some secluded spot in the countryside and put himself out of his misery.

It just happened that on that particular day, there was a hitchhiker standing in the rain and freezing wind, thumb out in an impossibly remote spot, a road that led nowhere but the abandoned quarry where Jim had intended to dispatch himself. So exasperated was he by the apparent hopelessness of the sodden hitchhiker's situation that he had pulled over and enquired (somewhat testily, no doubt) where the blazes the chap thought he was heading. On being told that the befuddled hiker was aiming for a town some three hours away and in a completely different direction, Jim had come to the grudging conclusion that he might as well set the fool off on the right road at least. He had driven the hiker back to the main highway; but as the rain was still coming down in buckets, it seemed a little heartless to eject him into the elements and so, one thing leading to another and having nothing on the agenda but killing himself – and with a fair amount of petrol still in the tank, which it would be a pity to waste – Jim had eventually driven the bedraggled fellow all the way to the distant town. After dropping him off, Jim realised that such a sense of purpose and good will had stolen over him that he thought he might postpone the trip to oblivion for a bit and do something similar the next day.

From that time on, Jim had spent his days touring the country in his station wagon, picking up hitchhikers. He would take them to wherever they wanted to go, having his own little joke with them all the way about just going to the next bend. At the end of the journey, all he asked was that they allow themselves to be photographed for his album and that they sign his visitors' book. As we stood there in the little inlet, Jim proudly showed me two things. The first was his album, full of surprised but beaming hitchhikers – some looking a little pale with shock and relief – and a wealth of comments written by people from all over the world. In fact, that very day Jim had received through the post a slice of wedding cake from a Danish couple who, a year before, had considered his startling generosity so propitious that they had proposed to each other in his car. Breaking the moist, crumbly slice in two, he proudly pressed half into my hand; it was rich and dark and reeked of brandy. The second thing he showed me, opening the boot to do so, was his shotgun. 'It's still there, and still loaded,' he said, 'but I don't think I'll be needing it now. Still,' he added cheerfully, as he balanced the camera on the bonnet of the car and set it to automatic, then joined me in the picture, holding the shotgun casually at his side while the camera whirred and went off, 'you never know, do you?'

As he munched on his slice of wedding cake, he promised through mouthfuls of crumbs to send a copy of the photo he had just taken of me to my parents back in Australia. I thanked him and wrote down their address, hoping they wouldn't think it was some sort of ransom note.

Just as he was putting his shotgun back in the boot and preparing to leave, a thought struck me. 'You don't know a Les McLeod, do you? A chap on a yacht hereabouts?'

Jim straightened up. He looked me straight in the eye, all the sparkle draining from his face.

'It's always bloody Les McLeod, isn't it? I dunno, bloody hitch-hikers! Hah!' He then lowered his voice to a malevolent hiss and, spitting crumbs, whispered somewhat mysteriously, *'He's not the bloody pope, you know ...'*

Before I could ask any further questions, Jim, surly manic farmer once more, had jumped into his car and taken off. I stood looking after him, my mouth hanging open, my thoughts churning slowly. I replayed the last hour or so in my mind. Then I walked off, determined to find a nice, soothing cup of tea and somebody sane to talk to.

*

Manganui was a quiet, hill-ringed harbour with a grey stone seawall and one little road that ran below a wooded bluff. There was a fine old hotel and pub, a wooden jetty, a general store, a row of Moreton Bay figs and hoketi trees with scarlet blossoms, and a hostel, the Old Oak Inn. Everywhere I went, I asked if they'd heard of Les McLeod and everywhere I went, people looked at me blankly. One concerned old lady in a tea shop asked why I was so sure that this Les McLeod would be in Manganui, but I didn't have the heart to explain that I was following hunches based on stray goldfinches. Perhaps I was thinking of Mang-o-nui, with an 'o', not Mang-a-nui with an 'a', dear ...

'Is there a Mang-o-nui with an 'o' somewhere?' I asked.

'Oh yes, love,' I was told. 'Just outside Auckland.'

I could do nothing but have another cup of tea.

But the goldfinch trail wasn't a complete dead-end. That afternoon I wandered down the quiet Sunday street to the wharf and there found a figure I had been searching for all my life. He was simply a busker, a young Dutchman dressed in antique clothes, but he was the very person I wanted to be, the living soul of the dream

I was pursuing in this odyssey of mine. If the old tales are true and the Pied Piper still walks the daylight earth, if the Dancing Fool of the Tarot has an earthly representation, then I have seen him. His shoes are buckled with silver and on one leg he sports a leather strap hung with bells that jingle at his knee. About his neck hangs a polished black wooden flute, tiny, no longer than a fountain pen. The tunes he plays on it are enchanting, as sweet and lively as a tree full of songbirds.

He also plays an accordion, brightly painted with suns and moons and stars. It is like the toy accordion held in the hand of a jack-in-the-box, looking somehow both as if it were painted that morning – tinny and cheap – but also fabulously antique. Playing a rollicking dance-tune on that accordion there in the sunlight, he holds the firmament, all blue and silver and yellow, in his hands.

Tomorrow shall be my dancing day
I would my true love so did chance
To see the legend of my play
To join my true love in the dance.
Sing O! my love! O! my love!
To join my true love in the dance.

When he starts playing on it, you can feel your feet beginning to shuffle and tap. You feel that it is the very music that turns the round world on its axis.

For the only time on my voyage, I wished that I had a camera to capture the scene. But there's the word – 'capture' – so alien a notion to his elusive quality. I am glad now that I didn't end up with a photo. Even if I had, I suspect it would have captured nothing. A magenta bloom of some flowering shrub, perhaps; a fallen doll in ragged patchwork in the gutter; the rainbow-glimmer of a garden sprinkler straying onto the footpath.

But did he know Les McLeod's whereabouts? No, he didn't, though he did know a good song about a mermaid if I cared to listen. I stumped off back to the hostel.

I went for a walk that evening up to the Maori Pa, the old hilltop fort above the village, reminiscent of English earthworks with its distinctive ridged shape and little sheep-tracks criss-crossing the grassy hillside. There, all my preoccupations faded. Why was I so anxious to leave this enchanted place? From the hill's summit I looked down 300 feet to the sea and across an expanse of glittering water to far-off peninsulas on the horizon, or to nearby bays and inlets laid out like a map below me. In the rich golden light of late afternoon, the colours glowed like oil paints. The hill itself had the magical quality of English hilltop forts: a loneliness, but crowded somehow with something, like a lighthouse built of air and lark-song.

There was something about the place that reminded me of Iona. With this thought, the despair returned. For a pilgrimage to the other side of the world, I hadn't got very far.

The next morning, a great wave of maudlin melancholy came flooding in after the enchantment of the last few days, leaving me as drab and lonely as the sand-flats that I looked out upon from the verandah of the Old Oak Inn. Gulls picked over the remains of washed-up fish and a chill little wind ruffled the salt tide. It was time to pick myself up, find an airport and fly my way out of here. I had seen the Dancing Fool and now there was nothing left to do but get to England with all speed.

Chapter 6

Now Fiddler's Green is a place I've heard tell
Where all sailors go if they don't go to hell.
If you look for the captain upon the bright blue,
You'll find that he's down making tea for the crew ...
So ... wrap me up in me oilskin and jumper!
No more on the docks I'll be seen.
And tell me old shipmates
I'm taking a trip, mates,
And one day I'll see them in Fiddler's Green!

—Sea shanty

Fate, having played me around for a bit, zooming me up and down the coast like a demented tern, finally relented. I found myself in the quiet little town of Kerikeri on my way south and wandered into a shop to buy a pie. As I stood at the till, one of the women behind the counter said to a co-worker, 'That Les, he's a gentleman and no mistake.' When I asked if they happened to be talking about Les McLeod, she replied with a broad grin, 'Yes, love. He's right behind yer.'

And indeed he was.

Les was a wizened gnome of a man with a soft North Country accent, a skin like old bacon and a gentle approach to life. After picking me up off the floor and patting me gingerly on the back to stem my tears, he explained that yes, of course there was a crewing position onboard *Meilani* for a passage across to Australia in the next week or so, nowt to cry about, lad, and that I was more than welcome to join him. The boat was moored in the inlet just down the hill and I could move onboard immediately if I wished.

And so it was that I found myself onboard a yacht, in an official crewing position, with a captain who actually wanted me there and who was not likely to run the boat onto the nearest reef. I wondered if I ought to confess that my previous sailing experience had been limited to pootling around an inland lake in a Mirror dinghy. But I needn't have worried overmuch, either about my competence or the chances of hitting a reef. The yacht wasn't going anywhere in the foreseeable future.

Les McLeod, bless him, had all the sense of urgency of a Zen oyster. Five weeks later, we were still sitting in the Kerikeri Inlet where I had first come aboard and my soul was slowly sinking into the mud and the mangroves, possibly never to revive.

Don't get me wrong. Les McLeod was truly a saintly man, gentle, warm, kindly and positive in everything he said and did. I think that it would be literally true of him that he never said an unkind word about anybody. He certainly didn't about me, despite me giving him every opportunity to do so over the five weeks we spent aboard *Meilani*.

It started the very first night. We had just settled down to sleep, Les in the main saloon and me in the tiny cabin aft. This was so tiny that it was not possible to stand upright; one had to slide into the bunk like a parcel into a letterbox slit. My first night aboard a yacht – let the adventures begin! After about ten minutes I could hear Les gently snoring in the saloon, but I could also hear something else: a sort of crackling, spitting, hissing noise. A fire! A fire aboard! It was the sound of twigs and kindling taking hold before bursting into full flame. I leapt out of bed, gave myself a cracking blow to the head on the low ceiling, and stumbled through to wake Les.

'Les! Les! Sorry to wake you, but the yacht's on fire!'

Les leapt out of his bunk, stared wildly around and dashed for the fire extinguisher, crying, 'Where? Where?'

We looked everywhere, up on deck, in the fore-cabin, the galley, everywhere, but not a thing could we find.

'Did you smell smoke, lad? Well done, you! Now where can it be, eh?'

I explained about the crackling noise I had heard, and there was a little silence.

'Ah, crackling, eh? That'd just be the crustaceans on the hull, lad. Nowt to worry about, they can't get in. But well done, you, for spotting it. Back to sleep then, eh?'

I was far from convinced, but as we couldn't find any evidence of fire and the mysterious crackling had stopped, I went warily back to my bunk.

Twenty minutes later, I was convinced. There *was* a fire, there had to be. The unmistakable sound of splitting twigs, licking flames and crackling timber was coming from close at hand, and it wasn't remotely like the sounds of crabs or whatever Les had said was trying to eat through the hull. Again I got up resolutely, again I cracked my head and again I tiptoed into the saloon. Les opened an eye resignedly.

'Yes, lad?'

'I'm sorry, Les, but there really *is* a fire somewhere, I can hear it, plain as day. Sorry, but …'

'Nay, don't fret, lad, I'm sure you're right, let's have another look round, shall we? Good thing one of us is alert and awake, isn't it? If this were me by myself, I'd be burnt to a crisp by now, like as not.'

*

'If there were a fire, that is,' he added ten minutes later when we had explored the whole ship thoroughly for the second time. 'Never mind, lad, fools a lot of people, that does, on a boat first time at night. See you in the morning then, but if there's anything at all that you're worried about, just let me know and we'll sort it out, all right? Better safe than sorry, eh?'

That was my first sample of the utter patience and saintliness of this man; the first of many. (I later, by the way, came to understand what that strange igneous noise was. Apparently all the tiny barnacles and crustaceans on a ship's hull become active at night and spend their time sucking and clicking on the steel body of the boat. This, magnified by the drum-like nature of the hull, produces a most unwatery sound of dry crackling and hissing and spurting.)

Les's next display of patience came after I had helped him paint the decks, a task he thought we'd better get done before heading out across the Tasman Sea. He took the front half of the boat and I took the back, and after three hours, all I can say is that it was not as easy as it looked. At morning tea, we took a break and Les came and surveyed my handiwork. There was a moment's blanching, and then his kindness kicked in.

'Well done, lad. Goodness me, look at that. Goodness. All that … paint,' he finished lamely.

'Yes, sorry, it's a bit difficult to make it go where you want, isn't it? I mean, you probably didn't want those portholes painted over, did you, or those ropes?'

'No, no, no, you've done a good job there, lad. And those ropes will come clean in a jiffy, and as for the portholes, well, there's always a little bit of paint going astray in these jobs. No, you've done a fine job there.' A pause. '*Have* you ever painted anything before, lad?' 'Well, some set-painting, you know, for plays and things.' 'Really? Really? By gum, I expect that takes some talent, I bet it does. That explains your … style, I expect, eh? Lots of flair in set-painting, I imagine. You've done well.'

He sent me off into town to buy some groceries, and when I came back I found that he'd quietly got on and scraped all the excess paint off shrouds and windows, neatened up all the wobbly edges and thick sticky patches, and it was drying nicely in the sun. At my apologetic look, he explained that he was just touching up a few bits, just putting the final touches to a fine job, my, look at that, what a team we were, me doing the hard graft and him coming along to do the icing on the cake. As he was explaining this and I was edging around being careful to avoid the wet paint where I'd been working all morning, I became aware that the deck beneath my feet felt unaccountably slippery; I skidded about as though on thick grease for a few agonised seconds, clutching the rail, and then looked down. I had skidded straight through the paintwork that *he* had been working on that morning on the front half of the deck, leaving what had been an immaculate coat of fresh paint in ruins.

I turned to face him, my mouth hanging open in horrified apology.

'Now then, now then, lad, it's nowt but a slip. All that front bit has got to be done again anyway, I reckon, because I don't think I did a very good job on it this morning. Just look at it, all streaky and smeary, deary me, what was I thinking?'

After carefully removing my paint-stained shoes to soak clean in turps, and carefully retiring to the saloon, where there was no paintwork to sabotage, I carefully made lunch for us both. We sat eating in silence, broken only by Les occasionally saying through a mouthful of tomato sandwich, 'My, my, these *are* good, lad. What did you say they were called? Tomato sandwiches, eh? My goodness, delicious, you did well.' After some time, he went up on deck and I could hear him repainting the entire front deck while I cringed below, wondering how long such niceness could last in the face of such incompetence. At last he poked his head down the hatch and announced that all the paintwork was now dry, fore and aft, and that I might want to come up and enjoy some fresh air while the light lasted. As my shoes were still soaking in their bucket, I slipped on my only other pair of footwear and went gingerly out onto deck. Yep. Dry. Completely dry. With renewed confidence, I went tripping lightly up to the foredeck, where Les was enjoying a well-earned pipe in the still evening air – and stopped dead as I saw him gazing philosophically at my feet. I glanced down. There, right along the fresh dry paint, the black soles of my riding boots had left great dark streaks of rubber ingrained in the deck. There was a pause, longer and heavier than any there had yet been that day.

'I am so sorry,' I whispered. 'I will now go away and kill myself.'

'No, no, lad, goodness me, a second coat … er, third coat will cover those marks up in a jiffy. My, my, what sturdy boots, eh? I bet they're useful for all the hiking you must do, a fit young feller like you. Lovely big black boots like those, they're a fair treat.'

He paused.

'You might want to get something a little lighter for onboard, mind you, just for comfort like. White-soled things, like sandshoes, just for example.'

The next morning, I woke up a little later than usual, put on my original pair of shoes – the non-deck-marking shoes, all clean and dry – and went gaily up onto deck. I skipped a breezy five paces before stopping dead, aware of an awful stickiness under foot once more. Les was crouched over a now-familiar tin of white paint.

'Cup of tea?' I enquired brightly.

'No thanks, lad. Just got another little job to do.'

*

After this inauspicious beginning, life aboard *Meilani* settled down to be soothing and uneventful and very, very pleasant. We were moored in the Kerikeri Inlet, where the river narrowed to a quiet snaking stretch of water between low wooded hills, on one bank of which was an overgrown Maori earthwork, a maze of ditches and dykes among the flowering broom. Just up the hill was a little whitewashed weatherboard church called St James, and down by the water's edge sat a gracious old tea-house with wide verandahs set in neat lawns. It was a thoroughly tranquil spot to spend one's days, if one didn't have a Kathmandu deadline to meet.

Each day was spent doing a few odd jobs, walking up the hill to do some grocery shopping, sitting in the local library writing a novel that I'd started in a fit of optimism, and sitting chatting to Les over a simple supper in the cabin. He was a fascinating man, though very modest about his achievements. He had once sailed solo across the Pacific, most of the way with a broken arm. On that trip, it being too painful to steer very well to port, he ended up going further and further to starboard – that is, south – and thought that he had bumped into Antarctica at one point. By then he was so cold, he had no feeling in his arm, so could steer whichever way he liked. He was married (he thought), but as he hadn't seen his wife for twenty years or so, he wasn't sure of the current status of this. He was also a very knowledgeable fisherman and spent a few hours daily harvesting the riches of the sea. We would sit down most nights to fresh mussels, pipis, cockles or fillets of fish, which he would pull out of the harbour with considerably more ease than most of us pluck things from the supermarket shelves.

Each evening, over a late-night cup of tea, we would sit and do the cryptic crossword together, at which he was both very skilled and typically modest. When I got a clue, he was all praise for my cleverness, my education, my ingenuity of thought. When *he* got a clue, he attributed it to a lucky guess. His commonest phrase was 'You did well there, you did well,' an observation he applied as enthusiastically to the preparation of a three-course meal as to the successful placing of a used teabag in the rubbish bin. Aboard *Meilani,* it seemed I could do no wrong. If only we were actually going somewhere.

Soon three weeks had passed, and with every day the chances of leaving seemed to diminish. Then one morning, in an uncharacteristic fit of decisiveness, Les decided that it was time we upped the anchor and set off. But first, a quick trial run up and down the estuary to try out the old girl. Les went to start the engine, there was a bang like a very junior Krakatoa, and something large and made of iron blew straight through the cabin roof. (Coat of paint number five coming up.)

Somehow the engine had had seawater sluiced through it, and this apparently doesn't do engines any good at all. I stood on the foredeck praying that it wasn't something I had inadvertently done, though no doubt if it had been, Les would have turned around and praised my initiative in reducing greenhouse gases. Les spent the next four days bashing the engine with mallets, pouring boiling vinegar down the cylinders and sacrificing spotted sheep to the god of engines while I stood by and tried to remember which was the grease-nipple adjustor wrench when called upon to hand him one – but all to no avail. Eventually we spent a day lifting the entire engine (three tons) out of the hold with a Heath Robinson arrangement of ropes and tackle, and left it sitting on the deck, ready to be lowered into the dinghy and rowed ashore. I was sorely tempted to topple the whole thing overboard and blame it on a freak tidal wave. Then we could have no more excuses for delaying and could just *sail* away like they did in the old days before the invention of engines and grease-nipple adjustor wrenches.

For me, of course, the timing was getting tight. In response to my letter to Newton, I had received a postcard back from him, terse in tone but nevertheless agreeing to put our Himalayan rendezvous back to the beginning of July. Even so, I would have to sprint most of the way if I was to make it in time.

In the meantime, Les kept coming up with new ideas to try with the engine. At one stage, when he was suggesting a plan involving Vaseline and a small firecracker, I decided this would be a good time to go to the post office to mail a few letters. The Irish post-mistress, when I mentioned that I was with Les on *Meilani* and that we were due to leave any day now, laughed merrily and said, 'Les? Les McLeod? Ah, bless him. He's been saying that very thing for a while now, to be sure.'

When I replied that yes, I knew, I'd been with him for four weeks, she said: 'Four weeks? He's been saying that for twelve years.'

Twelve years? Les McLeod had failed to mention that he had been sitting in the Kerikeri Inlet dreaming of foreign shores for twelve sodding years!

It was time to reconsider my options.

When I returned to the yacht, I found that Les had perfected his Vaselined-firecracker idea with a set of roughly drawn diagrams and was optimistic about the chances of us sailing within a week.

Les had all sorts of plans for the trip. For a start, he wanted me to teach him how to play the tin-whistle, and any day now he was going to go down to the nearest town and buy one to learn on. Mind you, I knew that any day now in Les-speak meant sometime that century, so I tried teaching him a few techniques using a rolled-up newspaper with the holes drawn on with felt-tip pen. It was not a great success, but Les was his usual encouraging self.

Two days and a small explosion later, the engine had cracked in two and I knew for a certainty that our departure date had now receded to somewhere beyond the year 2020. I would be ninety-five and on a Zimmer frame before I ever got to the Well to halt the march of time. I hated the thought of being disloyal, but I thought I'd better start looking elsewhere.

*

When I woke up the next morning and administered my customary crack to the skull, there was nothing to indicate that this would be my last day in New Zealand. I decided that in order to see the Batemans once more, I would hitch the forty miles back to Opua. I arrived about lunchtime, sat and listened to four husky anecdotes from George and devoured a plate of Dorothy's date-and-cashew loaf, but the news was not good. In fact, they intimated to me gently that while I had been idling away the weeks on *Meilani*, every other yacht in the region had been fitting themselves out with crew for the Pacific race that was due to start tomorrow.

'Tomorrow?' I yelped in despair.

'Oh yes, Sandy. They're all off at 9 a.m. tomorrow, I'm afraid,' said George. 'Most of the yachts will have their crews by now. Will you and Les be joining them on *Meilani*, do you think?'

'Not unless we paddle it,' I said bitterly, and explained about the exploding engine and Les's timeless approach to life.

'We're so sorry, Sandy,' both George and Dorothy murmured as I took my leave.

I wandered down to the wharf in the bright sunshine where three new yachts were taking on supplies. 'You don't need crew, I suppose, do you?' I asked wanly.

'No thanks, we've just taken on our last three crew members half an hour ago,' called one chap heartily. 'Half an hour ago, would you believe it!? Good thing they came along, otherwise we'd have been really stuck for tomorrow, eh?'

I could hardly bear the thought of it. But then a fourth yacht pulled up right in front of me and threw me a line. I took it, half thinking I could do with a good sturdy rope right about now. It was a French yacht, going by the name *Philette V.*

'Don't need crew, I suppose?' I intoned glumly to the attractive young woman on the other end of the rope.

'Meh-*bee.*'

'Maybe? Heading?' I enquired, my voice brightening.

'Nouvelle Calédonie.'

'What time?'

'To-*mor*-roh meuh-*ning.*'

There was a five-second pause while it sank in.

'Can I come?'

And after a short interview, yes, I had a passage for tomorrow. It was contingent on just one thing – I had to obtain a visa for New Caledonia if I needed one. I sprinted up the hill to the Batemans'. No, no date-loaf, thanks, Dorothy, the French Consulate, quickly ...

Ring ... Ring ... 'Do I need a visa for New Caledonia?'

'Oui, m'sieur.'

'Damn. Okay, how can I get one?'

'Ah, zis is simple, m'sieur, a mere matter of a few forms to fill out, and we can have one for you in a fortnight.'

'A fortnight!'

'Ah *oui*, m'sieur, c'est très rapide, n'est-ce-pas?' The French voice was positively beaming on the other end of the telephone.

No, c'est bloody lentement, actually.

Damn!

But then one of the Batemans' visitors said, 'Visa? You don't need a visa if you're going as part of the race. It's all organised at the other end.' I kissed her, kissed the Batemans, kissed their elderly dachshund and danced back down the hill to tell the French yacht I would be able to join them after all.

I was leaving first thing in the morning and there was a lot to do. In the next twelve hours, I had to hitch forty miles back to Kerikeri in the dusk to fetch my stuff off *Meilani* and then, at an ungodly hour the next morning, hitch another forty miles back to Russell to register with the race co-ordinators. Finally, I had to hitch another fifteen miles to Opua along a quiet country road to meet with the yacht before she departed thirty minutes later.

When I got back to Kerikeri, it was dark already and Les was on the deck of the yacht waiting for me. I shouted across the water to him that I had to go and see a woman immediately about something important – a woman called Myra had some mail for me – and he called back that I should use his bike, chained to a nearby post. As I was hurtling off up the hill, I heard him call out something like 'You can't come back late!' which I remember thinking at the time was uncharacteristically bossy of him. The road up out of the inlet is a long and steady uphill haul and I was sweating and shaking with exertion by the time I reached the top. But as I looked down into the quiet valley where *Meilani* lay at anchor in the darkness, I was jubilant. I was leaving New Zealand by sea as planned, and nothing could stop me now.

Except perhaps a fractured spine. It was only on the steep downhill run to Myra's place by the river that I realised two things in rapid succession. The first was that when Les had called out to me earlier, he might conceivably have been saying, 'There aren't any back brakes!', as this was in fact the case. Nor indeed front brakes, it would seem. The second realisation was that I was about to fracture my spine. At the bottom of that steep hill was a T-junction, beyond which lay a strip of shrubbery and then the dark waters of the Kerikeri River. I went down that hill like an oiled sardine on a slippery-dip, the last quarter of the descent with my shoes jammed firmly into the tarmac, sending great plumes of smoking rubber up on either side. Even this did not halt my progress. I went over the kerb on the far side of the junction, bounded bike and all through half a dozen hibiscus bushes and ended up suspended over the river in a nest of broken branches and shredded foliage. When I limped into Myra's house a few minutes later, I looked like a minor forest deity who'd been through a logging mill. No snapped spine, but it had been very, very close.

I returned to *Meilani* at a somewhat more sedate pace and found that Les, in his usual thoughtful way, had rowed the dinghy out to meet me. As we glided across the still dark waters to where *Meilani* lay, I summoned up the courage to tell him my news; namely that I was abandoning him and taking off with some French strangers the very next morning. In the darkness, as he rowed, I could not see his face but I knew what was coming.

'Really, lad? Well, well, who'd a-thought it? Well done, you! You've deserved this, I reckon, putting up with a messy old chap like me for all these weeks and me letting you down. I'm right glad for you, lad, right glad. No doubt about it, you've done well.'

When we had climbed aboard and gone below to put on a kettle and have a last cup of tea together in the cosy saloon, I saw what lay on the cabin table. He tried to hide it under the cryptic crossword but I saw it anyway. He must have bought it that day, ready for those promised lessons. A gleaming new tin-whistle.

The next morning, I woke very early to depart and found that Les had got up to make me a farewell breakfast of boiled eggs and toast. Amid the crumbs, I jammed in a quick tin-whistle lesson – *look, you blow in that end, move your fingers up and down like this, it's simple, really, you'll pick it up in no time* – and, racked with guilt, said my goodbyes.*

The next few hours I don't want to relive, even in memory. I reached the little harbour of Russell purple in the face with exertion, only to be met by the race commodore, who said, 'Oh, haven't you heard? *Philette V* isn't racing anymore, sorry.'

My mind reeled. Purple spots blotched before my eyes. I beg your pardon?

'Not going, I'm afraid. Withdrew last night. A pity but there you are.'

I seethed. I *knew* this would happen, I just knew it. My last chance of leaving this country as I had planned, and it had been quashed by the fickleness of a couple of bloody French yachties.

Stifling my anger, I asked the race commodore if there were any other boats leaving who might need last-minute crew.

'At this eleventh hour?' he snorted. 'You've got to be joking. You should have started looking months ago, son,' he said before turning

---

* Since leaving that morning, I have never seen Les McLeod again, and I wasn't able to write to him to let him know how grateful I was for his warmth, his gentleness and his saintly encouragement of my every move. I returned recently to New Zealand and went down to the Kerikeri Inlet, fully expecting to find *Meilani* still there, floating above her unmoving reflection, with Les aboard doing the crossword and thinking perhaps of sailing off one day soon. I was saddened in a way to find *Meilani* gone – nobody could tell me where – saddened but also pleased to think that Les is at last on his way to find Fiddler's Green, tasting the salt air and playing his tin-whistle all the way.

away, thereby avoiding the lethal clubbing blow I aimed at the back of his smug, patronising neck.

I have never been angrier. Three months of searching for yachts had come to this. In half an hour's time, every single cruising yacht would have left New Zealand for good and I had missed them all. Three bloody months!

Bloody, bloody, bloody, *bloody* yachties.

Well, they weren't getting away with it, that's all. I might not be going anywhere except back to Auckland airport but these Frenchies would not be sailing off into the blue without hearing a few home truths. I took a deep and angry breath and set off down the Opua road with my thumb out. For the first time since leaving Australia, the beauties of the landscape were as nothing to me. Lantana and hibiscus rioted in the hedgerows for nothing. A red sunrise painted the quiet inland waters of the estuary with scarlet bars, and geese and slender-legged waders stood silhouetted against the crimson waters unheeded. Even the sudden liquid song of a tui high in the trees made no impact on my seething soul.

Twenty minutes later, I was cursing. Early morning commuters drove by, unwilling to pick up somebody so unhealthily purple in complexion. Nobody stopped, nobody slowed down. The minutes ticked away. Under my breath I was planning exactly what I would say, working out in French some vitriolic phrases with which to tell the faithless froggies what I thought of them, and the rest of the yachting world, for raising the hopes of innocent people like myself.

Finally a car slowed down enough on a bend for me to reach through the window, grab the motorist by the epiglottis and ask firmly but politely to be taken to Opua at all speed. I arrived at the wharf with about three minutes to spare. Ropes were being coiled, sails shaken out and the motor was ticking over. I sprinted down the jetty and wheezed out some breathless, and fortunately incomprehensible, malediction to the young woman with whom I had spoken yesterday.

'Ah, here you are,' she responded coolly. 'We wondered if perhaps you weren't coming. Australians are so unreliable, I zink.'

To my spluttered question, she explained in perfect English that, yes, of course they were going to New Caledonia, they just weren't going with the fleet, zat is all. And now that I had arrived, we could depart.

My mind reeled. At the same *time* as the fleet, in the same *direction* as the fleet, but not, by some obscure definition, *with* the fleet. The morning's emotional roller-coaster ride had left me in no mood for semantics. It was probably just some arcane point of French linguistics that we could have a jolly time unteasing around the cabin table to pass the time at sea. I stepped aboard and went to put my rucksack in the main saloon. When I popped my head up two minutes later, New Zealand was at long last *going away*. For a place so beautiful, so friendly, so full of treasures and fond memories, I have never been so relieved to see a country disappear. I was on my way.

Only one question troubled me: where the dickens was New Caledonia?

Chapter 7

Trickortreat was the captain of our ship, saying, 'We are only
going to be in this port for a short time. I want all of you to go
ashore and have a good time. Just remember, we sail on the
morning tide.'
My God, he was right! We sailed on the morning tide.
—RICHARD BRAUTIGAN,
Trick or Treating Down to the Sea in Ships

Sailing at last! Sailing on a yacht out on the broad bosom of the
Pacific, crewing, working my passage, doing that which I dreamed
of doing when I had set out ... er ... four months previously. Ocean
sailing, what's more! I drank in every detail and relived a dozen different books each day: *Peter Duck*, *Missee Lee*, *The Voyage of Joshua
Slocum*, *Moby-Dick*. And I told myself each night as I snuggled into
my little bunk that I had known all along this was possible, even in
this day and age. I nair-ver dooted ye for a minute, Capt'n Main-
waring, nair-ver for a single minute, ye ken.

I was fortunate in my first sailing experience. *Philette V* was
beautifully appointed, a sleek thing of gleaming white decks and
polished mahogany below, and a great contrast to *Meilani*, which for
all the saintliness of its skipper had been rather like living in a half-
finished guinea-pig hutch. As we surged northwards, every day
brought some new treasure. Once we had dolphins following the
boat, beautiful creatures which played around us for fifteen minutes
or more. They had large, liquid, intelligent eyes and when I heard
them breathe out as they surfaced, it was such a puffy, warm, cow-
like blast of air that for the first time I saw them as mammals, not
just super-fish. We also had flying fish skimming across our bows,
slim silver-sharp darts with pearly wings, gliding from one crest
of a wave to another. And for our whole seven days at sea, we had
following us two large smoky brown birds which in the absence of
any bird book I labelled sooty albatrosses, pretending I was some

eighteenth-century ship's naturalist and taking taxonomy into my own hands. They skimmed low over the waves both day and night, each the shadow of the other, never resting as far as I could see, and never moving their wings.

The first two days were fine breezy sailing days, which settled into a two-day dead calm, during which we motored along steadily. The sunset colours over this glassy molten sea were superb: rich mango-yellows gliding into true indigoes, and persimmon-reds melting into bright turquoise, all the colours of the sky made glossier by their being reflected in the curving mirrors of the Pacific swell. And after dark was no less enchanting. One night we had phosphorescence in the water, which left a bright luminous trail of green fire streaming from our bows. An apple core thrown overboard in the darkness became a little bomb of green-gold light, fizzing and sparkling astern in the midnight ocean.

Once I had spent a few days drinking in the sheer excitement of sailing at last, I was able to turn my attention to my three companions. There was the skipper, Paul-François, his mate, Nanette, and a fellow crew-member called Kenny. Paul-François was a white-haired, mahogany-skinned Frenchman of about sixty-five who spoke not a word of English. When I tried to ask him what he had done for a living, the only answer I could make out was that he drove a BMW. I found out later from Nanette that the apparent misunderstanding was mine alone. He didn't own *a* BMW; he owned BMW, the company. I was suitably awed and maintained an obsequious silence for the rest of the trip. Nanette herself was thirty years old and could have been Paul-François's daughter, wife, niece, lover, masseuse or interpreter; I never did find out. She spoke English quite well, but spent most of the time throwing up or cleaning up, the last obsessively. She would wipe down the hatchway steps two seconds after I had descended them, and then re-wipe them when I had gone back up, a habit that by the third day had reduced me to near-immobility. It was Kenny the New Zealander to whom I looked for conversation, only to discover after the first five moody

75

silences in response to my cheerful questions that he was almost totally deaf. Then there was me.

Meals were partaken in a sort of Trappist silence, broken only by odd mangled snippets of conversation.

Me: Um, could I have the salt please, Paul-François?

Paul-François: *(puzzled, very rapidly to Nanette)* Ah, je-te-ne-riens-qu'est-ce-que-c'est-je-ne-sais-pas-vive-la-France-allez-oop-d'entente-cordiale-le-fromage-pour-quoi?

Nanette: *(to me, frowning)* Pardon, what eez eet you say?

Me: Um, sorry, the salt … could I have … um … le sel, s'il-vous plaît?

Nanette: *(to Paul-François, very rapidly)* Ah, c'est la vie, le plus ça change le plus c'est la même et le jardin de mon oncle est plus grand que la plume de ma tante, n'est-ce-pas?

Paul-François: *(to me, slightly puzzled)* It is a type of cheese, but for why do you need to know zis?

Me: What? No, please, the salt … there! … le sel, in front of you, oh never mind. Kenny, could you reach across for the salt, please?

Kenny: Sorry?

Me: The SALT! Could I have the S-A-L-T, please!

Kenny: Yeah, 'tis a bit for this time of year. It'll get warmer as we head north though.

And so on.

It was considerably easier up on deck on my own, being burped at by dolphins and christening passing seabirds black-capped Mackinnon terns.

Over the last three days, the wind became steadily stronger, until by the last night it was almost a gale, with waves crashing over the coamings and the yacht bucking and heeling. It became impossible to do anything but steer when it was my watch, sleep when it wasn't, and grab the odd apple for meals. Steering was difficult, but it was also great fun. By day I would steer by the compass swinging and floating in its binnacle under a globe of glass – north-west … north-north-west … north-west … west, oops, too far, back again, north-west, that's better, west-north-west – and so on. At night I would pick a star, place it firmly in a square of the rigging between, say, the mast, the spreaders and the upper shroud, and then steer to keep it there. As the boat reeled and swung through the night, the star would dance in sweeping arcs like a drunken Tinkerbell and occasionally swirl out to the left of the stays or behind the mainsail and

I knew I had to get back on course. But then there she'd be again, framed in her airy cage and leading the little ship on through the darkness.

When the waves were high, it was marvellous to watch them race up behind us, a four-metre wall of blue water with a crown of seething foam. They stood looking over our shoulder for a second like some soft-footed giant and then, just as I feared the whole wall was about to topple, the stern would lift gently but quickly, the giant would shoulder his way smoothly and firmly beneath the keel and reappear ahead of us, striding away to the horizon.

On the last night, we came in sight of the Noumea Reef lighthouse. The entrance to the harbour was very narrow here and the winds were too strong to risk entry in the dark, so we decided to heave-to outside the reef for the night. This meant setting the sails one way and the rudder another; theoretically, the boat would stay dead still. However, the sea-motion becomes ten times worse because, instead of rolling with the waves, one just sits going *bish-bash-bingetty-biff-splosh-crash* all night long. Trying to sleep through all this was a trial. I found that the only way I could stay in bed was to anchor myself to my bunk by spread-eagling myself face down and sticking my claws into all four corners of the mattress like a determined cartoon cat.

At one stage things got so rough that I staggered up on deck, executing a neat somersault over the saloon table on the way, and saw a most marvellous sight. Although there was a strong wind blowing, the sky was cloudless and moonlit. Even in the darkness I could see where a mile away the sea was battering itself to shreds on the fangs of black reef. This was throwing such volumes of fine spray into the air that there was a perfect moon-bow arcing across the night sky – that is, a rainbow, but in silvery colours: the faintest of silver-pinks like the glimmer on a trout's flank, the palest of pearly greens, the shimmering powder blue of the specula on the necks of doves.

*

That was my first taste of real sea voyaging. But as Peter Duck was fond of saying, 'Seafarin's fine. It's land that makes the trouble.' And so it proved. On arrival in Noumea the next morning, gliding through the gap in the reef over turquoise-green waters, we were confronted by Immigration in the form of a large islander with

tightly pursed lips and a fetching snake-skin handbag. In between bouts of grooming himself with a bright-pink hairbrush and a small mirror, he went through our passports. When he came to mine, his languid look of boredom sharpened somewhat.

I didn't have a visa.

You will remember that I had been told I didn't need a visa if I was part of the race. What none of us had realised was that because *Philette V* had declined to sail *with* the race, there was no automatic visa for me. I was an illegal immigrant. As such, I was the responsibility of the captain who had brought me. For a while, Paul-François and Nanette looked grim, and there was an awful lot of shrill, rapid French with an occasional 'What?' from Kenny, until finally the Immigration official snapped his handbag closed, eyed me up and down speculatively, and spoke.

'Let the boy stay.'

Then he explained that if I were a good boy, a nice boy, he would give me five days – five days, did I understand? – to find another yacht leaving New Caledonia. I didn't at this point reveal that my current record for finding yachts stood at four months. I simply nodded, thanked him and stepped ashore. His last words were 'Got anywhere to stay, sweet boy?' to which I replied that yes, my great-aunt owned a mansion just out of town, big place, lots of fences and guard-dogs, and she would of course be wondering where I had got to.

Noumea, the capital of French New Caledonia, was not quite the small collection of grass huts and coconut palms I had been expecting. I soon found myself sitting amid the dim light, dirty ashtrays and blaring accordion music of a small bistro. Before me sat a lump of flattened gristle and slabs of oily potato, masquerading as the steak and chips I had ordered three-quarters of an hour earlier. It was accompanied by two yards of dry French bread that had the texture of asbestos.

'May I have some butter, please?' I asked a lounging waiter.

'*Non*,' he spat and went back to doctoring the absinthe behind the bar with crack cocaine.

Ah, *oui*, of course, silly me. Butter is not available, having been off the menu since some time soon after the French arrived last century, along with such things as hygiene, native wildlife and common courtesy.

The sort of grubby temper I found myself in sitting there in that little bistro is in fact the natural state of the traveller – tea not made how you like it, insecure about the exchange rate, feeling ripped off and sweaty from lugging around an overstuffed rucksack and desperately hoping to meet someone cleanish and relatively sane to talk to. All this had been heightened by my false expectation that a Pacific island could at least *try* to live up to its stereotype. A few coconut palms would not have gone amiss, I thought to myself, or a Gauguin maiden bearing bananas and a bowl of massage oil.

I wandered out into the night-time streets to see if I could find a more congenial part of town, but everywhere I went it resembled a Parisian slum transplanted to the tropics: grey concrete; windows barred and slatted; seedy cafés and nightclubs with badly spelt neon signs; tired-looking jacarandas; and fan-palms that had been unaccountably lopped to look like poodles' tails. Hundreds of off-duty young men in military uniform lounged in the streets, toting guns and whistling at girls from sidewalk bars. I had five days to find a passage out of there, and so far all I had seen in the harbour were two yachts and a supermarket trolley. I didn't fancy my chances.

But chance, like the Immigration officer, seemed to fancy me. I went down the next morning to the water, sat on a bollard and played 'The Wild Rover' on my tin-whistle. Three men on the nearest yacht joined in the chorus with gusto, and ten minutes later I was crew. The yacht was called *Morwennol*. Its owner, a white-haired man who looked like the Skipper from *Gilligan's Island*, told me he was leaving the next day for Gladstone, on the coast of Queensland. I was bound for Australia. It was a big backward step, but at least I was on my way once more.

Chapter 8

The heavens themselves run continually round, the sun riseth
and sets, the moon increaseth, stars and planets keep their
constant motions, the air is still tossed by the winds, the
waters ebb and flow, to their conservation no doubt, to teach
us that we should ever be in motion.
—ROBERT BURTON, *The Anatomy of Melancholy*

On *Philette V* everything had been rationed – water, food, breath-
ing, smiling – whereas on *Morwennol* things were free and easy –
wet parkas, mugs of hot soup, knock-up meals, games of cards and
chatter. There were four of us aboard: Bill the skipper, straight off a
Birds Eye fishfingers ad, Les, his lanky weathered brother, Mike,
his son, and of course me.

Two days out, Mike caught a fish over the stern, a beautifully
coloured dorado about five feet long and slender, tapering from a
blunt head to a graceful tail. Dorados mate for life, apparently, and
I was later told that people who have caught one often find its mate
following the boat for days afterwards, mourning for its partner.

Its back was a deep ultramarine blue, speckled with turquoise
blots, and its flanks and belly were a rich gold. It looked like the sort
of magical fish that in a fairytale will grant the fisherman any wish
in return for its liberty. But this particular fish didn't get much of a
chance. Just as he was opening his fishy lips to start the bargaining
process, Bill got it through the gills with a gaff, there was suddenly
a lot of scarlet blood in the gunwales, and I had to go for a wander

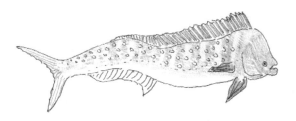

up for'ard to get some fresh air. So much for fairytales. Half an hour later it was lying sliced into neat fillets in the freezer. Two days later we got its mate.

For much of the time on these voyages, I continued to play my private role of eighteenth-century ship's naturalist, Joseph Banks perhaps, observing with wonder the hitherto unseen species of bird and fish. One bird that caught my attention was a tiny fluttering species of petrel I called a Jesus Christ bird, due to its habit of walking on the water. As it skimmed in tight circles over the waves, it would occasionally reach down with one foot and flick the surface, rather like someone riding a scooter pushing himself along with one leg.

Another bird was far more alarming. This was a frigate bird, a huge great thing that appeared out of nowhere and hung about us waiting for disaster to strike. These birds will attack other birds in mid-air and force them to regurgitate their food. They are as stiff-winged and motionless as a balsa-wood pterosaur on a mobile in a Munster baby's nursery. The one that floated above us for three days had a great rounded chest, a long, long beak, and a forked tail like two chopsticks.

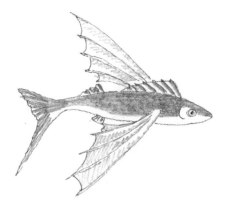

The flying fish were bigger now, not the tiny silver darts I had seen before, but heftier specimens the size of trout. They were a smart navy blue above, silver below and had a long downward fluke on their tails. With this, they could give the water a deft flick at the end of a long flight and go flying off in a different direction without ever re-entering the water. I watched them do this up to three times in a row, making flights of nearly 400 metres, zig-zagging across the waves. At dawn they would catch the early light, flashing across the sea like strange iridescent swallows. Sometimes they would land on deck and end up joining the dorados in the freezer.

One night, to stave off the boredom of a long night-watch, I borrowed from Bill his walkman and a couple of cassettes. What a difference it made! I'd steer along, up, down, side to side, a bit of wind in the rigging, when *click*, suddenly thundering through the night came *The Barber of Seville* and the whole scenario was transformed. Suddenly it seemed that the steady waves had become plunging combers, the wind a galloping torrent and the stars were streaming away in tatters on the rushing sky while the ship bucketed and hurled along on a desperate chase into the black night. Rossini was best; but play Puccini and the air turned silken and the scent of lemon blossom wafted across the balmy waves in the Aegean night. Or Bizet, and every breaker became an enraged bull and our sails clapped with the whip of a scarlet matador's cloak.

For three glorious days, we ran before the wind with twin headsails out. This meant we had two jibs, one on each side, and no mainsail, so the wind blew us along like a big white balloon. It

reminded me of an Arthur Rackham illustration I had once seen of a ship being towed across a windy sea by two great white swans.

Until one of the halyards snapped, that is, after which we had one giant magical swan pulling us along and the other stowed in a canvas bag in disgrace. Shortly after this, things began to get serious. There was a severe weather warning on the radio; I heard the word *cyclone* somewhere in the crackle and fuzz. Bill looked thoughtful, and even let his pipe go out. I stopped cloud-gazing and taking notes on seabirds; we knew we were in for stormy weather.

Over the next two days, the waves grew bigger by the hour. They were no longer the gentle, slow-rolling Pacific giants we had ridden so far. These were wolf-grey and had an uneasy menace to them, wrangling beneath the keel like pit bulls in a sack. The yacht would judder and halt, slapped viciously by the combers. Bill concentrated hard on the steering and the radio reports. It seemed a cyclone was brewing further north and within twenty-four hours was due to reach its full height of fury. We braced ourselves for the worst. Sails were reefed in, hatches secured and every rope checked and rechecked.

That night was the longest, darkest, wettest night of my life. We had the lot: pitch-black sea and starless sky so that we couldn't tell one from the other, except when great gobs of ghostly phosphorescence came flying out of nowhere across the coaming. The waves would rear out of the blackness and then launch themselves straight into your left ear-hole like so many playful wet black Labradors. There was seething rain, pelting out of the sky as hard as hail, making of my face a streaming wall of water so that I had to be continuously licking and slurping it off my lips, knowing that if I didn't drink it, I'd breathe it in and drown. And there was nothing to break the wide, wild darkness but the faint red goblin's glow of the compass in its globe of solid glass, the only fixed mark in that black chaos of night.

Coming off a two-hour watch and heading below was a wonderful relief, even though it meant climbing into a sodden bunk. Ten minutes after I climbed into bed, the yacht gave a great heave and a thump and I was flung hard against the ceiling. I was too tired to examine the knock I had received on my head properly, but when I woke six hours later I found that I had bled profusely. It wasn't that bad a cut, but, combined with the general wetness, the blood had spread in a thin layer over my face and hair and neck and sleeping bag; I emerged from the cabin looking like a minor character from *Macbeth*.

For two nights the storm raged, gradually subsiding by the dawn of the third day. We hadn't gone through the eye of the cyclone, but we had certainly caught a lashing by its tail. We spent a day repairing the damage, drying the bedding, cooking up a hot meal – our first in forty-eight hours – patching up the wounded and hearing disturbing reports on the radio. The loss of a boat called *Roger Rook* made me especially thoughtful: it was a boat I had seen often in Russell and Paihia. Three people, the reports said.

A day later, a white-capped noddy dropped exhausted out of the sky and spent ten minutes dozing on my arm. We must be near land, said Bill, and within three hours Lady Musgrave Island drifted into sight. We were nearing Australia.

And then, one morning, there it was: a eucalypt-green smudge on the horizon, and Gladstone a plume of nitrous-orange factory smoke. Our last night at sea was spent checking Admiralty charts and tide-tables and counting the white flashes of lighthouses and channel buoys, which reminded me irresistibly of the lady who applied for a job and ended up manning the Eddystone light for twenty years. You see, she had thought the ad in the paper said 'a little light housekeeping ...' When I shared this with the others, I was nearly thrown overboard.

I'm rather glad I wasn't. When I looked into the chemical-tainted waters of the Gladstone River, gliding between poisoned mangroves and the aluminium smelter, I didn't think I would survive the dip. As I was thinking this, I saw, swimming alongside the yacht, a pink dolphin. The others didn't believe me, but there it was, surfacing for air right at our bows. It was a sort of scaly pink, as though it had been scalded, and its white poached-egg eye looked blind to me. It had horrible yellow teeth. The Gladstone River was even more chemically corrosive than I had thought.

And then suddenly we were tying up in a pleasant little marina and stepping ashore. I had made it back to Australia; Adelaide, where I had set off from all those months ago, was only down the road. Well, a thousand miles down the road, but that didn't seem too far. My sister Maggie was living further up the coast, outside Rockhampton. I would set my sights northward once more and go and surprise her.

Chapter 9

The bushmen, who walk immense distances across the Kala-
hari, have no idea of the soul's survival in another world.
'When we die, we die,' they say. 'The wind blows away our
footprints and that is the end of us.'
          —BRUCE CHATWIN, *The Songlines*

Most people, when they think of Queensland, picture the fabulous
diamond glitter of the Gold Coast or the lush resort islands of the
Barrier Reef, all coral and glittering blue lagoons and suntans. But
vast tracts of the Queensland coast are less glamorous. Hundreds
and hundreds of miles of sugarcane territory stretch in a splintery
smoking swathe, sparsely dotted with small run-down towns melting in the sticky heat, each dominated by the rusting monolithic tin
edifice of a sugar mill. At night the cane burning makes the landscape look as though Ghengis Khan has just passed through, and by
day the thick yellow smoke blears the air with an acrid fog. Cane
toads plague the backyards at night and are licensed sport for a variety of cruelties practised upon them by otherwise respectable citi-
zens. Dettol is poured over them to make them writhe, or petrol,
which is then set alight; they are batted with hockey sticks over
neighbours' fences, or blown up with straws and used as hacky-sack
balls by schoolkids. Hippies, looking for a cheap high, scrape the
flattened and dried remains of the toads off the baking tarmac of the
interstate highways, put them in bongs and smoke them. Apparently the hallucinogenic effects can be spectacular, though you'd
have to be pretty far gone down the road to La-La Land to try the
experiment in the first place.

Not only in landscape is Queensland a world apart from Adelaide.
In culture, Queensland is to the rest of Australia what Texas is to
the rest of the United States: raw, rich and redneck. The people are
more Australian here than anywhere else, more confidently ocker
in their accents, more contemptuous of anything they might regard

as soft or Southern, and I wasn't quite sure if I would survive. An educated accent and a predilection for poetry might just bring out the Dettol and the hockey sticks. There had even been reports of a hitchhiker murderer operating along the coast in recent months. I had therefore been wary hitching north along the Bruce Highway to Rockhampton. Huge cattle-trains thundered northwards but rarely stopped. Drivers who picked me up tended to have machetes lodged down by the handbrake and overalls smelling of blood. I was relieved finally to make it to the small coastal town outside Rockhampton, where Maggie was able to take two months' worth of dirty laundry off my hands.

It was bliss to be in a domestic setting once more, safe from the perils of the world, sitting on the verandah of a house in the seaside hamlet of Emu Park. As I sat and regaled Maggie with my adventures, the floorboards beneath me gleamed in the lamplight. Past the passionfruit vine and beyond the flywire, a billion frogs were tuning up in the dusk. My rucksack was packed with freshly laundered clothes for the next leg and I would be off again in the morning.

I was telling Maggie about visiting Royal Albatross chicks near Dunedin: 'They're huge great things, fluffy and grumpy and long-billed … a bit like Big Bird who's swallowed Oscar the Grouch by mistake.' Off in the distance was a low musical moaning, a hollow keening that came and went on the night air. Werewolves? Maggie seemed not to hear anything, so I continued. 'Of course, they say to shoot an albatross is bad luck. I reckon it might be. If one of these things landed on you from any height, it would snap your spine in three places.'

I stopped again. The noise was quite distinct now, and it was the most unearthly thing I had ever heard. It sounded sad and musical, like the songs of mermaids lamenting the death of the Dolphin King, but as I listened more intently, it rose and shrieked like some monstrous creature out on the headland baying at the moon. It seemed that the domestic setting did not preclude night-time terrors, after all. Maggie saw my distress and took me out for a walk in the moonlight to show me the source of this weird sound: a curious and beautiful sculpture called the Singing Ship, on a knoll overlooking the sea. It was a curved structure of white cement, hollow pipes and taut wires, and looked insubstantial in the silvery moonlight, like a yacht under sail. It was designed to catch the slightest of breezes and thereby to strum, vibrate and resonate, producing a haunting music.

'It must drive the locals insane,' I commented.

'It does,' she responded shortly.

Before I took off again the next morning, Maggie took me to one side and gave me another of her stern sisterly talkings-to. 'You are not to hitchhike, Sandy,' she said. 'You are not to take so many risks. Mum and Dad didn't like to say so on the phone the other night, but they have been worried sick, first with the cyclone and now with this hitchhiker murderer about. They didn't know which boat you were on, they thought you could have been on one of the ones that sank, and now this new girl's been found in a culvert. You've got to start being sensible, Sandy, and stop worrying them to death. Promise, or I'll break your kneecaps.'

So I did. When I arrived in Townsville, the first thing I did was go down to the nearest bus station and book myself on a nice, reliable bus to Darwin, feeling tired of living on the edge.

*

Travelling by coach across the deserts of Queensland and the Northern Territory is not for the discerning traveller who enjoys being transported in comfort and style. Anyone who has done a long-haul coach trip in Australia's interior will probably tell you of sitting in a seat with as much legroom as would be required by a corgi; of finally dozing off at one in the morning, only to be woken by the cheery tones of the driver announcing the last refreshment stop for the next 600 miles; of neon-lit roadhouses selling weak tea in polystyrene cups; of groping, lurching 3 a.m. trips down the lightless aisle to the restroom, and slightly more lurching retreats to one's seat because the infirmities of the previous occupant have made the restroom unusable.

Actually, I am being unfair about the roadhouses. At one, I bought a chicken sandwich. To my surprise, it was not the dry margarine-and-processed-chicken comestible I was expecting, but a succulent gourmet creation that would have done credit to a Manhattan deli. In fact, it looked so good that I decided to keep it for the morning, so that I would have something to dream about all the long night through.

I dozed fitfully for the next five hours and then decided that the faintest of flushes in the eastern sky was good enough for me. It was officially morning and time for my mouth-watering chicken treat. I retrieved it tenderly from my bag, peeled back the paper wrapping, smelt once more the savoury tang of chicken and mayonnaise and, in the glow of approaching headlights, noticed with pleasure that there were even some nice crackly bits of roasted skin. I opened my mouth to bite and ... BANG!

The next thing I knew we were careering wildly along the road's verge and then off the road itself and down a sloping bank of low scrub and red boulders. Scratchy branches tore past the windows. There was a swerve, a jolt and a vicious smash as a big red anthill splintered the driver's side window and sent glass shards flying. Still the bus careered on, bucketing up and down as it thundered down the incline. Then, with a great crunch, the front of the bus ploughed into a mess of boulders and tree stumps and came to a halt.

A few seconds of utter silence. From outside came the thin dawn twitter of a small bird in the desert thorn-scrub. Then, something in the engine let off a great plume of hissing steam and the windscreen caved in. There was a querulous muttering from dazed passengers and somewhere close behind me a baby started screaming. The driver was slumped over the wheel unconscious, a woman was sprawled in the aisle motionless just beside me, and I had only one thought in my head.

Where's the chicken sandwich?

I have learnt since that, in moments of shock, the brain's reaction is to close down and focus on some trivial detail to keep its grip on a world that has slipped out of control – the soldier noticing how the buttons on his dead comrade's tunic are askew or the fighter pilot in a death-spiral trying to get that irritating smear off the windscreen – but I had no idea of the power of this impulse. Not only did I *notice* the loss of my chicken sandwich, my beautiful chicken sandwich, but I got up out of my seat, carefully picked my way up the aisle, peered under seats and over shoulders and asked anyone still conscious, 'Sorry, has anyone seen my chicken sandwich?'

I found it about five rows back, lying in the aisle between a stockinged leg and a fallen suitcase. I carefully retrieved it and held it aloft. I picked my way equally carefully back to my own seat – sorry, excuse me, could I just skip through? thanks awfully – and sat down again. I adjusted my seat to a comfortable position, took a deep breath and prepared to tuck in. Mmmm, chicken. It was only then that I noticed that half the sandwich was soaked in something dark.

Something red.

Blood, in fact. My brain finally caught up with events. I dropped the sandwich to the floor and, like my more up-to-speed fellow passengers, started to do the right thing and panic.

Time sped up again. Outside, a desert-red light was suffusing the sky and it was possible to survey the damage. A few of us got everyone else out of the bus, but the driver still lay slumped unconscious across the wheel, too injured to risk moving. Someone else clambered back up through the scrub to the top of the bank to wave down any vehicles that might be coming along behind us. There was then a period of waiting, a strangely peaceful time, in which I wandered off a little way, sat on a rock and thought, *My parents must never know, my parents must never know, my parents must never know* ...

Breaking my reverie, a small bird hopped out of the scrub and started flitting about in the dry grass and red soil, oblivious to the wreckage. It was a species I had never seen before, with a tiny round body, spindly legs and two long tail-feathers sticking straight up like those of a wren. Instead of the cobalt blues and jet blacks of the splendid wrens I was used to, this one was a delicate cinnamon, speckled and striated with sesame-coloured dots and stripes and a little cap of coppery green. Fascinated, I watched it peck around my feet. When it moved off behind a tuft of spinifex further up the bank, I stalked it carefully, the crash forgotten entirely. It could, I mused, be a grass wren, or perhaps an emu wren – both frightfully rare, if I was remembering correctly. What I really needed was a bird book. I wondered if any of the fellow passengers had one. I kept following the tiny atomy of feathers up the bank, my eyes glued to the ground, so that I hardly noticed I had reached the red dust of the main road. The wren hopped on, picking at tiny seeds or insects in the roadside grass until there was a tinny clanking from nearby and the bird flitted off in alarm. I looked up, annoyed at whoever or whatever had disturbed my quarry. Ah, there it was, an aluminium can of Tooheys beer rolling across the road in the morning breeze. Litter, right out here, I thought to myself crossly. And there was another one, bowling off along the road. And another, and another, and then a whole pile of clearly unopened cans spilling from a carton lying in the road beside the overturned wreckage of a white van. And a ragged bundle of what looked like dark clothing, flung half into the spinifex by the roadside, where already a couple of crows were gathering to feast.

I straightened up, realised what I was looking at, and went weak at the knees. Then I turned and threw up into the saltbush before hurrying back down the bank to let the others know what had sent us off the road in the darkness.

Within twenty minutes, a bus had pulled up and we were herded aboard. We had got off remarkably lightly – most of us. Much of the blood, it transpired, was from various blood-noses and the inert stockinged leg I had clambered over on the bus turned out to belong to a healthy young woman who was just a very heavy sleeper. The oncoming van we had hit, however, had been written off completely, and with tragic consequences, as I had already seen. Another corpse, I was told later, had been hidden from sight beneath the crumpled mass of the overturned van.

There followed a two-hour trip on the bus into Mt Isa, a mining town in the middle of that vast red desert. Here we were met by reporters from the ABC. After recording me muttering incoherently about blood and chicken sandwiches, emu wrens, bus-crash victims and the relative merits of hitching, yachting and bus travel, the reporters went off to find somebody more reliable who could tell them what had actually happened.*

Still shaking, I found myself at a loose end in Mt Isa for the next twelve hours, filling in time until a replacement bus could take us on to Darwin. I fell back on that reliable time-filler, the laundromat. Once I had washed my clothes as many times as could be usefully done, I found that I still had eight hours to fill. I took myself off to have a haircut.

As I sat in the old-fashioned barber's chair of green leather and old chrome, swathed to the chin in a black nylon sheet, I let the shock of the morning fall away with each lock and curl snipped from my head. There was something soothing about the process, something tranquil about the filtered, aquarium gloom of the shop, something homely about the morning radio and the fragrance of Old Spice. I was just thinking how very good it was that my parents would be spared the shock of knowing how close I had come to dying, when my ear picked up what the radio was actually saying. It wasn't only the ABC who had got hold of the story.

'... and that was Radio 87.3 morning news, the main item being the tragic bus crash in the Northern Territory in which it is believed that there are no survivors. Over to you, Richard.'

'Yes, thank you, Tony, and it's appalling, isn't it? I mean this is a McAllister's bus, right, and tell me if I'm wrong but isn't this the third such crash they've had in the past year? What's going on here, listeners? There are reports already that there's strong evidence that the driver had been drinking and half asleep and that he's walked away from this, leaving the rest of the passengers dead, and what

---

* I found out later that my garbled report, broadcast on ABC radio, woke my parents from their morning slumber some 2000 miles to the south in Adelaide, leaving them convinced that if not actually killed in the crash, their son was at least suffering dementia from the shock. So much for them not finding out.

can we do, listeners, to stop this sort of appalling carnage on our roads? Phone in with your comments after the break ...'

'Ah, a terrible thing that,' said the barber as he applied the clippers. 'No survivors, they say. Bloody McAllister's!'

It is a bizarre experience to hear over the radio reports of one's own death and I was nearly speechless – but not quite. Never quite. I was soon in full flow.

'Reports of my death have been greatly exaggerated,' I started off.

'What?' said the barber and added, as my head wobbled in disbelief at what I was hearing, 'Keep still, sir, if you don't mind. I nearly had your ear off then.'

'You know,' I continued, huffing a little, 'I've always shared the reasonable man's scepticism about what one hears through the media, but here is confirmation at last of their reckless unreliability. Less than half a day after this crash, some idiotic shock-jock broadcaster is telling the world with a degree of relish, and perfect inaccuracy, a pack of nonsense! It's outrageous!'

'But it's on the news, sir, it just said—'

'Look!' I expostulated, and then proceeded indignantly to tell him the facts of the case – leaving out my heroic rescue of the chicken sandwich, I confess – namely, that *all* passengers of the bus had survived, that the driver was neither asleep nor drunk nor on the wrong side of the road at the time, and that, if anything, he had been *extremely* skilful and heroic in keeping the bus upright as we plunged down the bank. Had he not done so, it might well have been a mortician instead of you, my good man, doing the grooming at this very moment. There!

I was a little too indignant in tone, I think, because very shortly afterwards the barber whipped away the cloth, held up the back mirror and I was out of there. I only noticed the next day in Darwin that he seemed to have stopped halfway through.

I meant what I said about the driver and his handling of the bus down that terrible bank. I never found out what happened to him, although a later rumour hinted that he had died in hospital. I sincerely hope that this was as untrue as the radio reports. The crash left me unhurt apart from a touch of whiplash and a tendency to flinch at oncoming headlights over the next few weeks, but it did make me question all forms of public transport. I decided that for the next stage, sisterly advice notwithstanding, it would be yachts and hitchhiking all the way.

Chapter 10

Terror came ... I was ripe for death. My debility led me along
to a route of dangers, to the world's edge, to Cimmeria, the
country of black fog and whirlwinds. I was forced to travel,
to ward off the apparitions assembled in my brain.

—ARTHUR RIMBAUD, *A Season in Hell*

Well, it had to be yachts, didn't it? I was now in Darwin, on the
forsaken northern shore of Australia, looking out over the tepid,
croc-infested waters of the Arafura Sea to the maze of the Indonesian archipelago. Like the Bay of Islands in New Zealand, this
place was a hopping-off point, the very end of the pirates' plank
along which my refusal to fly was edging me, the sharp and rusty
cutlass of Time pricking between my shoulderblades. On my world
map, the chain of islands peppering the seas all the way up to Singapore seemed so very close, almost within swimming distance. But
although the cutlass of Time might be metaphorical, the sharks
and crocodiles were not, so swimming was out of the question. I
had to find another yacht.

The problem was that, as with the Bay of Islands, I had arrived
much too soon. I was coming to learn that the fleet of yachties who
sail the world do so to a rigid and unchanging schedule, as regular
and predictable as the seasonal migration of swallows. At the beginning of May they leave New Zealand, arriving on the east coast of
Australia a few weeks later. By mid-June they are dawdling up the
Great Barrier Reef before summoning up the courage to thread the
treacherous straits off Cape York. It is not until the very end of July
that they gather in a nervous sail-flapping flock in Darwin Harbour,
ready to launch themselves across the Arafura Sea to Java and
beyond. With my hitchhiking and bus travel, I was skipping ahead
far too quickly and would now have another tedious wait for them
to catch up again and sweep me onwards.

I booked into an airless and noisy hostel, visited the post office to collect mail, and found only one letter. It was from my mother and was along the following lines:

Dear Sandy,

For God's sake, get a move on, will you. I keep telling my tapestry circle about my intrepid son who's off for a year of adventurous travelling, doing it all by land and sea, left five months ago, and when they ask where you are now, I have to keep lying and telling them you're in Mongolia travelling with the horse-monks of Utor, or climbing Kilimanjaro on the back of a white rhino. They are beginning to collectively doubt me, their sworn leader-in-needlework. Dorothy's son got married last week to a Tongan bus-conductress and she's getting all the limelight.

So for goodness' sake, get your skates on and have some proper adventures. Get trampled by wildebeest, or shot by a poisoned curare dart or something, even if you have to book it through a package tour.

Your ever loving,

Mum

I couldn't help feeling she had a point, but I didn't reply. Instead I wrote several hundred letters to other people to make them feel guilty for not having written to me and went off busking with my tin-whistle in Darwin's main shopping mall to wring some cash out of the local populace.

And then, after a few hot and frustrating weeks doing the rounds of the yacht clubs, I had some luck. It was time to write another letter.

Dear Newton,

You know how we said Kathmandu? We couldn't make it Cairo, could we? The thing is, I'm off to Africa now, not India, and people round here tell me that they're two quite distinct places really. And could we make it more November-ish than July?

Look, in all seriousness, I'm not going to make it to our rendezvous this side of Christmas, and by then you'll be in England and not wanting to up sticks again, I expect. I really am sorry about this. I'm writing this from Darwin, by the way, which, yes, I know, is back in Australia and not that far away from Adelaide.

But I have had an unusual offer. There's this chap called Alec whom I keep bumping into, and he is sailing to Africa in his yacht in about four weeks. Africa!

He seems friendly enough, but oddly cagey about everything he does. After a fortnight of negotiations that have at times resembled a Middle East disarmament summit, we've agreed on the following. He is prepared to take me with him when he sails to Africa in a month's time if I come up to scratch. To test this, we are about to depart for a ten-day trip around the Kimberley, exploring the coastline, which by all accounts is spectacularly rugged, remote and beautiful, accompanied by two girls from a nearby backpackers' hostel who are coming along for the ride.

At the end of that trip, we will return to Darwin and decide whether we get on well enough to endure the two-month crossing to Cape Town together.

My one worry is this. You may or may not be aware that for years now I have had a series of recurring nightmares, very vivid, very real, about crocodiles. In my dreams I have been chased, devoured, disgorged, mutilated and even rather sassily chatted up by crocodiles in every shape and form. And now I am accepting a lift on a yacht of unknown provenance to a place where three people have been devoured by crocodiles this year alone. The crocodiles of the Kimberley are the biggest in the world, I have been told, and I now feel like those doomed characters from legends – Oedipus, Merlin, Macbeth – who have been told perfectly clearly by an oracle precisely how they are going to meet their doom, but still go right ahead and blunder into the lethal trap. I have known for fifteen years that, like Captain Hook, I am going to meet Death in the jaws of a gently ticking crocodile and here I am, sailing off to the one part of the world where man-eating crocodiles, by all reports, subsist on a staple diet of steersmen, snatched from the decks of passing yachts with a simple lunge and snap of their jaws.

But am I worried? Not a bit of it. Who can impress the forest bough, bid the tree unfix his earth-bound root, and march upon Dunsinane? Ha!

Godfathers! I'd better go. I have just realised the time and I was due at the yacht ten minutes ago! Sorry again about Kathmandu. I'll post another letter when I get back. I'm only going for about ten days.

Cheers,

Sandy

*

So it was that I found myself sailing out of Darwin Harbour on a yacht I shall call *Meropë* under the direction of a skipper whom I shall call Alec. Neither name is real: I don't wish to be sued if Alec reads this, or – more likely if you knew Alec – hunted down with a spear gun and harpooned in the kidneys. The voyage, although full of extraordinary beauty and adventure and made bearable by the sanity and sweet nature of the two other crewmembers, whose names I have also altered, slowly turned into a nightmare. In fact, it started with an attempted abduction.

I arrived panting at the harbour to find Alec and the two girls already on the beach, waiting to load into the dinghy for the final trip out to *Meropë* where she lay at anchor some way out in the harbour. I had barely time to find out their names, Sally from England and Jutta from Denmark, because just as we were clambering aboard the dinghy, a rather dippy girl in a big sunhat and platform shoes came yoo-hooing along the sand and introduced herself as Belinda. She was in a summer frock covered in red poppies and looked as though she usually carried a small Pekingese under one arm. Could we, she asked, be sweet enough to give her a lift out to one of the anchored yachts in our dear little dinghy? Alec grunted agreement and she hopped in, pointing out a large blue yacht some hundred yards from shore. She burbled happily on about some party she had been at the night before as we chugged across the bay to the yacht, but when we drew closer, she said, 'Ooo! Er, no it's not that yacht, sorry, I think it's that one over there.' She pointed to a bigger yacht further out. We changed course, Alec maintaining a sardonic silence as Belinda chattered gaily on. 'It's my boyfriend's yacht, it's ever so nice, I went and left my handbag on it last night at this party I was telling you about.' But as we neared the bigger yacht, again her voice faltered. 'Ooooh, no, I don't think it's that one. I think it starts with an S. *Sunburst* or something. *Sunny Boy*, p'raps. That one's called *Jaws* and I'd remember if it was called *Jaws*, cos it's like the film, innit? I think it must be that two-masted one back there. Or what about that one with the awning over there? I seem to remember an awning, all stripy it was. I'd had ever so much to drink, I had, and everything looks different in the dark, don't it?'

At this stage, Alec's patience ran out and instead of zig-zagging around the bay like a blowfly on a windowpane, he headed the dinghy straight towards *Merope* and a minute later we all climbed aboard. He started rapping out orders to the two girls and me, ignoring Belinda, who was still brightly pointing out possible candidates for her boyfriend's yacht and telling us how good he was at making kiwi-fruit daiquiris. Jutta, Sally and I glanced uneasily at one another, but Alec seemed oblivious to the fact that we now had an extra person onboard. It was only when he asked me to help him haul the dinghy onto deck that I thought I'd enquire what was to be done about getting Belinda either to her boat or at least back to shore. Alec's reply was short and crisp, thrown over his shoulder as he busied himself with a rope.

'She got herself onto this yacht, she can get herself off it.'

'Well, yes, that certainly seems … fair enough but I wonder if …' I started to stammer, but Alec threw me an armful of sodden rope and barked out an order to Sally, who was hovering nervously in the cockpit.

Belinda seemed to become aware for the first time that we were all being busied into some form of departure. A flicker of uncertainty crossed her face, but then she brightened at the possibility of adventure.

'Oooo!' she said. 'I'm free till tomorrow morning. Where are you going?'

Alec's reply was again crisp. 'Western Australia.'

And to me, 'Sandy, get the anchor up. We're off.'

Belinda's *joie de vivre* collapsed. 'I can't go to Western Australia. I've got the cat to feed and … and … Western Australia?!' she said and started taking off her clothes, ready to fling herself into Darwin Harbour and swim ashore.

'Um, look, Belinda, is it?' I said, attempting to cover her up with a bit of spare sail. 'The harbour, it's not really safe, and I'm sure we can arrange something. Alec, why don't I drop her ashore in the dinghy? I won't be a jiffy.'

Alec's reply was dangerously curt. 'Nup. You're not using my dinghy or my fuel. She's wasted enough of our time. Now get that anchor up on the double.' After such a short acquaintance, there was already a hint of keel-hauling in his pebble-green eyes and I found myself scurrying to the prow.

Belinda clop-clopped her way up the deck to follow me, tears beginning to spring in her big Betty Boop eyes, while Sally followed, clutching the discarded poppy dress. What the blazes were we going to do? Then Sally spotted what we needed. A man in a motor-dinghy was chugging by a hundred metres away. Sally started screeching across the water. Belinda quickly caught on and added her own wailing yoo-hoos to the din. Mercifully the boatman heard us at the last minute and, just as Alec hauled up the mainsail and we glided away from our mooring, the tearful Belinda was able to leap overboard half-naked into the arms of the startled dinghy-driver. Sally flung her clothes after her. As the wind filled the sails and we glided on into the late afternoon gold, Sally and I shot each other a look that spoke volumes about the sanity of our skipper.

Yet Alec that first evening was charm itself, carefully taking us over the yacht and explaining the workings and our respective duties. Over an excellent supper, he regaled us with amusing stories of yachting life and, as the moon rose, spoke knowledgeably of the area we were off to explore: the ancient Kimberley, a vast area of coastline that few people ever see. The straits are treacherous, the shoreline inhospitable and the whole region almost uninhabited except for a few remote mission stations far inland. But far from being forbidding, it was painted by Alec in glowing hues – great winding gorges, vast mangroves and secret lagoons, ancient cave paintings, deserted beaches and abundant birdlife. By the time we toppled into our bunks, Sally, Jutta and I felt proud and excited to be aboard *Meropë* with Alec as skipper, and the foolish Belinda was almost forgotten.

Over the next few days, there was plenty of time to get to know my fellow crew. Alec was in his mid-thirties and was what might be described in an old-fashioned novel as a handsome brute: light-brown hair, bronze tan, hazel eyes and a poker face. I was later to learn that he could go from sardonic calm to unreasonable rage in half a second. Then there were the two girls, both of whom had answered an ad for crew in a backpackers' hostel: Sally, the English girl, was a little like Barbara Windsor of the *Carry On* films, though not quite so top-heavy. She had blonde curly hair, a wicked giggle, a Londoner's voice and quick, sharp movements, although she was soon slowed down by seasickness and tropic heat. Jutta was a Danish aristocrat, with straight brown hair, a wide serene face, beautiful grey eyes and a stately build; she looked as though she'd be very much at home cantering around some Jutland estate inspecting the water-jumps. She told us that first day of the time she was dancing with the King of Denmark and the top of her strapless gown popped off, leaving her exposed to the entire court. The King had whisked her courteously behind a towering salmon-mousse arrangement to allow her to adjust herself before dancing on. Alec's eyes boggled, but my naivety in such matters made me blissfully unaware of where things were heading.

Meropë had no inside shower, so ablutions were carried out by waiting until nightfall, going to the foredeck, stripping naked and then flinging a bucket on a rope over the side to catch a pailful of water. One hauled it aboard, emptied it in a shuddering sloosh over one's head, gasped a bit – although the water was rarely cold, more a tepid tropical coolness – applied special saltwater soap, and repeated as many times as necessary. We had all undergone this on the first night out, but the following afternoon something happened that should have set alarm bells ringing. We were sitting in the cockpit relaxing, I reading some murder mystery, Alec at the tiller and the two girls idly chatting. Alec suddenly set the tiller on autopilot, whipped off his shirt, dropped his board shorts, yawned and stretched luxuriously and sauntered stark naked up to the front of the yacht, where he proceeded to have a long and very public washdown. The girls stopped in mid-sentence, shot each other looks of alarm and rapidly disappeared below deck. As for me, I kept my eyes firmly on my book and wondered where this was going to lead. Some time later, Alec returned with a skimpy towel draped over his loins, flung himself down opposite me, grinned lazily like a panther thinking about a spot of lunch and shouted below, 'Okay, Sally, your turn. Shower time.'

Sally bobbed her head up from below and politely explained that she'd wait until nightfall, thank you very much. Then she bobbed back down out of sight again.

'No,' said Alec, with an edge to his voice. 'There's a storm coming and it's too dangerous to be on the foredeck at night. Come on, girlie, don't be shy, we're all grown-ups here.'

Sally reappeared from below like a small, determined marmot facing a team of bulldozers. In slightly crisper tones, she replied that in that case, Alec, she wouldn't shower at all until the storm had passed, and if he didn't mind, actually, she very much preferred not to be called girlie, but preferred Sally as that was her name, actually, if you don't mind, thank you very much, Alec.

Alec sat up, thunder gathering in his eyes. He shot me a look, clearly inviting me to share his exasperation with the unreasonable scrupulousness of women. Bloody tarts, all of them, eh? Think we're all only after one thing, eh? Which would have been more effective if I hadn't been so very absorbed right then in what Miss Marple was deducing from the vicar's habit of leaving the fish-paste sandwiches to one side, a fact I had now read about twenty-seven times in the last five minutes.

'I'm not having people onboard who are going to stink out the ship 'cos they're too up themselves to take a shower when they need one,' called Alec to the retreating Sally.

'Well, just drop us off at the next roundabout then, Alec, much obliged, I'm sure,' called back Sally, her voice as crisp and light as iced lettuce. 'And if you could give us a little warning in future before you strip off, Jutta and I can make ourselves comfortable and grab our opera glasses for the show, all right, Alec?'

There was a seething pause of about a decade.

'Well, send Jutta up then,' Alec called, but it was said half-heartedly and there was no reply. There didn't need to be. The battle had been won, and not by Alec.

I looked up from my book. 'I'll have a shower, if you like,' I said innocently.

Alec turned on me a long appraising glare that would have blistered oak and then flung himself down into his cabin, from which he didn't emerge for another six hours. And neither did the predicted storm, funnily enough. Daylight showering was never suggested again.

After three days' sailing across the flat and tepid seas of the Joseph Bonaparte Gulf, we came to one of the most superb anchorages it is possible to imagine, the head of the King George River. This was the start of the Kimberley proper, and here the mood onboard lightened as we surveyed the ancient surroundings. Nosing our way along the cliffs, we had come to a break in the coastline where a wide sandy bay opened out. Negotiating the sandbars and shallows of the bay brought us nearer and nearer to the beach, until suddenly a gap opened in the sand and we were slipping through into a broad river-mouth backed by high red-gold cliffs. A huge gorge lay ahead, narrow, sheer-sided, with a broad green ribbon of water snaking up between tottering skyscrapers of orange sandstone. This was our way ahead.

For six miles we glided up the green lane, slipping from purple shadow to bright sunlight while the cliffs towered over us, ten times, twenty times higher than our tall mast, the river gorge narrowing all the time. In the deep green water were huge jellyfish in delicate mauve and pink which floated beneath our bows. Some were spotted with transparent white. A lone grey heron flew ahead, slipping between the clashing cliffs as for Argo in the Hellespont of old.

So we wound on, deeper and deeper into a land that was utterly silent. Then ahead of us, the river really did end. There was no petering out, no lessening of the cliffs; just a great towering precipice that ended the gorge. This in the wet season is a roaring waterfall, 150 metres in a sheer drop. Now there was nothing but a smear of dampness down the immense black face. No sunlight touched the water here except at noonday, and it was purple with deep shadows. The apricot-coloured cliffs were cut and seamed across and up and down in a hundred places so that they looked less like solid walls than like untidily stacked books in a giant's library: ledged and coigned and buttressed, golden-orange where the sun fell, deep wine where shadow lay. Here, twenty feet from the cliff wall, we anchored, black water below us and a hundred metres of hanging rock above.

I shouted 'Hoy!' and back came an echo, 'Hoy!' Then, two whole seconds later, came another more distant 'Hoy!' and then another, and another, echoing away back down the gorge until it died away to nothing. I noticed for the first time the ceaseless, echoing slap and lapping of water on the cliff walls, repeated and magnified and carried on by the canyon walls speaking to one another eternally.

The water looked very inviting, but Alec told us that even right up here, huge sharks and crocodiles lurked. At this very spot a girl had been eaten earlier this year by a crocodile as she swam from her boat. The only comfort in the horrid tale was that she was stoned on marijuana at the time, so perhaps found the whole experience a bit of a giggle, who knows? I didn't do any swimming, I hardly need say.

*

On the following day we climbed up to the top of the cliffs via a gully of tumbled stone and bushes. At the top we found ourselves in a landscape of low scattered trees and scrub, interspersed with patches of pinkish-white rock flats and tough grass. Diamond doves sat tsu-crooing in the scrub and ants as fat and green as pear drops scurried in the pink dust. The yacht lay like a toy 300 feet below us, and we were a thousand miles from the nearest town. I had never been in an area more remote.

The river that in the wet season feeds the waterfall was a series of waterholes amid the flat jumbled rock of the creek bed. At first the pools we came across were little more than scummy green ponds of still water. Dragonflies darted, but these dragonflies were not your usual peacock green; they were from head to tail-tip bright, bright scarlet, the colour of a red-hot poker or a burning coal.

As we progressed up the river bed, the pools became more and more frequent and began to join together in long stretches of shallow blue. At last we came to one that was deep and cool and surrounded by rock ledges – perfect for swimming. All this time, I had been very conscious of crocodiles, scrutinising every floating log and low rock for telltale eyes or nostrils. For their part, the others had been earnestly pointing out that there were in fact two types of crocodiles, saltwater and freshwater, and that only the salties were dangerous. Then they proceeded to contradict each other: 'If you see a freshwater croc around, you know that there can't be salties around as well, because the salties eat the freshies,' and 'No, no, if you see the salties around, it means there *must* be freshies for the salties to live on,' and 'Every river in the Kimberleys has either freshies *or* salties but not both,' and 'If one of us is lying, then the other two are both correct, but if Alec is the liar then both Sally or Jutta are either also lying or are going to be eaten by a saltwater crocodile.'

Despite all the fun afforded by this sort of thing, I didn't relish standing around juggling Boolean logic tables while all the crocodiles in the region queued up for a Mackinnon Sandy-wich, as Sally put it. In the end it was the sun that decided me. In those parts it was blazing in the afternoon and a week of saltwater washing had left me feeling stiff-skinned and ashy. Throwing caution to the wind, I flung off my clothes and plunged into the pool.

It was bliss. It was cool silk on the skin. It was a week of salt and sweat and itch being soothed away by fresh, clean water. It lasted a good twenty-one seconds, exactly one second longer than it took for Jutta to call out, 'Ooh, look everybody! A crocodile!'

In the very pool where I had been gaily disporting was a crocodile, its wicked golden eyes and green snout lying on the surface, its body and tail hanging down almost vertically in the clear water. My nightmare. My terror. All of six inches long.

So this was the mighty crocodile, was it? This was the creature that tore people limb from limb? I doubted it could inflict anything much more disfiguring than a light pedicure. Henceforth, I would swim where and when I liked.

That night we lit a bonfire on a wide ledge, right at the foot of the cliff where a beaver's nest of bone-dry driftwood had collected, and roasted pieces of marinated fish over it. We sat half the night by this bonfire, drinking wine and eating chunks of juicy, dribbling fish, while our shadows danced on the ochre-lit cliff-face above us. I had found some star charts aboard, so I sat a little away from the others, outside the blaze of firelight, and searched the skies for stars. Some of these were old familiar friends, but I also found a host of new bright stars with strange Arabic names like spells: Alioth and Schedar, Al Na'ir and Procyon, Ophiuchi, Rasalhague and Zuben-el-Genubi. I determined to learn every major star and constellation in the sky before my travels were over.

*

After leaving the King George River, we spent our days nosing along the Kimberley coast, sometimes staying close to the shore and stopping off at sandy bays, but sometimes forced out to sea to avoid a patch of reef or bypass a huge indentation in the coastline. The weather was very hot, so much of the day was spent snoozing, writing, sunbathing or swimming. Unfortunately, Alec's idea of bringing culture to the Timor area was to play very, very loud rock music from the yacht's speakers for ten hours a day, so writing became impossible. Alec began to call me 'Professor,' in a tone that made me uneasy. Here we were in the tropics, and tempers were beginning to fray. At the same time, I was conscious of having to maintain good relations. This was, after all, a trial run, and a congenial and helpful attitude might earn me a ticket to Africa. I had spent five months maundering on the shores of New Zealand searching for a sea-passage, and I couldn't face the possibility of spending another five months in Darwin if I blew this chance. So when Alec called me Professor, even though it was in the tone in which other people say, 'Oy, Four-Eyes,' I smiled, gave a little wan laugh, put my pen down and tried to appreciate Def Leppard's contribution to the tranquillity.

I kept seeing wonderful and bizarre creatures. A Long Tom, for example, is a fish with a most peculiar habit. It is very long and thin with a pointy nose and a powerful tail, which it uses to launch itself out of the water and rear upright. In that position it flicks its way across the surface for a hundred metres or so before collapsing again into the sea. It looks rather like a hockey stick being wielded by a skilled but invisible player, skittering across the playing field to score a phantom goal. Alec told me of a woman swimming in these parts who was so intent on looking out for crocodiles that she got in the way of one of these Long Toms in full flight. Its nose went straight into her ear-hole and she had to have it surgically removed. Just as he was telling me this, I glanced down to notice a sea snake nosing its way along the hull, inches from my idly trailing hand. It was striped in ivory and black and appeared to be trying to come aboard. Their venom, I later learned, is about the deadliest thing in the entire marine kingdom. This was no place for the casual or unobservant.

Despite the wildlife, I found myself descending into an irritable, frustrated mood. The trip seemed to have become aimless. Why couldn't we just turn around and sail back to Darwin? I had lost count of the days, but surely our allotted fortnight was nearly up. We'd seen nothing in the past three days except rocky coast and stupid little islands and black reefs that popped out of nowhere, frightening the living daylights out of us. We came within inches of hitting one of these reefs at full tilt one particularly snappy afternoon; the clear aquamarine of the sea was suddenly an ugly black-purple, and Alec lunged at the tiller, using language that would have made Quentin Tarantino blush. The near hit reminded me of going out sailing on Lake Jindabyne as a boy. I used to make things more exciting for myself by negotiating the straits between the bare little islands, watching carefully for the sudden loom of amber rock through the green water, ready to pull up the centreboard with panicky fingers. Well, such was this coast, but magnified a thousand times. And on this yacht, there could be no quick pulling up of the centreboard and no sheepish trot home to confess a slight bump to the paintwork.

Here, if we bumped, we'd die.

That same afternoon, a coastguard plane flew overhead, quite low. So relieved were we to see anything or anybody else that Sally and I went out on deck and waved. Alec came out a second later, shouting savagely at us to go below and stop being idiots, and very firmly switched off the radio. 'Nosy bastards!' he muttered and went off to his cabin. Odd behaviour, I thought at the time. Knowing now what I do about marine etiquette and the rules about radios and coastguard officials, it was nothing short of criminal. He seemed more irritable than usual, but we all were to some extent. It was very hot and there was not much wind.

One afternoon Alec called me on deck, sounding pleased and excited about something. He had caught a big mackerel. Usually Alec was the one to pull the fish in, gash it through the eye with the gaff-hook, stab it in the head several times with a knife and then go about the whole ghastly process of decapitation, gutting and filleting, while I turned pale and retired below. But on this occasion, he insisted that I do it. Fair enough, I thought, pull my weight – and besides, I suspected he saw it as a much-needed lesson in manliness. With him watching on and instructing, I set to. A decade later, and after apologising to God and to the fish itself, I had converted that lovely sleek shining creature, whose sides were silver rainbows and whose blood streamed bright-dark in the gunwales, into a Tupperware container of pinkish fish-fillets.

At the end of the nauseous, slipping, sweating, slimy struggle, I felt terribly Australian and intrepid and as though I ought to light up a Winfield. I was also quite sure that I had satisfied Alec's need to bring the Professor down to earth. I scrubbed the filleting knife clean of scales and blood, washed the deck and chopping board down with detergent and put the fishing gloves to soak in a pail of soapy water. I then went below to resume writing a letter. A minute later, down through the window-hatch dropped the stinking gloves, still dripping wet, straight onto the page on which I had spent considerable time drawing coloured marginalia of seabirds and curly heraldic fish. Smeared across the paper was a stinking mess of dark blood and a yellowish fluid that made all my colours run and turned the ink into a discoloured puddle of indecipherable smears. The gloves were followed by a stream of invective even more pungent than the gluey slime. Alec was making a point about the proper cleaning-up procedure after fish-filleting, a process that apparently does not involve soaking gloves overnight in a bucket of soapy water.

After this incident, the girls and I became seriously worried about Alec's increasingly violent temper, although it was hard to compare notes when he was always within earshot. Darwin seemed a very long way away, and nobody liked to ask why we were still heading westward.

*

With every day that passed, I was more and more convinced that this trial voyage had only one possible outcome, that being a blunt refusal on Alec's part to take me as far as the corner shop, let alone to Africa. I had, after all, spent the last two weeks tripping over things, getting flustered at his bad language and failing to support Alec in his perfectly reasonable attempts to get the girls to lather themselves all over while naked on the foredeck. I had also failed to cook any appetising meals whatsoever – having told Alec that I could cook like a dream.

But for all this, Alec in one of his rare sunny moments came up to me one night and offered me a lift to South Africa. I could hardly believe my ears. A load was lifted off my mind. He wasn't exactly best-chum material, but anything was better than five months in

Darwin busking in the mall. Best of all, we were to leave a week after we returned. Nice fellow, Alec, did I mention?

With my newfound confidence, I began to appreciate things about *Meropë*, namely its stylishness and neatness. The saloon was gleaming in mahogany panelling, the upholstery was maroon leather, and we drank our nightly sundowners out of what appeared to be Tiffany glasses, each one decorated with a lustrous design of kingfishers in opalescent glass.

Meanwhile, Jutta and Sally and I plucked up the courage to ask when we were thinking of heading back. Jutta had a plane ticket to Denmark in about a fortnight and Sally a job to start in London about the same time. Alec, in a particularly buoyant mood, explained that we were only heading one more day westward, to a place called the Prince Regent River. He had been telling us about some Aboriginal cave paintings a couple of days' walk inland, which he wanted us to see. After that, it was homeward bound.

The news came as a great relief; we were all happier for knowing what the future held and sat each evening before dinner in the cockpit playing cards and drinking gin and tonics. We also opened up to each other in the long hot evenings: Jutta talked about her boyfriend Claus back home and her father's illness. Sally regaled us with stories about her work as a tour operator on package holidays to Corfu. Only Alec remained as cagey as ever about his past, though he seemed excited about the prospect of the cave paintings, which, he said, were seen by very few white people. We were now about 2000 miles from anywhere. We were also being forced to tighten our belts. That night's supper was three pieces of salami and a tomato. Thank goodness we had tons of water. We also had a freezer full of mince, but we were saving that for the return trip.

*

Two days later, we turned into the Prince Regent River system, a huge tidal wash full of sandbars and whirlpools. About twenty miles upstream, the river widened out into a vast triangular inland lagoon, the St Georges Basin, a body of water thirty miles across and ringed by mountains all around; real mountains, knobbed and peaked and table-topped in reds and oranges and purples and clothed with eucalypt forest, the first proper tall trees we had seen for weeks. We continued up the river to its highest navigable point, a muddy stretch between mangroves, where we finally anchored. Here for the first time we saw crocodiles worthy of the name. Every few minutes there came floating by a log with eyes and nostrils just protruding. Usually we saw only the head, but occasionally one would allow its whole body to float to the surface and waggle its tail to swim from bank to bank. Only then did we realise how huge they were; fifteen, even twenty feet long. I became ridiculously wary of standing too near the rails of the yacht at night. After our first morning there, I was taking no chances. They knew I was there, you see. They'd smelt me, they'd smelt me.

On that first morning we had rowed in our dinghy another two kilometres up from our anchorage to where the river stopped at a low wall of the usual reddish-bronze rock and a little cascade of fresh water. The dinghy was about the size of a budget tub of Blue Ribbon Dairy ice-cream. All the way up there were crocs to either side of us, drifting in the water, lying on the mud banks, and it suddenly struck me how very fragile and eggshell-like the sides of the dinghy were. When we were about twenty feet from the rock wall, we grounded on a mud bank under the water and, as the tide was going out, Alec realised that we might be high and dry unless we did something quickly.

'Sandy,' he barked. 'Get out and push us off!'

I looked over the side into the muddy depths and the girls glanced around in alarm at the log-strewn banks just metres away.

'Er … when you say, get *out* …,' I stammered, but Alec cut in again.

'For Christ's sake! Out now and push like buggery or we'll be stuck here for the night. Jesus!'

I was more scared of him than I was of the crocs so I was out of the dinghy, pushing it off with one almighty heave, and back into the boat before you could say 'dinner time,' thinking in that split second, which seemed like half an hour, 'Ah well, this is it, this is where all those premonitions come true, this is Nemesis.' In my haste, I brought back with me into the dinghy half a ton of mud and debris and a few small fish. Alec's only comment as he rowed us the last ten feet to the bank was, 'You'll be scrubbing this dinghy clean, you moron.' I was pleased to see that one of my mud-smeared trainers seemed to have caught him a fair whack across the face, judging from the slash of mud that now marked him like an unkempt raccoon.

But I didn't really mind what his mood was. Sally told me afterwards that within half a second of my splashdown, she and Jutta saw three logs get up onto legs and slide into the water. This put Alec's insanity into some perspective.

We clambered ashore to find ourselves in a landscape dotted with deep black billabongs, cool beneath ancient gums and surrounded by cycads and palms. These billabongs were covered with little waterlilies, each white petal fringed with a ragged series of pink fronds or tassels, giving the whole bloom a curiously hazy or insubstantial appearance. We didn't swim in these larger pools for fear of crocs, but there were plenty of smaller pools where we were able to have a dip and sunbathe on the satin-bronze rocks. We wandered further up the gorge but found it pretty tough going. Where the rock petered out, the ground was covered in a wiry grass. This was lemony-green in colour, and exceptionally sticky, making wading through it a continual process of strenuous dragging, leaving the calves covered in a tacky gum and hundreds of tiny sharp seeds. It made me think carefully about the proposed expedition inland to see the cave paintings.

One bizarre find had me puzzled, and I remain so to this day. At the foot of a cliff on a huge flat slab of rock was, inexplicably, an enormous iron double bedstead, fully sprung, brass-knobbed and only slightly rusty. How on earth had it got there? It must have weighed a ton, would barely fit on any yacht, and, sitting as it was on the only smooth, traversable patch of land for miles around, could hardly have been carried – and even if it had been, for what reason? The only explanation I could think of was that it was conclusive evidence of a final tragic and unpublished chapter of *Bedknobs and Broomsticks* in which the three children carelessly wish themselves into the Kimberley Ranges with a fond desire to see some kangaroos and end up as croc-fodder, leaving the old iron double bed to moulder slowly into the outback wilderness.

Within the hour, I could have done with a magic bedknob to whisk me out of there. After we had returned to the yacht, Alec started talking about the trip to the caves. He estimated a two-day walk in, and a two-day walk back again. He wanted, he said, to start immediately. He asked Jutta whether she felt up to the walk and as soon as she said yes, sent her down below to pack a bag. Then he asked Sally whether she wanted to tag along, stressing that she really didn't have to and that it would be quite tough going. Sally, having spent most of her life negotiating nothing more threateningly botanical than the Chelsea flower show, had a thing about thorns and long grass. When she replied with some relief that she was very happy to stay and mind the boat, Alec clapped his hands and said briskly, 'Yep, good idea, no worries. Just duck below and check the freezer, would you, Sal?'

As soon as Sally had scurried below, Alec helped Jutta down into the dinghy, passed down his backpack and climbed down himself.

'Untie us, Sandy, will ya?'

'Yes, of course. Here's my rucksack. Could you …?'

'Just untie us first, do as you're asked,' Alec said curtly, settling to the oars.

'Yes, sorry, here we are,' I said, handing Alec the untied painter. 'If you could just … I mean, I *think* I can jump, but …'

'Yeah, about that,' said Alec from the dinghy, now some metres from the yacht, 'I think Sally'll need someone to look after her. She can't stay here on her own.'

'Well, of course, but—'

'So be a gentleman, Professor, won'tcha? We'll be back in four days.'

'Um, Alec?' I called to the rapidly retreating dinghy.

'Can't hear ya,' he called back cheerfully, and then added, 'Oh yeah, and don't use any of the food. We're running short. See ya!'

And at that, Alec and an alarmed-looking Jutta motored away up the crocodile-streaked river.

As a neat bit of abduction, it left his last attempt for dead.

Sally emerged from below and was surprised to find me still there. 'Wot's goin' on?' she asked sharply. 'Where are the others?'

I pointed silently up the river; the dinghy was now just a black speck on the bright silver skin of the water.

'What?'

'Alec said you needed looking after so took off without me.'

'Joo mean to say, Sandy,' said Sally, with more than a hint of rat-trap in her voice, 'that you've let Jutta, poor bleedin' Jutta, go off alone for four days in the bush with that ... that ... reptile?'

'Um ...'

'You moron! You utter bleedin' imbecile!' she snapped, and punched me in the arm. Then she turned and marched down below.

Sally might have had me to protect her from the dangers of the wilderness, but who the blazes was going to protect me from Sally? It was going to be a long four days.

Once Sally had calmed down enough to realise that we had both been outmanoeuvred, we put the kettle on and talked it over. Ah, the sheer relief of unguarded speech! For the first time since Darwin, Sally and I were able to talk freely and lost no time in sharing our frank impressions of the last fortnight. In a breathless torrent of indignation we covered the entire voyage in minute detail. For two weeks now, we had each been in our own private world, making the best of a bad job, determining not to be the one to upset the apple-cart, convincing ourselves that our discomfort was the unreasonable bristling of an over-refined sensibility, and gritting our teeth in a rictus of politeness – not out of a sense of hypocrisy but out of a real sense that perhaps we were the ones being oversensitive to a broader, blunter set of manners than our own.

But now that we were speaking freely, we wondered how we had not spoken up long ago. Cowardice certainly played its part, but I like to think that there was also a genuine desire to be friendly at almost any cost. Besides, as Sally pointed out, if things had blown up onboard, there were not many places to go.

Having exhausted an analysis of Alec's character and his dealings with us, we had other things to worry about. The first, obviously, was Jutta. Alec's disappearance with her was so obviously engi-neered that we feared for the outcome. Quite apart from that, the fact that they seemed to have taken off into the most inhospitable terrain for four days of hiking through forty-degree heat with only the scantiest of preparation and equipment was cause enough to worry. We wondered if we would ever see either of them again.

However, without a dinghy or any way off the yacht, we could do nothing about Jutta and had to trust her to look after herself. Besides, we had other things to worry about. Sally's rootle around in the freezer had revealed that there was precious little food left any-way, and we would need every bit of it to get us back to Darwin.

'I could go ashore and forage for berries or mushrooms or some-thing,' I suggested brightly, but Sally pointed out that as we had no dinghy, getting past the crocs put paid to that idea, and anyway, where did I think we were, *Wind in the Willows?* While I retreated into silence, Sally rummaged around in a locker and hauled out a fishing rod.

'Ever used one of these before?' she asked.

'Is it a dry fly rod?' I asked. 'My father's a bit keen on trout fishing.'

'No, Sandy, this is not a bleedin' dry fly rod, this is not bleedin' 'Ampshire and I am not bleedin' Izaak Walton,' said Sally. 'Gawd 'elp us, I'll catch the buggers meself, just watch me.' Then she added, somewhat slyly, 'You can kill 'em, mind you, being the big man round 'ere 'n all, and me just a little woman 'oo needs protectin'. I've never killed a livin' fing in me life and I don't intend to start now.'

She added as an afterthought, "Cept that Alec if 'e lays a finger on Jutta.'

At that, she settled on the deck, impaled a dried piece of salami onto the hook and cast the line expertly into the murky depths.

Despite my experience with the mackerel a few days before, I felt far from confident about dispatching a fish and expressed my doubts. Sally's only reply was an unhelpful suggestion along the lines of 'Tell it one of your jokes, Sandy, it does for us every time,' so I stalked off to see if I could find a weapon of some sort. Oh yes, and something to use on the fish as well.

The catching was not the problem. Three seconds after dropping a hook into the river, Sally was hauling up a small mud-grey fish with a wide mouth, googly eyes and whiskers: a type of catfish, I thought. This was a relief, as I knew I wouldn't have to kill it, for the very good reason that, as I assured Sally knowledgeably, members of the catfish tribe are completely inedible due to toxins in their flesh. Besides, there wasn't enough flesh on this one to feed a mouse. We must, therefore, regrettably, throw it back. Pity, better luck next time.

But first, to extract our one and only hook from the creature's jaws. I had always assumed fish to be lissom things, frail, fleshy and tender, the animal equivalent of custard apples. Well, this thing wasn't. Its top lip was constructed of something resembling Tupper-ware and it took half an hour to pull the hook from its lip, and only then when I resorted to using a pair of pliers. I took away half the wretched thing's face before finally releasing it with a long sigh of relief back into the river. I was sweating, slimy, bloodstained and shaking with the effort; the catfish, on the other hand, seemed as fresh as a lemon sorbet when I finally threw it riverwards.

Half a minute later there came another bite at the hook. Sally reeled in the line excitedly, only to find another wiggling catfish.

Wait.

Another catfish?

No. The same one, evidenced by the fact that half its face was newly missing. It had clearly enjoyed its time with me so much that it had neatly caught the hook through the other half of its face on the off-chance of another bout of playful wrestling. This time it only took fifteen minutes with the pliers and the removal of another quarter of face before I was able to throw it back again.

And wham …

Yes, another bite. And yes, somehow, old Smiley was back on the line, having caught the hook with incredible deftness through the last remaining fraction of its upper lip. I sighed and went to dig out the pliers once more.

By this time, Sally had fetched from below a book on the fishes of Australia and together we looked up this peculiarly kamikaze species. The book told us that contrary to my belief, there *was* reasonable eating on this fish, thank you, Professor, and furthermore, there weren't many other species likely to come our way in these waters. Catfish stew it would have to be. Smiley could fulfil his death-wish after all.

Despite my expressed misgivings about dispatching a fish, I wasn't really that worried. How hard could it be? I placed him on the chopping board, held him tightly around the gills in a most professional manner, took a sharp knife and went to cut his head off. I had seen my father cleanly sever a trout's backbone and send it painlessly on its last swim to the depths of fishy heaven, but when I tried this with Smiley, I found it impossible. The catfish's head was covered with a bony plate the consistency of Lego and utterly impervious to my knife. It was also impervious to a bigger breadknife, a chisel, a screwdriver, a hammer and a carpenter's saw, all of which I mustered over the next sweaty, stinking half-hour. It was while I was attempting unsuccessfully to saw through the plate and stop the damned thing from grinning up at me that I discovered the other amazing thing about catfish, namely that they talk.

Killing anything is a beastly business but at least with fish, you expect them to die in dignified silence. But no. For forty-five minutes, Smiley kept up a continuous stream of grunts, whistles, ooohs and aaahs with each new phase of my increasingly frenzied assault.

After that first one, Sally hauled three more catfish out of the river. By the time I had finished off the last, I was convinced I was going to Hell. And if Alec happened to return suddenly, I was certainly going to have my own head sawn off, because the deck looked as though we had re-enacted the Battle of Trafalgar. Finally Sally managed to catch a different species of fish, a wonderfully large and mercifully flabby thing, which the book said was a Mangrove Jack. It didn't utter a word and, as soon as I showed it the hammer and the pliers, it died instantly in my hands. My sort of fish.

Two hours later we were sitting out in the cockpit as dusk fell over the river. Five big crocodiles had glided by over the last half-hour and I had checked each one carefully to see if it had any bits of Alec or Jutta stuck in its teeth. In a nearby tree there were flying foxes, hundreds of them, chittering and wheeling and flapping like dilapidated killer umbrellas, and they were terrifying Sally. I was rather enjoying having a more subdued maiden to comfort after an afternoon of biting badinage – though to tell the truth, the bats frightened the willies out of me too. Dinner had been superb. Sally had somehow turned four muddy little catfish carcasses and one Mangrove Jack into a superb curry, and now we were sitting back relaxing and feeling full-fed for the first time in days. The absence of Alec was like the lifting of a thundercloud. Neither of us said anything out loud, but I was wondering what lay out there in the darkness of the Kimberley and how Jutta was faring. For her part, Sally was looking thoughtful and tense and I guessed it was not really the bats, after all.

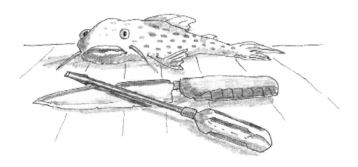

To our intense relief, Jutta and Alec returned the next day, having decided for mysterious reasons to cut short their trek to the caves. Alec reverted immediately to his moody, suspicious self. Jutta oscillated between being very quiet and thoughtful and then manically cheerful. She and Sally closeted themselves together for a long private talk. Alec clearly hated their doing this, but over the next week spent more and more time on his own in his cabin, which was no bad thing. I remained maddeningly cheerful, just to irritate him, and started using big words all the time.

The one encouraging thing was that at last we pointed our nose eastward and started the long haul back to Darwin.

*

A week later, we were drifting in a dead calm somewhere a hundred miles off the coast of Australia in the Arafura Sea. We had been due back in Darwin five days before. Jutta had missed her flight home, and Sally had missed the start of her job and was quite sure she had been sacked. We now had no idea when we would get back to Darwin. Three days earlier, the wind had dropped and dropped and eventually died away to nothing. Alec had gone to start the motor but it had coughed, sputtered and died to nothing. It transpired that we had run out of diesel.

Hmm, serious stuff, we thought; let's make a nice cup of tea. I lit the stove, put the kettle on and waited for it to boil. Twenty minutes later Sally asked how it was getting on and I went down to find the kettle only warm. The stove had gone out. We had run out of cooking gas.

Check stores of food. We were right out of fresh food, and had been for a week now. We had plenty of pasta and raw mince, but without gas to cook with, both were inedible. Besides, now that we were unable to run the motor, the freezer started to defrost, spilling a smelly pool of water over the cabin floor. In the soaring heat, the mince began to fester before the day was out. All we had to eat were two packets of dry crackers and a small tin of pineapple chunks. We had not, however, run out of music. Megatrash and The Vomiters still kept us entertained twelve hours a day with their *Cacophony for Pneumatic Drills and a Rabid Hyena*. Perhaps somebody from the mainland a hundred miles away would hear it and come and rescue us.

Tempers shortened. We really were getting very hungry indeed. Brunch one morning was a single soggy cube of pineapple on a dry cracker, for example. I began to worry about how this was going to end.

One morning, we nearly lost Alec for good. It was so hot and calm that he lowered a rope ladder over the side so that we could swim off the yacht. The water was very clear, very blue and very deep. I dived over the side and had a wonderful splash around. Then I climbed back aboard and it was Alec's turn. I idly watched him, peering down into the deep, satiny water. Something caught my eye. What was it? It looked for all the world like one of those catfish – small, grey, flat-headed. Then I looked again. The little fish was growing. It was swelling visibly as I watched. Some sort of puffer fish, I pondered. It had gone from about one foot long to two feet in seconds, then four feet, then six feet. I realised what I was seeing. This was no small catfish swimming six feet below the surface. The sea here was so much clearer than I was used to. This creature had been much deeper down when I first spotted it and was in fact about twelve feet long, clear to see now that it had risen to the surface. In fact it was ... it was ... should I bother telling Alec? So easy to say nothing. Damn my conscience.

'Alec ... sorry to bother you, but ... shark! Shark! Bloody great shark coming your way, Alec. Shark! Don't panic but there's a shark!'

Alec was aboard in three seconds, just in time to see the creature surface a few yards away, a sleek tiger shark with a wicked mouth and tiny eyes. It spent the next hour circling lazily, while we tried to work out ways to capture it and use the pineapple chunks to turn it into Hawaiian shark fondaleo.

We didn't do any swimming after that.

There was nothing much else to report. Alec won thirty-six games of gin rummy, Jutta seventeen and I twelve. Sally won 357 games and then we didn't play anymore because Alec banned it. This was on the fifth day of the calm. The rapidly rotting mince had gone overboard two days before after some discussion as to whether it was worth trying to salvage the less green bits and cook them over the paraffin lamp. Sanity won the debate and we held a brief but touching sea-burial for the whole soggy mass. No sign of land, no sign of wind, no sign of a decent meal ever again. We were all going to die.

Jutta was the plumpest of all of us, but if it came to eating any-body, Alec was going to be my first choice because he was a complete bastard. If he called me Professor again, I was going to kill him.

*

Like most trials in life, this one was simply a waiting game. On the seventh day, the calm broke and we were on our way once more. The day began as had the previous six: absolutely still, windless and stiflingly hot. We had been joined by a character from *The Rime of the Ancient Mariner*, namely a large albatross-like bird that had wheeled … is wheeling … I think I might write in the present tense just for dramatic effect … in slow, maddening circles around the mast and has been doing so for the last three days just waiting for one of us to die. (It isn't really an albatross; it's a blue-footed booby, but I can't imagine Coleridge getting that particular species into a poem destined to become a classic, can you?) We have out on a long line a lure, a bright fluorescent-pink plastic squid, in a vain attempt to catch something to go with our last spoonfuls of pineapple chunks. We are singularly failing to catch anything. I am on watch while the others are languishing below. The sails are up in a vain attempt to catch some air, but they hang limp and lifeless with only the odd slow creak and thump as the gentle ocean swell rocks the boat infinitesimally from side to side. Only that and the slow wheeling of the booby overhead like a cross of doom. Doom!

I look up to scan the horizon for a sign, anything that might save us, and am puzzled to see off on the horizon a long low solid line. Land!

But surely that's the north, and the only land around should be over yonder on the southern horizon? Unless somehow we've drifted all the way up to Java?

'Alec? Can you come here a moment? There's something puzzling me.'

By the time he has popped his head out of the hatchway, I am even more puzzled, as the bank is now twice as dark and twice as thick on the horizon.

'Alec,' I start, 'I was just wondering—' but I get no further.

'Christ almighty!' he cries. 'Sally! Jutta! Get up here immediately. Sandy, help me get the sails down. Jutta, close all the hatches. Sally, go below and stow everything you can lay your hands on. Step on it!'

Before he has even finished speaking, three things happen at once. First, out of nowhere, three Harrier jets pass overhead, seemingly five feet above the top of the mast. They make no noise. They pass over as silently as drifting clouds. The sheer irrelevance of them, coupled with the total absence of appropriate roaring jet noises, makes me wonder if I have slipped sideways into some giant movie screen with the sound turned off. I am just about to comment on this when I am knocked off my feet. The sound of their passing, lagging some fifty metres behind, hits me like a twenty-foot baseball bat, a full five seconds in their wake; a searing, splitting, boom-crack of noise that tears the sky in half and shatters the senses like great panes of glass cracking. That is the first thing.

The second comes immediately after: the onslaught of the storm, a seething white squall of wind and rain that turns the world into a blinding, thrashing maelstrom, flogging the sails and sheets like thunder and making the yacht heel and lurch as though she is being physically buffeted by a great slapping hand. Down below I hear the crash of crockery and the clatter of pans and through the hatchway I see Sally tumble sideways under an avalanche of books and papers left idly around the saloon.

The third thing to happen is that as the yacht leaps forward, the luminous pink squid darts to the surface. The booby, the bird of doom, Coleridge's cursed albatross, pounces upon it and in a moment has a barbed hook firmly embedded in its breast-feathers. Squawking and flapping in fear and terror, it is suddenly in the cockpit on the end of the fishing line. The bird is about the size of a goose but with a bill like a blue dagger; while it thrashes around the cockpit, we cannot get near the tiller or the sheet winches to control the madly bucking boat. Alec manages somehow to grab it and pin its wings and hold its head, then sends me stumbling down to the galley for a sharp kitchen knife. I do think momentarily of educating him about the literary traditions concerning the killing of large seabirds, but think better of it. Fortunately, the knife is for more humane purposes. While Alec holds the bird, I cut away the sliver of breast-flesh that holds the cruel hook and though it bleeds a little, I do not think it is deep enough to have done any permanent harm. We throw the bird skywards, and after a brief ungainly struggle with the elements, it regains its balance on the wind and disappears astern, taking the storm with it.

Minutes later, all is still once more. We look around the cockpit and the tangle of sheets and lines. The rigging is awry and the saloon is a shambles – five idle days of calm have made us careless about stowing things safely – but we realise that the gust, almighty though it has been, has passed on its way southward, leaving just a rollicking breeze to take us back to Darwin.

*

The next morning, we sighted Darwin. Calculations showed that we had thirty miles to go, spanking along as we were before a fine breeze. The tide was with us. We held a jolly little competition to estimate our time of arrival. Some said 5.30 p.m., others guessed 7 p.m. Alec, who presumably knew about these things, put it earlier than all of us. We quietly rejoiced. We each had a nice wash and sat in the cockpit, eating the last of the dry crackers and talking about exactly what we were going to order at some bistro once we hit Darwin. Steak was high on my list, pineapple further down. We lightened up a little. I whistled a careless tune as I packed up my rucksack. We all smiled quietly at each other a lot. And then Alec, who was steering at the time, said, 'I know a short cut!'

Ten minutes later, we'd hit a sandbank.

If ever there was justification for a mutiny against a ship's captain, this was it. Even Captain Bligh, newly hauled from his ordeal at sea and having had no time for a quick shower and a gin and tonic, would have said, 'Yep, yep, fair enough. Due provocation, I can see that. Kill the bugger.' Or so I mused as we sat helplessly for twelve hours and watched the tide go all the way out, the yacht leaning over and over and over until it was on a sixty-degree angle, and then watched as the tide came all the way in again ... but not enough to lift us free. With an engine, of course, we could probably have churned our way off the sandbank, but we didn't have the diesel, did we? With cooking gas, we could have cooked up a pasta dinner to while away the hours, but we didn't have any cooking gas, did we? We could have torn Alec limb from limb, but he had locked himself in his cabin and told us to go to bed, so we couldn't commit murder, could we?

As the tide receded, the yacht began to heel over to an angle that made lying in one's bunk impossible. It was hard enough trying to move around a boat on such a steep angle. That afternoon I had lost my footing as I made my way crabwise across the tilted saloon and ended up slippery-dipping into the crockery cupboard, breaking a bowl. For Alec, it was the last straw. As we all sat in the cockpit later that evening, pretending to enjoy our sundowner drinks – a glass of water with a dried-up slice of lemon in it to make it posh – Alec started to lecture us. He berated us for our inefficiency, for our inability to learn about life onboard, for the wastefulness and extravagance that had led us to this pass, for our obstinacy in failing to obey instructions and for the general wimpishness of our worldview. We sat there very solemnly, nodding our heads and letting him rave, occasionally sheepishly whispering, 'Sorry, Alec' like naughty schoolchildren. He finished with a flourish and a last point.

'And,' he fumed, 'I cannot believe the carelessness of some of you here. Only this afternoon Sandy broke a bowl! Over the last few weeks, we've had other things broken, gone missing, sadly abused. This is *my* yacht and it deserves, as I do, a little respect! Is that clear?'

'Yes, Alec,' we mumbled. 'Sorry, Alec, won't happen again, Alec,' we dutifully chorused and Alec sat back, satisfied that he had made his point. Just then, Sally downed the last of her pretend gin, went to throw the lemon-slice dregs over her shoulder into the sea – and her hand slipped. Not only the lemon but the glass itself, one of Alec's Tiffany kingfisher ones, flew over her shoulder and disappeared with a splash overboard. For a frozen second, we watched Alec. With a barely audible snarl and a face of stone, he vanished below. That was the last we saw of him that night.

*

The next day, sure enough, the tide floated us free of the sandbank and we limped into Darwin Harbour, starving, desperate and with our nerves scraped raw by the tension onboard. Both Jutta and Sally had indeed missed their flights home, Jutta was desperate for news of her sick father, and I was sick of being called Professor. Determined, however, not to leave on a sour note, we agreed to one last drink. We packed our bags and rowed ashore and sat in the main saloon of the Royal Darwin Yacht Club with false smiles of camaraderie hitched on our faces, trying not to show that we just wanted to get to the nearest bistro and eat a whole cow. We ordered and drank the smallest possible drinks, said, 'Well, here we all are' a lot, and then we were ready to go. All we needed was our passports, still held by Alec in his role as skipper. This is where we hit a last snag.

'Not so fast, girls, not so fast, Professor,' Alec said. 'You owe me money.'

As our jaws dropped, Alec explained. We had been told before setting out that the trip would take fourteen days. It had actually taken twenty-five. Although we'd paid Alec an agreed sum for the fortnight, he now expected us to pay him almost the same again for the eleven extra days. Sensing our outrage, he held up our passports and refused to hand them over unless we paid up. In sheer dazed exhaustion, we wearily pulled out our wallets. But as I was about to hand over the cash, I finally let rip. Weeks of conciliatory politeness gave way to schoolmasterly sarcasm.

'What exactly are we paying for, Alec?' I asked in a ringing voice, loud enough to turn heads. 'Just so we're quite clear, eh?'

'Shhh!' he hissed. 'You're disturbing people. Keep your voice down.'

'No, no,' I went on, notching up the volume a little. 'I think we'd all be interested to hear, Alec. Is the extra cash for the eleven days overdue, Alec? The fact that two of us have missed our flights home? It can't exactly be for all the extra food, can it, seeing we ran out *six days ago*. Hmm?'

'Look, keep it quiet, will ya?' Alec whispered again and tried drawing me into a quieter corner. By this time, a number of people were staring and raising enquiring eyebrows. Incompetent or dishonest yachtsmen get short shrift in the yacht clubs of the world.

'Nor could it be for all the extra diesel, could it, since that ran out as well, didn't it? And the emergency tanks were empty, weren't they? Never filled, in fact?'

'Look—'

'Like the cooking gas, in fact, Alec,' I continued, riding on a tide of indignation. In all my years of performing onstage, my elocution and voice projection had never been better. 'Perhaps we're just paying you extra for your delightful company, prolonged even further when we hit that sandbank and stayed an extra eighteen hours aboard, hmm? What did *you* think of the company, girls? Tell the whole club. Did you enjoy being asked to share your showering pleasure with the captain, I wonder? Did you appreciate the—'

But before I could finish, Alec had flung the passports at me and fled. That was the last we saw of him.

Once he had gone, Jutta rang home from a public phone in the bar, and returned to us with a white face and appalling news. Her father had died just a few days before. In tears, she babbled out a barely comprehensible explanation. She should have, as we knew, flown home almost a fortnight before. When without any explanation she had failed to turn up in Denmark, her parents had begun to worry. Her father, she said, had even had the Australian coastguard out looking for us. I thought of the plane we had seen, and of Alec turning off our radio, and wondered how much the worry about his daughter might have contributed to the failing health of a man already seriously ill.

By now it was late and the restaurant bar, too dark, too modern and too loud, had become oppressive. Jutta was finishing up her sad news and Sally was packing away her things. Jutta would fly straight back for the funeral, leaving tomorrow. Sally had to go and sort out the mess left by her own failure to catch her flight home. After a sombre and scrappy farewell, I was left sitting alone over a beer and eight packets of crisps. What were my plans? Although Alec had not said as much, I suspected that the offer of a trip to Africa had been retracted. I munched my way ravenously through a ninth packet like a morose termite. Tomorrow I would start looking for another yacht out of here.

Chapter 11

Proceeding eighty miles into the north-west wind, you reach the city of Euphemia, where the merchants of seven nations gather at every solstice and equinox. The boat that lands there with a cargo of ginger and cotton will set sail again, its hold filled with pistachio nuts and poppy seeds, and the caravan that has just unloaded sacks of nutmegs and raisins is already cramming its saddlebags with bolts of golden muslin for the return journey.

—ITALO CALVINO, *Invisible Cities*

My unscheduled month's sailing in the Kimberleys had brought me neatly to the end of July. Over the next five days, a fleet of yachts was departing for Indonesia in what was called the Ambon Race. Consequently, many of them were advertising for crew to get them as far as Ambon – about seven days' sailing. From a glance at my world map, the chain of islands looked enchanting: here were the Cinnamon Isles, the orang-utans, the leafy huts and the fishing nets and the green bottles washed ashore, the crescent-moon beaches, the turbaned pirates in leaky junks, all in a great necklace of rich jewels, rare and strange, lying on the silk of the Timor Sea.

I trotted off to the yacht club and put up a notice on the board there. This had my room's phone number on it. By the time I wandered back, the phone was ringing and I found someone on the other end saying, 'Hello, saw your notice, why don't you come to Ambon with us next week, good-oh, bring your toothbrush.'

I met the skipper that afternoon, a fitter and turner from New Zealand called Skip. The yacht was called *Moonshine*, a small but sturdy vessel built out of steel by Skip himself in his garden. There was also his wife, Brenda, who seemed a bit nervous and fretful but friendly enough. After a brief interview – at least I could now claim some six weeks' genuine yachting experience – they offered to take me all the way to Singapore. I could not have asked for a better arrangement: now I had a clear passage to the Asian mainland. After this, surely there would be no major obstacles, the English Channel being the only stretch of water between me and the final few ferries to Iona. I was glad to be leaving Australia at long last. The next stop would be truly exotic, the old Spice Islands shrouded in legend and mystery. I might even be eaten by cannibals, which would be a turn-up for the tapestry circle and might put even Dorothy's bus-conductress daughter-in-law in the shade.

Packing my bags once more, I set off to board *Moonshine* for the voyage north.

*

Although we were supposedly in a race along with thirty other yachts, we didn't see any of our competitors after the first two days, days of stifling calm when we longed to use our engine but couldn't because of it being a race. Then a stiffish breeze sprang up, sending us skimming over the Banda Sea to Ambon. By the time we were nearing the finish – in about twentieth place, I think – we were not that bothered about the racing element. It was merely a quick way of getting a cruising permit for Indonesia, which was otherwise difficult to obtain.

On the seventh night, there came stealing across the water a new fragrance on the breeze, no longer just salt and ozone but an exciting, hot smell that tingled in the nose and made me think of mulled wine and Christmas ham. It was the aroma of cloves, of cinnamon, of nutmeg and pepper, and we knew that we were nearing land. Just how close we were to Ambon we didn't quite realise until, as we were gliding forward on a moonless night, a flare went up right under our bows and exploded in a dragon-star of blazing crimson flame, nearly taking Skip's eyebrows with it. We had crossed the finishing line. We had completed the race. We had officially arrived in the Spice Islands.

Waking the next morning I went on deck before Skip and Brenda were up, looked at the scene before me and breathed a long, silent 'Yes!' *Moonshine* lay in a long wooded inlet not far from a narrow strip of beach backed by a profusion of jungle trees. Coconut palms, classically slender; frondy banana trees; bright dense clove trees; many-branched banyans; great buttressed tropical fig trees with dark glossy leaves and massive horizontal branches splashed with scarlet blossom – and a hundred others of every shape, size and hue. A steep mountainside clothed in forest rose sharply up from the beach, so steep and high that its peaks were wreathed that morning in grey mist.

As I gazed out across the water, almost giddy with wonder, I struggled to take in the detail. Here on the beach, fishing nets were drying on poles or draped over native canoes; these were painted in battered blue and adorned with orange eyes. Down the one narrow road walked a group of women with top-heavy baskets of strange pink fruit on their heads, perfectly balanced. A man wandered past with two huge bunches of green bananas slung from a stout pole over his shoulders, while on the beach a five-year-old boy bashed a coconut over the head of a goat to try to dislodge the creature from the canoe it was sitting in. The goat seemed impervious to the bashing and was beginning to chew the boy's toy, which was simply a stick on a string. And still came those wafts of incense blowing in warm gusts from the land – the cloves, the cinnamon, the vanilla – though underlain now by other aromas: cooking fires, pigs and open drains.

Closer to the yacht, a youth was sailing a tiny sampan, an extraordinary craft, little more than a tiny canoe with outriggers on each side, a large triangular sail on a bamboo mast and spar, and an awning. Both awning and sail looked as if they had been stitched together out of old blue sugar sacks. The boy stood dressed only in faded red shorts, his brown skin gleaming in the sun against the sea-green. He had a thin band of gold and scarlet around one ankle and a blue tattoo on one arm. He waved and called a greeting as he glided by yards away.

Later that afternoon there was an official welcoming ceremony by the locals, the sort of thing that might have greeted one of Captain Cook's contemporaries 200 years ago (apart, I hoped, from the ritual spearing and eating of the guests of honour afterwards). Dancers in red sarongs, gold bracelets and head-pieces made of bird-of-paradise plumes leapt about the sands to the booming sound of a dozen conch-shells, blown like so many French horns.

Finally came a display of magic that to this day I cannot explain. Seven bare-chested islanders picked up a log of bamboo, all seven standing abreast and holding it at chest height. Out from the palms stepped an old man with a plumed head-dress and bone bracelets about his ankles and elbows. He started chanting an odd nasal song and swinging a brass censer, from which drifted a haze of smoke. Suddenly, the bamboo was alive and trying to escape. It bucked and swung, and dragged the men into the shallows while they strained with cracking muscles and pouring sweat to keep it from plunging into the water and swimming off.

Now the witchdoctor, releasing the seven islanders from their task, called for seven yachties to come forward and take their place. Seven men, all Westerners, picked up the bamboo log as the islanders had done. They stood looking at each other, clearly thinking, as I was, 'Well, we don't know the trick to making this thing seem alive. What do we do?' But when the witchdoctor started his chanting and his smoke-waving, there was a sudden stirring among the seven.

'Oy! Stop shoving!'

'I'm not. Hold your end up, would you?'

'I am, I am. It's too heavy!'

'Keep it still, will ya! Who's pushing it? Watch out! Let it go! I can't!'

In obvious consternation, the seven men struggled to hold onto the log, which again seemed to have a life of its own. It bore them to their knees. It tried to float them into the air. It galloped them around the beach in great circles, and finally, it tugged them down into the shallows of the sea and dunked them in an irate, wriggling heap.

The witchdoctor brought his chanting to a close and the seven men dropped the bamboo log as if it were a cranky anaconda and stood glaring and panting like men possessed. Some were cross at the state of their soaked trousers, others too exhausted to be coherent, but I managed to grab one and ask how it had happened.

'Buggered if I know,' he said. 'When I was watching them before, I wondered if it was something in the smoke stuff, something to make them act funny. But now I don't know. You could hardly get a whiff of the smoke, and my head's clear as ever. It's just ... just weird, if you know what I mean.'

Later, I asked a group of locals. They explained that it was magic, a forest spirit trapped in the bamboo and invoked to dance, but they said this without any of the smirking twinkle with which I tell small children that a vanishing silk hanky is real magic. It was just 'magic,' a curiosity of the region like beefeaters in London or koalas in Australia.

As we sailed onward through the Indonesian archipelago, I became more and more aware that we were sailing through a region where such magic was rife. Spirits dwelt in the forest and must be placated. Every well had its sacred eel, fed with eggs by the local priest. The island of Buru was inhabited by flying sorcerers who rode the thunderstorms. In case I was tempted to find this wholly enchanting, I also came across a grim side to the wizardry. A spiteful neighbour would make a traditional toy ship from cloves, hundreds of them all gummed together in exquisite detail. Then she would load it with curses and a lock of hair stolen from their neighbour's child. From the moment the ship was set afloat on the sea, the child would fall into a coma, her spirit marooned on the ship by sorcery. When the ship foundered, the child would die.

Part I

But returning to the sunlight world: did I mention the huge black and azure swallowtail butterflies that flopped ponderously like animated atlases among the jungle trees? Or the great mats of drying cloves and cinnamon twigs and vanilla pods laid out on the sides of the dusty road? Or, when we went into the town of Ambon one day, the huge, shabby chained eagle I accidentally backed into outside a shop and nearly lost an ear to? This was the other side of paradise. The filth in the gutters, the snarl of minibuses, the dogs eating unmentionable things in the concrete drains, the wailing of the great tin mosque and the throng of pickpockets and beggars and market-sellers made our occasional trips to town a harrowing experience.

*

As we sailed westwards towards leggy Sulawesi, I came to know my sailing companions well. Skip was a short, stocky man with wavy reddish hair, a pleasant freckled face and a pair of hazel eyes habitually crinkled against the sun. Brenda was taller, with a long face like a nervous ewe, a cap of dark curly hair and large brown eyes that often looked on the point of brimming over with tears. She had, at best, only a tenuous hold on her husband's affection. From snippets of conversation, I gathered that Skip's job as a fitter and turner had allowed him to spend seven years building *Moonshine* in his backyard, talking of the day when they would chuck in the rat-race and go off around the world. When the last bolt was in place, he had weighed anchor by himself, leaving Brenda standing on the quay, asking, 'When you said "we," did you mean me as well?'

'I'll give you a call if I need you,' was his reply, and he had headed off to Fiji for six months. At the end of that time, he had in fact sent for her, so she packed in her job and flew out to join him for what she hoped would be a prolonged second honeymoon in the palmy tropics. By the time I came aboard, however, this illusion was fading fast. Skip lost no opportunity to make it clear that if he could find any crew marginally more competent or better-looking, she would be off back home again. I had a feeling I might be meeting at least one of those criteria, and Brenda spent a lot of time eyeing me sideways with barely concealed jealousy.

I felt sorry for Brenda, but I could understand Skip's exasperation. Brenda's dithering insecurity moved me to tight-jawed deep-breathing exercises on an almost daily basis. And their relationship was frequently unsettling to witness. The most unnerving thing of all was that Skip could switch from polite, interested conversation with me to livid abuse of Brenda and back again in two seconds flat; as she dissolved in tears of humiliation in the front cabin, I would be left trying to think of the answer to his courteous inquiry as to what my favourite books were for Year 10 students.

But for all this, I had little cause to complain: I was sailing through the most beautiful archipelago at a gentle rate, stopping off at places one could only dream of, reading, writing, stargazing and hoping like blazes that Skip and Brenda didn't read the letters I was writing home about them.

When we reached the shores of Sulawesi – Celebes on the old maps – we turned southwards to run through the narrows of the Butan Straits. Here we anchored off a tiny humpbacked island of white sand, on which were seven palm trees, a single palm-leaf hut and a blue and orange canoe. We spent a day cleaning the boat, scrubbing off all the barnacles and weedy debris that coated the bottom and was slowing us down.

The water was not very deep, about twenty feet or so, and I took the opportunity to explore the reef. The seabed here flourished in delicate fans and flowers of stone, brains and mushrooms and antlers, in whites and plum reds, Monopoly greens and indigo blues, and in water the pale green of old Coca-Cola bottles. Seen through a snorkel mask, the backdrop was an unfocused retreat into dim blue depths, against which the fish and coral under my mask stood out with an intense clarity of outline and colour. All was lit, not with the ordinary seamless glare of daylight, but with rippling, shifting shadow and soft, bright beams, wavering in fuzzy pencils that highlighted a fish here, a coral stem there, the feathery tip of a purple polyp. And indeed the effect of the light was truly luminescent: even the skin on my arms and hands looked strangely luminous against the dim teal-blue of the depths, let alone the astonishing violets, the emerald greens, the iridescent roses and neon yellows of the fish.

I turned from fascinated absorption in the miraculous detail on a clownfish in apricot and ivory to realise that the dim blueness beyond was resolving into separate shades of blue and dark grey … and that the grey shadow was long and slim and torpedo-shaped, and looming closer all the while. As I watched, the shadow unhurriedly coalesced and became a shark, about seven feet long with tiny dead black eyes and a folded-down mouth. Not exactly Jaws, I thought to myself, but big enough to remove a limb or two, which might make the rest of the journey interesting. I'd always had nightmares about sharks, but now I felt oddly calm. It seemed the most natural thing in the world to be sharing the element with it, watching it clearly through the snorkel mask rather than thrashing about on the surface with cello music madly playing. So, I floated quietly and watched it curiously and impassively as it glided through the coral, in and out of the deep gloom. I was over here, and it was over there, and now it was weaving that way, and now it was weaving this way, and it seemed utterly – almost insultingly – uninterested in me, before it turned back into a dim shadow and dissolved into the blank blue backdrop once more.

As I floated there I felt that I had discovered something about fear: that when we confront the actuality of what we fear, it becomes a merely practical problem to be monitored, not an unseen bogeyman to hag-ride the reeling mind. Macbeth had put it well: 'Present fears are less than horrible imaginings.' There in the water I had felt perfectly in tune with the rhythm of the sea and happy to be part of Nature's great cycle – although, I confess, with one eye out for a handy lump of rock with which to club the shark to death if it came one whisker nearer than I liked.

The nearest village on the mainland, just a dinghy ride away, could have been a Hollywood model for *South Pacific*. There were palm huts on stilts, slender coconut palms, the usual collection of goats, hens and children playing in the sand, and, more alarmingly, giant palm crabs the size of dinner plates sauntering arrogantly

across the domain and sending the hens scuttling. Four hundred yards away, along a path that wound between lantana and jacarandas and cocoa trees, we discovered the main prize of the village: a freshwater stream that widened into a perfect bathing pool, deep and clean and cool. A sandbank shelved gently into one side of the pool, but a ten-foot wall of rock rose from the other, where a cascade of water fanned out to make a natural shower. The whole area was decked with ferns and mossy roots and palms; in fact, a Beverly Hills landscape gardener could not have achieved a more perfect effect.

It was here that the whole village came to bathe and wash each day, and for several days this was what we did too. Our ablutions were always accompanied by the village children, who begged shampoo and swung from lianas and did dive-bombs from the top of the waterfall, shrieking like monkeys. On one occasion we were joined by a couple of the young men of the village, who were fascinated by my safety razor. One of the youths watched in fascination as I lathered up my chin and applied the blade. Then, smiling shyly, he took the razor gently out of my hand and started to shave my chin for me. With some trepidation I closed my eyes and lay back in the pool, wondering if this might be the last the world saw of my ears. After some minutes, I checked in my little hand-held mirror and found that he had done a perfectly reasonable job – but when he started on my chest hair as well, I had to stop him before he gave me a full Brazilian.

From here it was a three-day haul southwards across a stretch of open sea to Maumere, the capital of Flores, one of the larger islands of the Indonesian chain, and years later to become famous for the anthropologically extraordinary discovery of the remains of miniature people, dubbed 'hobbits.' In fact, many of the islands we passed claimed that there were wild spirits in their forests, goblin figures akin to the African *tokoloshe*.

Flores was a turning point in my fortunes. For some time now, we had been travelling in a loose flotilla of cruising yachts of different shapes and sizes and nationalities. We tended each to go at our own pace, but we ended up at the same anchorages most nights and a social scene had sprung up. One night it might be Monopoly aboard *Moonshine*, and the next sundowner drinks aboard *Sitisi III*, a huge mustard-yellow yacht owned by a genial American couple in their eighties. Then there might be a pot-luck supper aboard *Arietta* or a salad lunch with the English couple on *Silver Ruffian*. It was very healthy, especially for Skip and Brenda and me, as even my blunted social antennae were beginning to pick up faint signals that where a marriage is concerned, two is company but three's a crowd. Any new yacht joining our loose flotilla was generally a welcome chance to widen our social gene pool and avoid the insanity of conversational inbreeding.

I woke up one morning to find alongside us a large, elegant ship called *Flying Dolphin*, two-masted and a deep sea-blue-green. There seemed to be a family aboard, Mum, Dad and two kids, and, from what I could hear, they were from the American Deep South. The father kept calling the mother 'Sugar Pie,' pronounced *Shugah pah*, and the little girl answered to 'Heathie-pup.' The boy seemed to have escaped a saccharine nickname, but was probably called Junior or Chuck. Both he and little Heathie-pup called their parents 'Sir' and 'Ma'am.' It was like being moored next to a continual repeat of *The Brady Bunch,* redubbed for the good folk of Tennessee. The letter I wrote that afternoon was scathingly anti-American.

Putting this new irksomeness aside, I turned my attention to our latest plan. All the yachties who had arrived in Flores together had decided to pool money and hire a minibus and a guide to take us on an overnight expedition into the highlands to visit some volcanic lakes, the coloured lakes of Kelimutu, one of the lesser known wonders of the world, we were told. That evening we gathered in a little eating-house in the town square. Our guide, who sat with us eating nasi goreng and drinking all the beer we could buy for him, was a pistol-toting bandit with a fat, smiling face and killer eyes who, I gathered, doubled as the town's police chief. He assured us through mouthfuls of rice that there was a lodge at the foot of the last ascent, the best on the island, a veritable five-star Hilton. At this, quite a few faces around the table brightened at the thought of double beds and honeymoon privacy. But my mind was elsewhere: I had noticed those Americans, those sugar-pie posers, coming down the street. I tried to erect a few menus to shield our faces, but too late. They had spotted us and were approaching the chop-house, all smiles and enthusiasm and an overweening certainty that they would be welcome at any gathering. And sure enough, a minute later, they had wormed their way into the expedition. Toying savagely with a hairy chicken drumstick in satay sauce, I wasn't sure I'd be able to stand their American howdy-doodiness for two whole days.

We gathered the next morning at the crack of dawn and jostled for our places in the minibus. As luck would have it, the seat next to me, the only empty seat left, was taken at the last minute by the American boy. I sighed and prepared to be stoic. If he chewed gum, I couldn't promise not to be rude, that was all.

Well, the minibus trip took ten hours, ten hours of winding, jolting roads through jungled hills, but I noticed none of it. Five minutes into the journey, the boy tentatively asked if I had ever heard of a book called *The Lord of the Rings*. He had just finished it, and there were one or two things he would like to ask about it. Could I help?

Could I help? I turned and gave the young lad my full attention. Aged eleven. Called Peter, not Chuck or Chester, which wasn't so bad. A courteous manner. Intelligent grey eyes. And the remarkable foresight to have packed in his knapsack a sheaf of blank paper and a set of pencils.

The next ten hours went by in a blur. Elvish alphabets, Dwarvish runes, discussions about what exactly an ent should look like. Narnia followed, and mazes and treasure hunts and how to make fireworks. My only fear was that I was mistaking politeness for real interest and that I was boring him terribly.

My mind was put to rest when we stopped at a tiny highland village for glasses of sweet tea. I found myself standing alone in the village square beneath an enormous spreading tree with blossoms like pink silk tassels. Here was a man tending a strange contraption resembling a top-loader washing machine, but without a lid. As I watched, a local came along carrying a live chicken by its legs. He handed a few coins to the keeper, who switched the machine on. The drum started spinning wildly and, without so much as a blink, the local dropped the chicken straight in. There was a brief cackle, a lot of horrid thumping and a cloud of feathers flew out the top in a whirlwind. A minute later, the keeper pulled out the chicken, thoroughly plucked. And thoroughly dead. I was appalled at the process – nasty, brutish and short – but six years of dealing with eleven-year-old boys had taught me something of their tastes, so I went off to find Peter, who was looking at some woven cloths with his mother. I dragged him away and back to the chicken-plucker just in time for another demonstration. The resulting squawk-thump-flutter of fountaining feathers sealed our friendship. Dwarvish runes and mazes were all very well, but this was pronounced 'neat,' and I knew he meant it.

On arrival at the mountain lodge, we found that it was indeed spacious, airy and well kept. The only difficulty was that although yes, there were beds for all of us and double beds for most, they were, somewhat oddly, arranged three to a room; that is, a double bed for the honeymooning couple and a single bed for an interested onlooker. As we allowed this logistical problem to sink in, I said brightly, 'Well, Brenda and Skip and I don't mind sharing a room, do we? We've been on *Moonshine* long enough together.'

Brenda shot me a look of pure poison and grabbed Skip's arm, whispering furiously into his ear. As we moved into the bedroom, Brenda was in tears of fury. Skip was, for once, anxious to make things right for her – and also keen, no doubt, for a spot of unobserved and uninhibited sex after months of abstinence. Once the truth dawned on me, and blushing like a pomegranate at my own naivety, I zoomed off to the other rooms and tried explaining the situation to the other couples. None of them seemed particularly keen to budge, until finally Fred and Nan, an older Jewish couple from New York, cheerfully said, 'So what's the big deal? You come sleep with us, boy, because at our age, are we going to get up to tricks? I don't think so!'

The next morning we woke at four o'clock, so as to see the sacred lakes by sunrise, and found Skip and Brenda strangely unrefreshed by their night of honeypots and love-birds, as Fred had roguishly put it. The fact is that the 'double room' provided at short notice by the management had actually been a staff bedroom doubling as a cleaning closet, hastily vacated by the cook and his assistant. It was where the hotel kept their mops, their leaky vats of disinfectant and their supply of cockroaches. The sleeping arrangement was not so much a double bed as a double bunk, suitable only for love-making of the more gymnastic sort. Even the implacably cheerful Skip was looking a little grim that morning, and as for Brenda, her face was blotchy and red with rage ... or possibly disinfectant fumes. Even Fred had the sense not to ask any saucy questions about how the night had gone.

We arrived at the peak of Kelimutu at five, while it was still dark. Nothing could be seen except a scattering of bright stars across the eastern sky and the morning star burning like a white jewel very low down. It was cold and a wind whipped about our ears and, although it was dark, we knew that we stood on the edge of a vast precipice. Then slowly a band of dark blue replaced the darkness. Threads of gold and scarlet appeared low down, and we could see the raw shapes of volcanic mountains silhouetted against the dawn, very far below us. An ancient hymn came to mind.

Stars of the morning so gloriously bright,
Sang with celestial music and light!
Then when was finished the first day's employ,
Then all the sons of God shouted for joy!

The whole tableau now began to show in sombre colours as the sky paled: dim umbers, blue-greys, charcoals, dull purples, and the lesser stars fading one by one into the blue until the morning star was left shining alone. Then suddenly, there was the sun, a red blood-orange cradled in a distant mountain saddle. It rose and rose, grew hotter, to orange, to fierce gold, to burning white when we could look at it no longer – and it was day.

We found ourselves standing on the sharp tip of a volcanic crater looking straight down a sheer precipice of white rock to a lake of vivid turquoise blue. A similar crater directly behind us held a lake of emerald green and a third smaller one held a lake of blackish purple. These were the three sacred lakes of Kelimutu – one for the spirits of the damned, one for the spirits of the blessed and the third for the spirits of the … um, the undecided, I suppose. We were at the highest point on the whole length of Flores Island, looking fifty miles to the sea. As I gazed down the giddying thousand-metre drop at my feet, I heard a rattle of loose stones behind me and turned to find Brenda at my back, her face still sour. I thought it wise to step away from the edge and leave her to her thoughts …

*

On our return to Maumere, I was invited over to *Flying Dolphin* for afternoon tea. The skipper, Mason, was a lean, tanned hounddawg of a man with a slow Southern drawl and a quiet, laid-back manner. His wife Catherine had long fair hair, wide grey eyes and was as beautiful as a mermaid. The yacht was the most gracious I had yet seen. There were plenty of flashier yachts around, but not many with deep brocade upholstery and what I suspect was a Burne-Jones painting on the saloon wall. The reason they had asked me over took me by surprise; they wanted to invite me to join them for the rest of the trip to Singapore. They had been worried about relations aboard *Moonshine* and although they didn't want to interfere with Skip and Brenda's plans, they were offering me an escape route if I needed one. Things had seemed a little tense, they told me with masterful understatement. Besides, they would love it if I could help with tutoring their children. How about it?

I was flattered and, for a moment, tempted. But for all my griping, Skip and Brenda had been very good to me and were relying on me as crew to see them through to Singapore. It would be unfair to jump ship now. Also, I explained, things weren't nearly as bad as they seemed. No, really, we were the best of friends.

At this point the ship's radio came crackling out of the saloon. '*Moonshine* to *Flying Dolphin*! *Moonshine* to *Flying Dolphin*! This is Brenda here. Tell Sandy to get our bloody dinghy back here straightaway. There are jobs to do, and that moron's not bloody getting out of them! Over.'

There was a silence as the Flying Dolphins looked at me.

'Ha, ha, best of friends, really,' I said weakly. 'Bark's worse than her bite.'

Catherine looked at me steadily. 'Honey, there's your bunk right there if you ever need it, you hear me now?'

With that thought in mind, I rowed reluctantly back to *Moonshine*.

*

Interlude: while in Maumere, I came across an old man squatting in the street selling something from a mat. What, though, it was difficult to identify. It looked like a heap of little irregular polished stones, mostly in whites, yellows, greys and browns. They were strangely familiar. Hardened corn-cob kernels? Too big. Quartz gravel? Too shiny. Dirty enamel beads? Too natural-looking.

As I was giving up, a woman arrived and squatted down beside the man. He started picking his way through his wares while she pointed to her gums and bared what were left of her teeth. Then the man picked out what he had been looking for, smeared one end of it with some deep purple glue from a little bottle and plugged the gap in the woman's mouth with – of course! – a second-hand tooth! Never mind that it was grey-yellow with age, furry brown with decay. It fitted nicely. The woman inspected the dental work in a small hand-mirror he held up for her and went away satisfied. I reeled away from this island dentist and his mound of used teeth, and ever since then have wondered where he got them all. There must have been more than 500 in his collection.

*

Four days later we were further down the coast of Flores and about to cross the straits to the next chain of islands. These lay strung out all the way to Java: islands as big as Lombok, as tiny as Komodo where the dragons are, and as famous as Bali. The straits themselves, we were to discover, were treacherous, full of reefs and whirlpools and rips.

Much had been improved by the neighbourly presence of *Flying Dolphin* and a host of other friendly boats. Most evenings saw us on and off one another's yachts and I got to know the children, Peter and Heath, better with each visit. Peter had fairish curly hair, his mother's wide grey eyes, and was as nimble around the decks as a monkey. He seemed as at home working out a message in secret pirate code as he was operating the Zodiac dinghy or diving off the bowsprit for a morning swim. Heath was eight years old and quieter than Peter, a mouse-child, neat and solemn and sweet, and rather looked as if she should be growing up in the Little House on the Prairie. The family had been sailing for almost three years by then, which accounted for the maturity of the children and the way they related to adults. It was 'Sir' and 'Ma'am' when they addressed you, and then straight down to good, sensible conversation about real issues; they gleaned as much knowledge as they could from the diverse people who drifted across their path. They were doing a correspondence course, which was giving them a basic education, but were starved for all the other stuff: the stories and games and tricks and magic and things you can do with a pair of scissors, a cork and a sheet of paper. I found myself filling that niche happily.

Meanwhile, Brenda's mental state had seriously deteriorated. As we rollicked along in the evening breeze off the coast of Sumba, I offered to cook a tomato bake for dinner. As I was doing so, she kept up a constant litany of complaints about how much bread it took, about how long it took to cook in the oven, about the dish it needed; when we sat down to dinner in the cockpit, she took a small mouthful, screwed up her face like a three-year-old eating Brussels sprouts and then pointedly and wordlessly scraped the whole lot off her plate over the side. There was a three-second silence before Skip exploded and ordered Brenda to her cabin in disgrace. He told her that if she didn't stop complaining and acting like a child, he would throw her off the boat at the first opportunity.

It was not only the domestic peace that was fragile. At times we were reminded that we were sailing through an archipelago where the political situation is never certain. One afternoon we anchored along with several other yachts off a tiny village called Labuan Bajo, nestled under the lee of desiccated yellow hills of dry scrub. Before we could even drop anchor, a motorboat came racing out from shore with five armed soldiers in it. They indicated that we should report immediately to the chief of police in the village. He was not happy.

With some trepidation we went ashore, where we found the other yachties, who had likewise been rounded up at gunpoint. We had with us our passports, our cruising permits and our wallets, ready to pay the inevitable bribe, but there was much head-shaking among the assembled skippers. There was something wrong about this place and we all felt uneasy. In the village we were ushered into the courtyard of a shabby concrete building in the shade of a wilting mango tree. Between us we had, among others, a couple of American tycoons, a retired judge, the owner of a major airline, an ex-Royal Naval officer – and me. One by one we were taken through the door to see the police chief. Each skipper came out shaking his head gloomily. Rank, wealth and former position in life seemed to be making no difference, and it looked as though we would all end up under arrest for breaking some local maritime regulation. The chief was keeping our passports and there was worried talk about a massive fine and having to sail non-stop to Jakarta to have our permits reissued. No-one could quite understand the problem – or rather, they all suspected that this was just plain piracy under the guise of officialdom.

Finally it was my turn – last, as befitted my lowly station as crew-hand. I stood respectfully before the desk while the police chief leaned back and regarded me with ill favour. Name? Passport? Nationality? These were demanded in rapid succession and I was asked to fill out the same form as my fellow yachties. I filled in the last space, which asked for my profession, and handed it back. His eye slid idly down the page. Then he sat up. 'You! You are a teacher?'

'Er … yes. Yes, an English teacher. Why?'

'A teacher? A guru?'

'Well, yes, a guru, I suppose. A teacher. Yes.' I knew that the Indonesian word for teacher was *guru*, but it hadn't until then struck me how venerable that sounded.

'Ah, Mister Guru! Welcome to this village! You are most welcome!' He rose from his chair and sent his aide running for a cigarette. 'We have no guru here in our village. We are too poor. But this, this is an honour!'

I sat up a little and went to straighten a non-existent tie.

'But wait,' he went on, suddenly thoughtful. 'These others, outside? Are these friends of yours? Friends of the guru?'

'Yes, yes, they are actually, but I only teach English you know. Verbs, prepositions, Shakespeare, What-I-Did-in-My-Holidays, that sort of thing.'

'Ah yes, I know this. I know what a teacher is. This is still an honour. You are a *guru*!'

And at that, he handed me the passports of my fellow yachties, wished us very good cruising in his beautiful country and offered me a cigarette. When I declined, he smiled, shook his head and said, 'Ah no, of course. The wise guru! Of course.'

And off we sailed that very afternoon, scot-free. I liked these people's priorities.

*

Leaving the westernmost tip of Flores behind, we sailed southwards and soon found anchorage in a blue bay set among the dry, golden, grassy hills of an island with hardly a tree in sight. So clean and lonely and sun-drenched was this place that I thought of Prospero's isle and looked for him along the wide shore. We stayed for a couple of days, and most of my time was spent with the Flying Dolphins. It involved me in quite the stupidest thing I have ever done in my life and I came closer to dying then than any time before or since.

An expedition in the Dolphins' Zodiac dinghy had us exploring a long white beach covered, every inch covered, with great pearly nautilus shells. Then we went nosing along the limestone cliffs and found to our delight a sea-cave. The entrance was low, but when we chugged tentatively into the darkness we found that it opened up to a great booming cathedral deep inside the cliff, floored with the sucking, sighing swell of the sea. Further in still we could see a glimmer of light coming from a distant passage; when we chugged over to explore this, we found ourselves winding out of the cave again into bright sunlight.

But what a find! We had emerged not onto the main coastline again but into the bottom of a steep circular well of light, sheer-sided and with a tiny moon of white sand forming a beach. Here a single slender coconut palm grew up the cliff-face. This had clearly once been a deep sea-cave like the first cavern, but long ago the roof had fallen in to create a hidden cove, open to the sky but accessible only through the water-cavern we had just negotiated. It was a perfect pirate's lair, secret and lonely, and Peter and I agreed that one day we would return to the place and bury a treasure worth the finding.

After enjoying the solitude of this hidden cove for a while, we turned the Zodiac back through the main cave. Before we emerged out into the ordinary world again, Mason killed the motor and we sat for a while in the hollow, booming darkness, enjoying the echoing susurration of the sea-swell slapping against the cave walls. It was then that Peter noticed a curious thing. There seemed to be light coming from the seabed below us, perhaps some sort of luminous coral or creature. I offered to hop into the water to investigate, and once I was in, realised that what we were looking at was a blurry glow of sunlight filtering in from somewhere under the water. There must be an underwater tunnel leading to a source of daylight somewhere close by.

Without explaining to the others what I was doing, I duck-dived down and, sure enough, saw a rocky submarine tunnel in the wall of the cave leading to somewhere brightly lit. With a kick of my legs, I swam down and off through the tunnel towards the light source. Mercifully, this tunnel wasn't very long and when I could see sunlight straight above me, I surfaced. To my astonishment, I was somewhere completely different. I was neither back outside the main limestone cliffs near the nautilus beach, nor was I in the secret cove with the palm tree. It seemed that I had swum in a third direction right through the main promontory and was now bobbing up and down in an ocean swell out at sea. The change in scenery was as astonishing as though I had stepped through a magical mirror and found myself in another world altogether. Above me towered a line of unbroken sea-cliffs with neither beach nor ledge to climb ashore. The anchorage was nowhere in sight, and was presumably around the corner of the cape far off to my left. By sea, it was probably two kilometres or more to the cave and the Flying Dolphins. On the other hand, they were a mere ten metres away through the underwater tunnel. All I had to do was dive down and along to rejoin them.

But this proved harder than I anticipated. On my first dive, I found no sign of the tunnel at all, just black shadows in dark rock,

and I surfaced spluttering and beginning to panic. The problem, I realised, was that whereas before I had been following the blue-golden gleam of underwater sunlight to find my way through the tunnel to open day, now I was trying to find the black entrance of a tunnel in a black cliff leading into the further blackness of the cavern. I wondered if perhaps the swell had swept me along the cliffs a way while I trod water. I tried swimming back a little against the waves and made another attempt. No, still no good, though I thought I had seen a darker patch of shadow between two patches of weed. Three, four, five more attempts went by and on resurfacing after the last one, I realised the seriousness of the error I had made. I was beginning to tire rapidly in the choppy swell and there was nowhere within a kilometre in either direction to climb ashore. I simply had to get back through that submarine tunnel. On the sixth attempt, trying not to think about conger eels and other dwellers of the deep, I scrabbled my way frantically along the underwater cliff-face, desperately searching for the tunnel mouth. Just as I was running out of breath I saw it, looming before my nose, and instinctively kicked my way forward, hands groping into blackness. This was it. This was the way through.

Within five seconds, however, I realised my mistake. Having found it, I should have surfaced first for a fresh lungful of air before diving again to make my way through. Too late now. My lungs were bursting, my eyes popping and I had no way of knowing if I could surface yet. I scrabbled forward for as long as I could and then kicked upwards.

Wham! The top of my head slammed into something hard. There was still solid stone above me. My head exploded in a burst of stars, prettier than all the coral in the world. I kicked desperately downwards again. Again I clawed my way onwards through the tunnel with arms that now felt like wet string. In my ears, the thunder, that deep and dreadful organ pipe, pronounced the name of Prosper; it did bass my trespass, and I in the ooze was bedded. My air was gone. I was going to die.

No. Here the water was surely infinitesimally lighter, a shifting pattern of shadows in the water. And yes, there was the blue of the Zodiac bottom. Once more I kicked upwards and felt the last lip of the tunnel slash at my thrashing heel. But that was fine, just fine. My head broke the surface and I breathed air again in great gasping gulps and lay limply in the water of the sea-cavern while Mason supported me. In the dinghy, Heath was leaning into Catherine, hiccuping sobs. Peter, his face a white, wide-eyed blur in the darkness, played the man by determinedly attending to the outboard.

'You've been gone quite a while, Sandy,' said Mason as he hauled me dripping into the Zodiac. 'We were a mite worried about you for a time there. Ah guess you found *somewhere* down there to surface – either that or you've got the biggest pair of lungs ah ever heard of.' As I flopped trembling and breathless into the dinghy, my heel left a smear of watery red across Peter's leg and Heath buried herself once more in her mother's shoulder. 'Welcome back aboard. Ah reckon we'll git you back to the ship and look at that heel of yours,' said Mason. 'Let 'er rip, Peter!' Peter gratefully busied himself with the motor, and we chugged out into bright sunshine once again.

And back we went, flying over the waters of the bay like Ariel released, to the deck of the good ship *Flying Dolphin*. Then there was homemade lemonade and peanut-butter and jelly sandwiches and a patching up by Catherine of my nastily cut heel; I bear the scar to this day. And of course, once I was back on *Moonshine* and reunited with my writing things, there was the ultimate joy of being able to write home about the whole adventure and horrify my parents. They remain horrified to this day.

Chapter 12

And the wild beasts of the islands shall cry in their desolate houses, and dragons in their pleasant palaces.
—ISAIAH, Ch. 13, v. 22

On old maps, cartographers would write across wild uninhabited areas the words *Here Be Dragons*. Nonsense, of course, unless you find yourself sailing along the stretch of water surrounding the islands of Komodo and neighbouring Rinca, in which case it happens to be the literal truth.

We were in Rinca and in a quandary. We were due to sail across to Komodo tomorrow, and a couple on another boat, *Arietta*, had invited me to join them for the crossing. They had a huge collection of classical music aboard and wanted to share some of it with me. The problem was that the strait between Rinca and Komodo is legendary for its ferocity, and Skip and Brenda would need all the help they could get. I was longing to get off *Moonshine* for a while (I kept stubbing my toes on the atmosphere aboard) but I realised that if Skip said no, then that was it. However, to my great delight, Skip said yes, and I went to bed that night looking forward to a day aboard *Arietta* and a musical passage. Vivaldi's *Crossing to Komodo* for keyboard and two violins. Brilliant!

On the next morning Mark and Laraine put on the Vivaldi as we set sail into the wild straits. Here several seas meet, the Java Sea, the Flores Sea and the Indian Ocean, swashing together between barren conical islands of grey-yellow grass. The meeting forms giant whirlpools; even with the engine driving at full and the sails straining, *Arietta* was swept up in a giddying waltz for several turns before she was released to glide onwards, patting her hair and smoothing her petticoats in outrage at the impropriety. No sooner had we escaped the whirlpools than we ran straight over the other oddity of these waters: a four-foot drop in the sea level. This is a giant step in the water level, not caused as far as I could see by any underwater ledge or reef, but sitting there in mid-sea, defying all those stuffy textbooks that say that water always finds its own level. Down we bumped and the worst was over.

We radioed behind to see how *Moonshine* was faring, but Skip and Brenda were having some engine problems so hadn't started yet. However, just before we went out of radio range, the message came that they had got it fixed and were on their way, and would meet us a little later on Komodo.

Once arrived, we decided to waste no time in hunting out the famous dragons. We anchored in a sheltered bay three miles from the main village, zoomed around the coast in a Zodiac and met up with a guide, Ari. He pointed out the tall stockade of wooden logs that surrounded the village and the masses of limestone rocks on the cemetery graves, precautions to stop the dragons disturbing the living and the dead. They are especially fond of digging up fresh graves, Ari told us with grim relish, and devouring corpses. They are mainly carrion-eaters, he explained, but a few years earlier, a Swiss baron had gone walking in the forest behind the village. All they found of him was his hat. So, yes, if we were wondering, they do kill live prey as well.

Ari took us into the jungle, picking up on the way a small, excited goat. It was clearly thrilled to be going on its very first picnic, skipping along the jungle path giving short happy bleats. As we walked, Ari explained further about the dragons. They are a type of monitor lizard related to the Australian goanna but a hell of a lot larger. As with goannas, their bite isn't venomous but is still deadly, owing to the virulent cocktail of bacteria in their saliva, a brew kept fermenting away by their carrion-eating habits. They need only inflict a flesh wound on an animal and then follow the creature around for a day or so before it expires from acute septicaemia. They will then devour it, hoofs, horns, bones and all, leaving not even a damp patch on the ground. By this stage the goat, who had been listening brightly to all this, was beginning to look dubious.

But too late. The path ended abruptly at the edge of a deep dry gully in which various dusty grey logs lay scattered about among low thorny shrubs. A terrible stench filled the air; it may have emanated from the blackened remains of something, possibly our little goat's aunt, dangling from a hook attached to a rope pulley running to a tree halfway across the gully. As we watched, and before either the goat or I could protest, Ari slipped out a knife and dispatched the poor thing with one neat cut across the throat. Then he slung it from the hook, hauled the hook out over the gully and waited.

At first nothing happened. Then one of the logs in the gully bottom stirred and materialised as a full-size Komodo dragon, some twelve feet long. I had been expecting something pretty big but not nearly this big. Then another log stirred … and another … and soon there were five dragons approaching the dangling, dripping goat. They started slowly, moving in a ponderous waddle, their skin hanging in heavy folds like chain-mail around their necks and hindquarters. But as they built up speed, they ran more and more smoothly until one was moving fast enough to launch its great bulk into the air straight at the dangling goat. It took one enormous bite out of the goat's stomach – the juiciest part, explained Ari – and then sank to the gully floor to gulp and snatch at its mouthful. Soon the others were wrangling and clambering over the remains, seemingly in slow motion, sending great wafts of stench from their sulphur yellow jaws; the stench of putrefaction. In a way the label 'dragon' was wrong for them. There was none of the golden elegance, none of the suavity or glitter of Smaug, none of the fire and thunder of the old Norse dragons of *Beowulf.* Instead there was a terrifying stony deadness about their eyes, a massively blind stupidity in their movements. They were dead dust and drought personified.

Once we got back to *Arietta*, there was still no sign of *Moonshine* and Mark and Laraine were looking fidgety. It turned out that they were due to meet somebody in Bali in two days' time, and it was still about two days' hard sailing away. It was with some relief that we finally spotted *Moonshine* on the horizon, a tiny speck some four miles away. Sensing Mark's anxiety, I breezily assured him that I would be fine sitting on the beach under a coconut palm for the next few hours, swimming, dozing and carrying on with my letter writing until *Moonshine* arrived. Mark still didn't seem wholly convinced about leaving me – it felt too much like the traditional crime of marooning – but as we turned to watch *Moonshine*'s progress once more, we could see that they had hauled aloft a yellow spinnaker which I didn't know they had. Now they would be here even quicker, I pointed out, and finally Mark and Laraine seemed happy. They took me ashore in the dinghy and set sail.

I settled down to some peaceful writing. It was very tranquil, the very picture of a tropical paradise, and I would make the most of it before *Moonshine* arrived, with its cargo of attendant prickliness. Poor Brenda. Poor Skip. It cannot have been easy sharing their married life with a stranger in the tiny confines of the yacht for weeks on end.

As I was thinking these idle thoughts, I was also lazily watching *Moonshine* way out there on the horizon. Despite the yellow spinnaker, it didn't seem to be getting any closer. In fact it looked a little off course. Those currents, I thought …

It *was* them, of course …

Oh God, I don't believe it. It wasn't them. I sat and watched in disbelief as the yacht sailed straight past the northern edge of the bay and out of sight, still three miles out to sea.

I was trying to make up my mind whether this was funny or alarming when I was relieved – or was it mildly disappointed – to see that *Moonshine* now really had appeared on the horizon. White sail, dark hull, heading straight this way. She would be here in an hour. A pity not to drop so neatly into a new adventure, to become the new Crusoe, but there it was. Time for a swim and a snooze.

*

An hour or so later I awoke to find that this second yacht was not *Moonshine* either. It had sailed close enough for me to see that it sported a dark-green hull where *Moonshine* was red and had then sailed on past the distant point like its predecessors. The horizon was now empty. Moreover, the daylight was fractionally dimmer and more golden and I realised for the first time that I might be stranded there for the night, if not longer. My mind raced. I was stranded on a desert island, and what's more, an island with man-eating dragons.

Where the hell was *Moonshine*? Suddenly I knew what it was, and this really *was* likely. Skip and Brenda, in trying to fix the engine, had had to move my stuff out of the way and had accidentally found the bundle of half-written letters which were sitting in my rucksack. They'd gone and read them and were bloody upset, as anyone would be – hadn't I described Brenda as a dim but determined sheep at some stage? – and had decided that as I clearly didn't enjoy being onboard, it would be a kindness not to come and pick me up. That was it, for sure. It must have been five o'clock in the afternoon by now; they should have picked me up by midday at the latest.

I considered my options. The village was three miles along the shoreline, not too far a walk in normal circumstances, but along a shore which, beyond the crescent of the beach I was on, consisted of scattered cliffs and rock-pools and treacherous banks of razor-sharp coral. The going would be tricky and slow – and what if the yacht arrived in the meantime and found me not at the rendezvous? Behind me, backing the beach, was thick and impenetrable jungle, already filled with the shadows of dusk, rearing steeply up to the near-vertical hills beyond. I was best staying put here, even if it meant sleeping on the beach. Darkness was approaching fast, but after all, the air was warm and the night would be fine. I wandered up the beach to see if I could find a particularly spreading palm to settle beneath.

Two minutes later, I was sprinting back down the beach as fast as my heels could take me. As I had approached the fringe of dense scrub at the top of the sand, I had heard a roaring noise coming from within the trees. It was the sort of noise dinosaurs make in Japanese monster movies, and was accompanied by some heavy crackling and rustling in the undergrowth. I had forgotten the dragons. Suddenly, things were serious. I stood as close as I could to the water's edge, but there were still only forty metres between me and the jungle. The light was fading fast and now there was more rustling, and a roar coming from further along. Not one but two of the damn things. I had nothing with me in the way of a weapon, having brought only a small knapsack, a bundle of writing paper and a fountain pen – hardly effective weapons in fighting off ravenous dragons. It did occur to me briefly that I might at least be able to pen a quick wish-list for anybody who found my remains: *Dear Mum, The Old Hundredth at my funeral, please, and since I am going this way anyway, 'Devoured by Dragons' might look rather good on the tombstone.*

It also occurred to me that perhaps the rustlings and roarings in the undergrowth were nothing worse than wild pigs. Surely the dragons didn't roam over the *whole* island? Just then a breeze sprang up, wafting down the beach, and I knew my fears were well founded. The breeze brought with it a smell I had encountered earlier that day, the foul stench of rotting carrion, the worst halitosis in the animal kingdom. It was dragons, all right, and they were coming to get me. I did the only thing I could think of and waded straight out to sea.

Three hours later, I knew I had made the right choice. Admittedly I had spent most of that time wondering if Komodo dragons could swim, a worry only occasionally interrupted by the thought of night-feeding sharks. Nevertheless, I was happy to stay exactly where I was, trying to keep my feet on the bottom and my knapsack on my head as I stood chest-deep in the tropic waters of the dark and starry sea. Although the night was moonless, I could faintly see by starlight the beach whence I had fled. I watched in horror as, sure enough, giant shapes, long, low shapes, shuffled to and fro across the sand. It was too dark to see properly, of course, but in my mind's eye I watched them as they paused, sniffed the air and wondered dimly if a night dip might yield a prey less knobbly than goat.

It was with an immense sense of relief that I eventually heard a distant splash behind me. Bobbing in the water, I turned and saw that a yacht had glided noiselessly into the bay. My first thought was that this must be *Moonshine* at last, but something about the lights made me doubt that. (Besides, I had by then, after hours of watery thinking, convinced myself that my theory about the letters was right and that I would never see them again.) I was dying to call out but I made myself wait until they'd gone through the whole noisy business of dropping the anchor and de-rigging before I sent a soft halloo across the dark water.

'Excuse me! Help!' I called softly, reluctant to rouse sleeping dragons. A few minutes later, by the soft glow of the riding lights, I saw a woman climb down into the dinghy and start rowing my way. Only when she rowed past me and headed for shore did I realise that she couldn't see me and had naturally assumed I was hailing from the beach. Bugger. It would be a blow for me if she were to reach the shore and promptly get eaten. I called out softly again and she checked her progress and looked about, puzzled to find a disembodied voice floating out at sea. Finally, she rowed up to me.

I am not quite sure what she made of finding a man standing up to his neck in the Java Sea in the middle of the night with a straw hat and a knapsack on his head, especially as I instinctively tried to raise my hat and apologise at the same time. Nevertheless, soon I was sitting in the cockpit of the yacht explaining my plight. Then it was a much-needed rum and coke followed by supper and then to bed on their saloon bunk, safe from dragons, safe from sharks and safe from the folly of ever writing acerbic things about people ever again.

*

Moonshine turned up at three the next afternoon, with Skip and Brenda worried sick about me. Just after we had lost radio contact, their engine had failed again and they didn't dare make the crossing of those terrible straits without it. That was the reason for their being so late. Or so they claimed.

And so to Bali. Shops. Showers. Hotels and telephones and post offices and bank machines and ice-creams and fresh supplies of gin. Both Brenda and Skip seemed happier on the last leg – until, that is, Brenda and I managed to put a huge great tear in the mainsail while hauling it up in a gale one night. Skip was furious, but for once couldn't be furious with Brenda alone, so remained civil. It forged a sort of bond between Brenda and me for the time being – partners in naughtiness. At any rate, she was not sent home in disgrace from Bali. She was, Skip magnanimously decided, to stay with us till Singapore. I was going to suggest we celebrate with a home-made tomato bake but thought better of it.

Interlude

Denpasar Harbour
Bali, Indonesia

Dear Newton,

Thanks for your letter from ... er ... Kathmandu. But didn't you get my last letter from Darwin telling you that Kathmandu was off the cards? Sorry. Hope you didn't wait too long there, though by all accounts it's a stunning place, especially the post office. I look forward to hearing about it when I see you next.

Anyway, the letter was brilliant from what I could make out, although it seemed in its travels to have been opened several times and was smeared with what looks a little like Marmite. Another oddity was the inclusion of twelve pages of completely blank paper. It was thickish, white, grainy paper, quite unlike the rest of the letter, and each page was numbered in the top right-hand corner in the same pen you used for the rest – and yet was quite, quite blank.

This isn't all part of some elaborate hoax, is it? You're not sitting at the next table here in Denpasar disguised as a Balinese taxi-driver, are you, ready to spring some terrible surprise on me, like you did with the candles and the vampire under the bed thingy? I do hope not. It has taken eight months of ocean cruising for my nerves to settle.

So, yes, I am in Bali. I am aboard a small yacht called *Moonshine*, which is taking me through to Singapore. Out of the skipper's wife and myself, one of us may not survive the voyage. I would love it if you could join me for the last part of the trip, the only difficulty being that I have no idea where I will be round about January. The plan is that once I get to Singapore, I will investigate the possibility of travelling overland up into China or better still through Burma and into India. Then there's the possibility of traversing all those odd countries that end in 'ekistan' and popping out somewhere near Turkey or Israel. That'd be a good place to meet, wouldn't it? Then we could do the trip across Europe together over a month or so.

How does that sound?

Goodness knows where I'll be writing from next. A lot depends on what I find when I get to Singapore. In the meantime, enjoy England – or Kathmandu, or wherever you are – and keep yourself free round about January for a quick flight to Uzbekistan. Thanks again for the letter, or those bits of it that arrived. It kept me going on the long night-watches as I sucked the Marmite off it. I do so very much hope that this letter reaches you.

Cheers,
Sandy

Chapter 13

He married a wife, O then, O then,
He married a wife, O then!
He married a wife, she's the bane of his life
And he longed to be single again!

—Folk tune

For those cruising through Indonesian waters, Bali is a place to restock, recuperate and recover from the stresses of the sailing life. It is in itself a remarkable island and rightly considered the jewel of the archipelago, even overrun as it is by Australian tourists who come there to get laid, drink too much and throw up on the pavements outside the noisy nightclubs along Kuta Beach. Away from the tacky madness, the charm of the island wafts over you like a scented emerald cloud, healing the soul and mind of even the dullest visitor.

After the Kelimutu fiasco, I felt that my absence from the yacht for a few days might not be unwelcome, so I took myself off to the hill village of Ubud. Here I stayed in a *losmen*, a bare room of polished red brick, with a large water-jar in one corner for washing and a simple bamboo bed covered in woven Balinese fabrics as gorgeous as peacocks. At night, outside the houses with their high walls and courtyards, little golden lamps lit up the laneways. I flitted from pool to pool of light, lured by the clangle-jingle-dongle of the *gamelan*, the Balinese orchestra, which sounds like a thousand wind-chimes in a house of bamboo. There was a shadow-puppet play being presented in an open theatre; I watched for a while but never picked up the thread of what was happening between the two angular, praying-mantis-like lovers, so I wandered back to the *losmen* to write by lamplight.

On Bali, religion is evident everywhere; they seem to live it out in the streets and in their everyday lives rather than confine it to Sundays and churches as we do. Everywhere I went were little woven palm baskets full of orange flowers and incense left as offerings to the Hindu gods. Young women stopped in the middle of the street to make offerings to an invisible deity, as unabashed and matter-of-factly as they might stop to greet an acquaintance. There is a great emphasis on calmness, tranquillity and light in the Balinese religion, which made Christianity's preoccupation with body and blood, suffering and darkness, seem a little morbid. I idly thought I might become a Hindu.

On my second day in Ubud I wandered out of the village and found myself ambling along a path between paddy fields. These were terraced all the way up steep hillsides in tiny emerald steps, a living contour map of the land. I had stopped to admire one particular slope when a rickety truck pulled up behind me. From it emanated a quite indescribable noise. It was the sort of croaking gibble-gabble you hear at a crowded cocktail party, but almost deafening in its volume.

As I watched, a little man emerged and opened the back of the truck. Out waddled a thousand ducks, which he herded to the edge of the paddy field with a bamboo stick. They waddled in a neat line straight along the lowest terrace, from left to right along the hillside. When the front duck reached the bamboo fence at the end of the terrace, it had no choice but to hop over the little strip of water onto the next terrace up and start wandering back, from right to left. As the others kept coming behind, soon we had two rows of ducks crisscrossing one behind the other. When the leader reached the leftmost edge of the field, it jumped up to the next terrace and started waddling back from left to right. Soon, the whole hillside was one

moving tableau of ducks, waddling in alternate rows as neatly as the mechanical ranks of yellow tin ducks in a fairground shooting alley. It was the loveliest sight, comic and earnest and endearing as only ducks can be. The next morning I went back just to watch them for another hour or so. I learned that they were used by the Balinese to eat the water-snails in the rice fields. Lucky ducks.

*

Yes, well, unlucky ducks actually. Hinduism may seem all sweetness and light and flowers and joss-sticks, but it does have its dark side too. That night there was a huge celebration down in the village. There were fireworks and lots of noise and the *gamelan* music was more maddeningly tuneless than usual. Next morning I went to see my friends the ducks and found that they'd gone. Every single one. Vanished. I asked a man working in the paddy field where they were and he beamed at me.

'You like duck? Me too! Last night, big celebration! Yum, yum. We call it Feast of a Thousand Ducks.'

I decided communion wafers were not so bad after all.

*

Once we left Bali, we headed non-stop for Singapore. As we sailed, I was smugly delighted to be ticking things off on my list. One late afternoon, for example, we had an encounter with a waterspout. It came twisting over the sea, a thin black hose connecting sullen sea and sultry sky, waving and gyrating some miles off our starboard bow. We kept a very close eye on it but it went off to molest some fishermen elsewhere and we could relax again.

As we lolloped northwards, the air became tropically humid. We kept passing extraordinary structures, clusters of houses on bamboo stilts, tiny villages on the open sea. It seemed that local fishermen lived here for weeks on end, feeding, as doth the chameleon, on dew and air. I was terrified of ploughing straight through one at night and kept a sharp look-out for the faint flicker of kerosene lanterns in the moonless darkness.

I didn't know what sort of ship's log Skip was keeping – a very accurate and practical one, no doubt – but there came a morning when I was able to make the following delirious note in a letter.

I have just crossed the Equator. I've done it. I am now in the Northern Hemisphere. I am no longer sloshing about in the Antipodes but am now gently cruising the … Podes. In one second I have sailed from a southern spring to a northern autumn. The water in the washbasin has just reversed and is now going down the plughole widdershins. I have left behind the be-penguined half of the world and am now anticipating my first sight of a polar bear. England is just over the horizon. I am going to make it, buddy! Hooray!

I know all this because the SatNav device, which tells us exactly where we are, now has a big N after the degrees rather than a big S. Mind you, I also know this for a much better reason, and one of which I am rather proud. On the long night-watches I have been learning all the constellations off by heart. Did you know that there is a star called Zuben-el-Genubi, which may sound like Obi Wan Kenobi's wiser and more mystical younger brother, but actually means 'the left claw of the scorpion'?

On these watches, you soon pick up the mechanics of the night sky. For example, I've noticed that as we go further north, the Southern Cross describes an arc that is lower and lower in the sky behind us. And each night, all the stars wheel across the arch of the sky, rising and setting like the sun and the moon. From this, it doesn't take a Galileo to work out that we are progressing around the sun and that the earth is round and we are crawling over its surface like an ant. (Well, yes, it did take a Galileo, and hindsight is a marvellous gift, but once you know these things, it all becomes pretty obvious to anyone up at midnight for ten weeks in a row.)

Anyway, just last night, a new star appeared on the horizon, straight ahead, very faint through the sea-haze. No great matter, you might think, and not particularly impressive in magnitude or luminosity. In fact it takes a few hours to notice the really extraordinary thing about this star, which is that no matter how long the night-watch, it never budges from its position. In fact, as you watch, you realise that the whole celestial dance revolves around this one faint star. I knew then that I was seeing Polaris, the Pole Star, and had therefore to be in the Northern Hemisphere. Now there's navigation for you.

*

One night away from Singapore, it all came unravelled. For weeks and weeks I had been keeping my temper, smiling, taking a deep breath. Brenda, it seemed, was the unhappiest soul alive: she had been sniping and complaining and whinging at every turn. The last straw came when, after a petty tirade about the way I had served up dinner – so appallingly, it seemed, that she had no recourse but yet again to scrape her plate of food straight over the side – I made the mature decision not to stoop to her level, not to let her know how childish her behaviour was, but rather, once I had done the washing up, to take myself off to another yacht for an evening of chocolate cake, Purcell and whisky. So I did. There aboard *Arietta* I congratulated myself on the thoughtful way I had given both Brenda and myself some space. Three generous glasses of single malt helped in the calming process.

Rowing back later that evening, I climbed aboard as softly as a drifting piece of swan's down, glided noiselessly into the saloon, brushed my teeth up on deck so as not to disturb Skip and Brenda, slipped silently into my bunk and slept content that my return had been ghostlike in its minimal intrusiveness.

But the next morning, my cheery 'Good morning!' was greeted with a 'Huh! I didn't sleep a wink after the bloody racket *you* made coming back last night!' – and I blew up.

'Well, I'm sorry to have woken you, Brenda, but I could not actually have been quieter if I were composed entirely of argon gas, which for your information is odourless, inert and completely undetectable

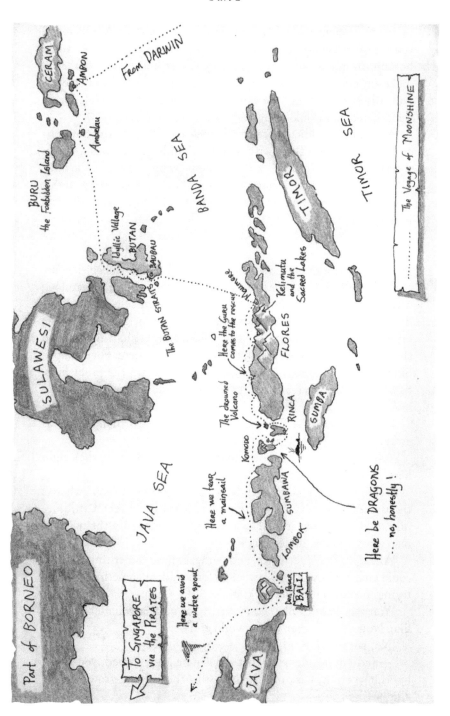

by modern science, but (*deep breath*) I knew, I just *knew*' – here my voice shot up a couple of decibels – 'that whatever I bloody did, you'd be complaining about it this morning. I don't know why I bother to make any effort at all, I should have come stamping aboard in bloody hobnail boots, dancing the can-can and playing the ukulele for all the difference it would've made.'

And on that ridiculous note, I stamped off up to the bowsprit and drank a cup of tea with shaking hands. There was a sixty-second silence, and then – *bang!* – Skip blew up as well. In the middle of his tirade, it came out, the reason she'd been so angry all this while. She'd gone and read my letters. God knows what she had found in them, but I remembered with horror the ewe comparisons. I felt slightly ill at the thought of what else she might have come across.

Anyway, it was out now and we were all feeling sheepish – no, sorry, Brenda, I didn't mean sheepish like that! – but it went a long way towards clearing the air. It also had an odd side-effect. After dinner that night, Brenda sat on one side of the cockpit, Skip on the other and me in the centre, and they both started chatting to me in the most cordial way as though the other weren't there. For example, Skip kicked off by saying in a rueful voice, 'Yeah, the problem is, Sandy, that I don't really fancy Brenda anymore. I'm just not sure how to let her know that, see?'

I glanced across at Brenda, who was sitting less than two yards away, on the verge of tears.

'Oh, er, well, I think she knows now, Skip, because she's right here, actually.'

'Yeah, but,' chimed in Brenda as though Skip were somewhere a thousand miles away, 'what Skip doesn't realise is that I still love him to bits and that if he'll let me, I could make him the happiest man alive. Do you understand?'

'Ah, well, that's very nice, and perhaps that's something you two could chat about while I ... er ... go for a walk or something,' I said, trying to edge out of the cockpit.

'You see, Sandy,' Skip continued. 'You've seen what she can be like. Now you're a man of the world and—'

'No, not really, Skip.'

'—and I'm not denying that she can be great in bed, you know, but is it worth it, I ask myself? Now that the kids are grown up and all?'

'Well, let's see now, it might be better actually if you ask Brenda that, which is convenient because, why, here she is and—'

'See, the only reason I get stupid when I'm around him is 'cos I'm trying to please him,' continued Brenda. 'I mean, you've heard him.'

'Mind you, she is the mother of my kids, I suppose, and a good little home-maker, but is that enough, I ask myself? What do you think, eh?'

I was left longing for the good old days of savage abuse and endless complaints about the way I served food.

I needn't have worried. On the final approach to Singapore, Skip caught a dorado. The afternoon in question was particularly hot. Skip had managed to fit up an ingenious awning over the cockpit to keep the midday blaze off, and Brenda was on watch. After hooking the fish, Skip struggled for half an hour to keep it on the line and then managed to get it aboard. Horribly enough, dorados change colour as they die. First the deep indigo flushes a rich emerald green and then wave after wave of colour washes down the fish's long body. Emerald turns to azure, azure to purple, purple to rose-pink, rose-pink to iridescent gold, and then, in the last throes, the gold pales to silver and finally to dead, flat white. The death-struggle is over.

Skip proudly showed the catch to Brenda. But Brenda wasn't interested. She was irritated that the sun was in her eyes. 'Oh, I don't care about your stupid fish,' she snapped. 'This bloody sun. I wish it would go where I wanted. I *hate* it being over there.'

I looked at Skip, and he looked at me. Singapore was just over the horizon. 'Go home, Brenda,' he said heavily, his voice as dead and white as the fish lying in the scuppers. 'Go home.'

And the next day, she did.

*

For by then we were in Singapore. We pulled into Changi Yacht Club on a grey afternoon, mooring beneath a giant marble statue of the Lion of Singapore – half lion, half fish. Surrounded by its steamy gardens and buffalo-grass lawns, I tried not to think too hard about Changi as it was for hundreds of Australian prisoners-of-war, for whom the name is still synonymous with Hell. For me it was time to say goodbye to all the people I had travelled alongside for ten weeks. There were Fred and Nan from Winsome, my good-humoured New York Jewish couple who said things like 'What, should I worry?' and 'Get out already!' and told lots of rabbi jokes about sex which I thought I understood. And, of course, my beloved Flying Dolphins, who had been the saving grace of the whole trip. And Brenda and Skip, of course, who got me there in the end and deserved a good deal more gratitude and tolerance than I have shown them here.

Having said my goodbyes, I heaved my rucksack onto my back once more – my shoulders tanned, my hair fair with salt and sun, my feet splayed and brown from the freedom of no shoes – and set off to catch a train into the centre of Singapore. Ten weeks it had taken from Darwin, but the biggest hurdle was over. I was now on the Asian mainland and nothing stood between me and Iona.

Or so, in my folly, I thought.

PART II.

Chapter 14

Travellers return from the city of Zirma with distinct memories: a blind black man shouting in the crowd, a lunatic teetering on a skyscraper's cornice, a girl walking with a puma on a leash. Actually many of the blind men who tap their canes on Zirma's cobblestones are black; in every skyscraper there is someone going mad; all lunatics spend hours on cornices; there is no puma that some girl does not raise, as a whim. The city is redundant: it repeats itself so that something will stick in the mind.

—ITALO CALVINO, *Invisible Cities*

Singapore is the hub of the world, and as I stepped ashore at the Changi Yacht Club in early October, it felt like the first footfall grinding on the Rest of the World. All Asia lay before me. Mandarins! Goldfish! Water buffaloes and rice paddies! Tibetan monks and yak butter, and gurus in saffron robes riding on the smiles of tigers. I had done all the fiddly island-hopping and there was now nothing, it seemed, to stop me before Calais. There were the Himalayas, of course, or the Mongolian Steppes, depending which way I chose to go, but these were trifles compared with the sea-crossings. Any chance of a rendezvous with Newton was long gone. Singapore was a good place to organise myself for the months ahead, but it was hard being back in the twentieth century again. I had been spoilt by ten weeks of rustling palm trees, the silken swoosh of water at the prow, balmy starlit nights and the gentle snarl of skippers chainsawing into their wives every couple of minutes. Now it was glass towers, metro stations, air-conditioning and traffic lights and the fever and fret of the modern world. Singapore has a sort of stainless-steel air about it, so the next day I hopped on a train and passed through Malaysia in a green blur to Bangkok, the brazen and heat-hazy capital of Thailand.

The sudden acceleration in pace was disconcerting. After months of the slow lolloping of sea travel, the clatter and speed of the train seemed obscene and terrifying. No wonder our forefathers, in the early days of the Steam Age, believed that the human frame could not stand velocities over thirty miles an hour. They thought we would crumple and melt to porridge if so tested. My body took the strain manfully, but my mind did indeed nearly unhinge as we roared from Malaysia to Thailand in a matter of hours.

Bangkok was choked with exhaust fumes, teeming with mad traffic, sweltering hot concrete and noisy neon-lit nights. There are parts of the city, to be sure, where canals cut their way through the sprawl, green avenues of water that might be expected to provide some relief from the overwhelming ugliness of modernity, and here can be found flashes of bright colour – the hot pinks and oranges of tropical creepers, the green swords of water-plants, the glitter of silk flags on crowded barges and the untidy charm of boat-dwellers the world over. But the canals themselves are foetid and soupy, smelling of open drains and drowned dogs. A malarial miasma hangs over them and one breathes shallowly, almost longing for the sterility of concrete again.

In the meantime, things did not look particularly auspicious for my quest not to fly. I waltzed cheerfully into the embassies of various neighbouring countries – and trudged out again soon after, my spirits dashed further each time. People in this region seemed to take international borders a little too seriously for my liking. Burma, for example, seemed the most obvious route but was a complete no-no. I could have flown in, the Burmese embassy staff explained, but I definitely could not cross the border by land. Seeing no doubt a hint of mischievous stubbornness in my eyes, they added that the last person to try was languishing in a Rangoon gaol and would be there for some time. Cambodia and Vietnam, meanwhile, welcomed overland visitors from the Thai side … but were closed at the Chinese border.

Perhaps this was the end of the line. In my lassitude, I didn't even mind that much. I was heartily sick of travelling. Sick of living out of a rucksack, sick of being unable to identify what I was eating, sick of airless rooms and tropical heat and of facing each day the awful prospect of yet another tourist site. I wanted to get to Iona, gulp down a swig of the water of eternal youth and then live out my days telling wide-eyed schoolchildren how I had fought off Komodo dragons with just a fountain pen.

In Singapore, I had had a huge clean-out of my goods and chattels, throwing out the junk I had collected along the way. Soon after, I discovered to my dismay that I had thrown out my hiking boots. Perhaps this was an omen to stop tramping. Sitting there in the Bangkok hostel, I had one last rummage through my pack to see if I really could have thrown out my boots. The pack was empty and all its contents spread out on the cigarette-ash-coloured carpet. No boots to be seen – but there, unexamined for many weeks now, was my map, the one my father had given me all those months ago on my departure from Sydney. I consulted it closely.

Wait a bit ... there did seem to be one other country there, a country called Laos, lying between Thailand and the vast mass of China. I had never heard of it. I went and found the hostel receptionist. Neither had he, nor had anyone else in the hostel's lounge, all of whom I consulted in a growing fever of impatience. In my optimism, this made Laos my only promising lead. The next morning, I tracked down the Laotian embassy and did my homework. At the end of the day, sweaty, dusty and near-dead from carbon-monoxide poisoning, but grinning from ear to ear with renewed hope, I wrote to Chris with some very specific instructions in case I died.

Dear Chris,

Tee-hee! I have a plan. But first you must promise, absolutely promise, not to breathe a word. Not to anyone at all, Chris, I mean it. My father has a set of antennae that can pick things up through lead-lined walls, across continents, down subterranean shafts. He has always had this irritating gift, ever since we were little. He knew exactly what we were plotting even before we'd got the final details worked out. He knew precisely when, for once in my entire studious school-days, I skipped my homework to play The Enchanted Wood with you in the cellar, do you remember? He knew before Tibby did that she was going to have a baby. I don't know how he does it, but I am determined that he does not find out about this plan of mine. And, Chris, I'm serious. You'd only have to mention it casually to a complete stranger in a street café in Adelaide and my father over in Canberra will have somehow heard about it before either of you has finished your cappuccino.

Anyway, here's the situation. Thailand is surrounded to the west by Burma and to the north and east by Laos. Beyond these two inscrutable lands lies the wide and traversable expanse of China. If I can just get myself into China, I am virtually home and hosed. The Trans-Siberian Express will take me all the way to Moscow, and even on to Finland.

Getting into China, however, is the problem. Burma is right out. You can only fly in and fly out. Laos is nearly as difficult but not quite, and therein lies the seed of my idea. One can travel by train to Vientiane, the Laotian capital across the border from Thailand, but apparently one cannot just wander around Laos at will. However, there seems to be nothing physically stopping you leaving the town – no walls or moats or fences – only the fear of being stopped by an official who will want to see a passport, and who will, no doubt, be highly susceptible to my whimsical charm and possibly a small bribe.

I have been off to a local library and obtained a photocopy of a very rough map of Laos showing a road leading straight from Vientiane to the Chinese border. This map has only about six lines on it in all, so not exactly the Ordnance Survey, but they wouldn't show a road if none existed, would they? Unless it's a tear in the original map. Anyway, my Laotian visa gives me fifteen days, surely enough to dash for the border? Dodging officials? Possibly.

But what, I hear you ask, happens at the border, you fool? Ah. There, I happen to know, informed by a highly reliable man I met in a bar, dwell hill-tribes who don't like the government much and have very little truck with red tape and bureaucracy. They tend, it is said, to side with the poor, honest traveller against the local gendarmerie and even have ways and means of nipping across into China themselves for a spot of tea-smuggling. These are, I feel, kindred spirits whose hearts beat as one with mine.

There is no physical barrier barring the border like a river or a Great Wall – that's further north, isn't it? – so what, I ask myself, is to stop me treading the nut-strewn road to within half a mile of the border post, then treading the banana-strewn jungle off to one side, looking sharpish about me, and then rejoining the road once safely into China, eh?

Well, the answer is obvious. Being in China, for starters, without an entry stamp or a visa. A problem, yes, but hopefully they won't find me until I'm well on my way to Beijing and then if they want to kick me out, why, the Trans-Siberian Express is almost the quickest way to see me off the premises. So, presto! On to Iona and immortality!

I shall finish this here. I have to go and pick up my Laotian visa. This I have arranged with a little man outside a travel bureau to whom I gave sixty dollars and my passport. He told me to come back today, and yes, it is only now as I am writing this, Chris, that I realise the idiocy of what I have just done and the unlikelihood of ever seeing my passport again.

*

And here I am back again, passport, visa and all. You've got to learn to trust people more, Chris. I never doubted him for a moment.

I depart for Laos tonight by train. I have been reading Paul Theroux's *The Great Railway Bazaar* and he says that the train trip from Bangkok to Nong Kai on the Laotian border is one of the ten great train trips of the world, so I am looking forward to it. Once I am in Vientiane, I'm sure I will be able to spy out the land a little more. Sorry that this is so brief. I will write again from Laos and let you know how things look.

Again, and sorry to go on about this, but please don't tell anyone what I'm planning. If on the other hand you haven't heard from me in, say, two years' time, you might want to drop Mum and Dad a line. All right?

BUT NOT BEFORE!

By the way, another thing you can avoid mentioning to my parents is a visit to the infamous Pat Pong red-light district, where young ladies do things with ping-pong balls and small fish to make the eyes boggle. Other bits sometimes boggle as well. I did have a wander down one gaudy street and was propositioned twenty times in as many yards, but came straight back here to the hostel to work on what I hope will become the best board game in the world. It's a game involving sailing around on a chequerboard sea from island to island, trading different coloured chips, red and yellow and green and so on. I think it's going to be brilliant, though as usual, the rules run to fifteen pages already, and I haven't even started on the combat rules.

Sorry to go on. You can see how very dull travelling gets at times.

Cheers,
Sandy

P.S. You will be astonished to learn that I have actually taken some health precautions. I went to get some malaria tablets today, and find that I am now protected by Malaprim and Chloroquin and all the Company of Heaven. Amen.

Chapter 15

To see where not only camphor, castor, colocynth and cocaine come from, but whence also the emerald, the chrysoprase, the topaz and the tourmaline; where impregnable forests brood, and the yellow fever skulks, and the Buddhist abounds ... all this can scarcely be acquitted of a romantic flavour.

—WALTER DE LA MARE, *Desert Islands*

If the Bangkok–Nong Kai train trip is one of the world's top ten, then I'm not keen to try the others. You board the train at 8.30 in the evening in Bangkok, climb into a bunk, fall asleep and wake up in Nong Kai ten hours later. Apart from the Thai family who spent the night slurping noodles in the bunk below, there was nothing to distract me from the blank darkness outside the window.

The destination was a different matter. Anywhere would have been nice after the fume-choked streets of Bangkok, but my first sight of Nong Kai was frangipani trees and hibiscus and the Mekong River. The train was met by a handful of boys with rickshaws, one of whom took me to the ferry crossing along quiet dusty streets lined with shady trees.

The Mekong is one of the great rivers of the world, flowing from the foothills of the Himalayas to the China Sea. As soon as I had crossed its wide brown breadth into Laos, I was told by a border guard to wait for a taxi to take me the few miles down the road into Vientiane. I later discovered that this was not a friendly suggestion but a direct order in line with the country's strict tourism laws, my disobeying of which was later to have strangely fortunate consequences. At the time, however, I was so happy to be out in the countryside again under a sunny sky that I mentally damned all taxis everywhere to blazes and started walking along the road between fields of tall reeds and cane. Very soon I was picked up by a local and taken into town. I booked into a cheap guesthouse. Very basic. One bed. One fan. Eight billion cockroaches. Bathroom down the hall.

Vientiane was charming. Ninety per cent of the traffic was bicycles and all the buildings were in the French colonial style, with faded yellows and greys hung with magenta clouds of bougainvillea. People smiled and waved as they passed and no-one tried to sell me a fake Rolex. One particularly lovely sight was the Buddhist monks, shaven-headed young men with sticky-out ears and orange robes, looking very mystical and enlightened were it not for the fact that a cigarette dangled from their lower lip, or they were standing in a stereo shop trying out headsets or sitting in a park reading Batman comics. I saw one riding along on an ancient bicycle, gliding down an avenue of plane trees, an old black umbrella held aloft as a sunshade. The saffron robes, the leafy-gold stripes of sunlight, the flash of the wheel-spokes and the solemnity of the young face made an unforgettable picture.

On the first night, I sat in an eating-house whose menu started off like this:

Grilled Moose Bleeding
Baked Sealy Ant-Eater
Half Cooking Moose Salad
Fried Wildboar Juicy with Vegemable

I ordered the last item.

I had read the previous night in Paul Theroux's *Riding the Iron Rooster* how he was surreptitiously offered 'forbidden food' at enormous prices in southern China. This turned out to be poached pangolin (or scaly ant-eater, see above.) Here there was nothing clandestine about it at all: it was printed on the menu. This was appalling. Pangolins are rare and unusual animals, something like a cross between a sloth and a pine cone, and you can't just *eat* them. As for Moose Bleeding – I shuddered to think.

Animals were not prized here. I had already seen in dim little stalls stuffed otters, pangolin skins and the mangy pelts of ocelots. The stuffed animals were dreadful. Their eyes had been replaced not with proper glass eyes but with cheap glass marbles, the type with blue-green swirls in the centre, so they looked as though they had died after ingesting some hallucinogenic drug.

I began to enjoy myself more once the gentle haze of Laotian sunshine seeped into my soul, and even went snooping about. There were interesting things to uncover, such as the imposition of an eleven o'clock curfew each evening. All good folk had to be in their homes behind barred doors after that time. 'Why?' I asked the lady in the bank.

'It is safer,' she said.

'Safer from whom, or what?' I pursued.

'Well, there's a big festival coming up soon and it's better this way. Security,' she hedged.

'Do you mean people might be rebelling or demonstrating?' I pestered.

'No, no, no,' she laughed. 'But it is good for us to be safe at home.'

'Are there patrols at night to check that people are at home safe?'

'No. I do not know. It is better not to be out.'

So. Also …

'Is it possible to go north?'

'Not for visitors, no.'

'Why not?'

'The road is not very good. It is dangerous.'

'Dangerous? You mean because of bad road conditions?'

'Yes. It is a very winding road.'

'What about being attacked by rebels? I heard in Thailand—'

'Oh, those Thais! They make mischief.'

'So there aren't any rebels?'

'I haven't heard anything like that. But it is unsafe.'

What was I to make of all this?

One morning I made the mistake of wandering into the official tourist agency, where I was confronted by a balding, vulture-nosed man in a green military uniform. A hard shiny label on his shirt declared him to be an officer of the Laotian Tourist Police.

'Ah,' I said brightly, 'could I trouble you for some brochures?'

'Name! Passport!' snapped the officer.

'Anything of interest, really, local temples, pretty waterfalls,' I went on.

'I asked you for your passport,' he grated. 'Passport, please!'

'Terribly sorry, but it must be at the hotel,' I said cheerfully. 'Now, if you could recommend a good bookshop, and where I might do some birdwatching. You must have some interesting species here, yes?'

But the Vulture was not to be put off his stride. 'You will fill in these forms. Your full name, what tour agency you are with, when you arrived.' He slapped down a sheaf of official forms and turned away to start thumbing through a grey filing cabinet.

Glancing around, I noticed there was a distinct lack of glossy posters and helpful maps on the walls. I read the forms carefully. 'Name I can manage, ha ha, and I arrived in Laos three days ago, but I'm not with any tour agency, I'm afraid, I'm just here flopping around on my own, I like to be independent, you know what it's like.'

At this the Vulture stiffened. 'But this is impossible. You must be with a tour agency. They would have met you at the ferry. It is not permitted to be ... independent.' He said the last word as though it were a bad prawn he wished to spit out as quickly as possible.

'Well, nobody met me, and I'm sorry to have troubled you, I'll leave you in peace now, shall I?' I didn't like the way things were heading.

'Wait!' he said, coming round from behind the counter and beating me to the door. 'Three days ago? You are Australian? Ha! Then you are the one I missed. I was to monitor you. You should have waited at the ferry for me as instructed.'

I was going to say something along the lines of, 'Well, you should have been on time, old bean,' but there was something in his look of triumph that I didn't think would be wise to deflate.

'Why were you not there?' he asked.

'Oh, sunny day and all that, don't like to sit still, decided to walk into town.'

He gave me the sort of look a real vulture might give a promising zebra carcase that had just got up and wandered off. 'Walk? Walk? In future, no walking. I will drive you. It is my job – and my pleasure to welcome you to our hospitable and friendly country, Land of a Million Elephants,' he added, suddenly remembering his role as tourist guide. This shift was accompanied by an almost audible clashing of mental gears.

'Oh, thank you, but—'

'Now, the name of the hotel where you are staying, please. That way I can report daily – to answer your every need.'

But I had made up my mind. It was obvious that an eye was kept on every tourist in Laos from the moment they stepped into the country, and this didn't fit in with my plans. It was by the sheerest good fortune that I had managed to dodge this overzealous official in the first place and I wanted to keep what advantage I had. 'Yes, right, the Mekong Hotel, lovely place by the river,' I lied sweetly, and backed out the door. 'And tomorrow, you can take me bird-watching. Cheers.'

As I was in fact staying at a tiny and anonymous hostel and rather thought that the Vulture would not be amused by my efforts to elude him once more, I spent the next few days creeping around town keeping a careful look-out, wishing I could curl up and hide in my room until he had forgotten all about me. But hiding was not an option. I had a serious purpose: to reconnoitre the road northwards. I soon met one or two people who provided me with a good deal of information. The first was an American, a Mr Doran Butts of Missouri who was working with the United Nations. He and his Laotian wife, Khamtoune, had me over to lunch several times, and I put my plans to them. They liked my spirit, they said, but they also shook their heads. The problem, it seemed, was that on one section of the road northwards there were rebels who, for some obscure reason, would occasionally step out of the jungle and blow up a passing bus with a bazooka. This was why the Laotian government forbade all visitors to travel northwards, except on official tours, which involved skipping over the trouble spots in a plane. It also meant that on the road out of town, there were officials checking to see that travellers had the correct permits.

However, Doran offered to introduce me that afternoon to George Scott-Ogilvie, the first secretary at the Australian embassy and a good friend of his. I rather expected someone with such a name and title to be a gruff, military type with a no-nonsense manner, a twinkle in his eye and a healthy disregard for local red tape, pass the port, there's a good chap. Well, he wasn't. He looked like Danny de Vito and when I put my thoughts to him over a gin and lime at the Australian Club, he squashed them flat. He told me categorically that the roads north really were dangerous, with rebel activity at an all-time high; even the Laotians no longer travelled the roads. A Danish lad had been killed just two months before, and he had even had a permit.

I still felt that if I could only get walking, there wasn't going to be a problem. Who was going to stop an amiable walker with a tatty rucksack and a pocketful of magic tricks, simply trying to see the world, eh? Especially if I travelled at night and able to nip off the road at the first click of a trigger. In fact, I could even try off-road completely! That'd be a bit of a lark, wouldn't it?

George Scott-Ogilvie fixed me with an oyster-eye over his gin and lime and said, 'No, it bloody wouldn't. We'd be the ones shipping you home in a body bag.'

I sipped my gin meekly and said nothing.

On the way back from the meeting, sitting in a motorised rickshaw, I was still thinking to myself, 'Yes, but surely,' and daydreaming about slipping through the jungle like a fleet-footed beast of the forest shadows. Just then, the rickshaw juddered to a halt and startled me out of my reverie. In the road, partially blocking our way, were two men begging for alms. And no wonder. One was without a left leg, the other was missing both feet. Landmines, Doran explained. The American pilots, returning from bombing missions over Vietnam, had strict orders to return with an empty hold. Consequently, on each return trip they would empty their bomb-bays over Laos – a country largely unconnected with the conflict – and someone has calculated that ten times more bombs were dropped on Laos than were ever used tactically during the whole of the Vietnam War. There were still thousands and thousands of them through the region and years later they were still going off, Doran explained. It was a tragedy and a disgrace, of course, and it also made me reconsider the sanity of my daydreaming. Fleet-footed beast of the forest shadows I may be, but not so light on my toes that I might not find myself being blown to soggy popcorn if I strayed off the path.

Yet I still couldn't believe it could be that difficult. I went off to the library to do more research. The Vientiane Library was situated in a French colonial building of crumbling yellow plaster, wooden shutters, a grand portico and two ornamental lions guarding the doors. Inside there was one huge echoing room to the left and another to the right. The room on the right had a wall of shelves lined with books, which I couldn't get at because there was a large, evil-looking bat swooping and scything through the shuttered gloom. It was the size of a small pterodactyl and yammered at me hungrily when I entered. The room to the left was identical except that the books were not on the shelves, but piled in a huge haphazard heap in the centre of the floor. They were lying as though they had been dumped out of a gravel truck and made a conical mound as high as my head. The mound was covered in yellowish dust. Curled up in the middle of them, like a dormouse in a nest, was the librarian, fast asleep, also covered in yellowish dust. When I entered he awoke, looked a little bemused and got to his feet. He stepped

out of his book-nest and said rather sadly, 'Yes, all for the shelves. Seventeen thousand books. One day I must put them on the shelves.' Then he hobbled off into the other room – the one with the bat.

I picked up a few books out of interest and found most of them to be from Russia and written in the 1950s. There were books about hydro-electricity plants and Soviet farming practices and lots of pictures of Stalin, and I remembered that Laos was a Communist country. There was nothing whatsoever on Laos itself.

I then went back into town and found the country's only bookshop, which was much more useful. In fact, I found a guidebook to Laos that said:

Northern Laos consists of mountainous hills, thick jungle, deep ravines and impassable rivers. Wild buffalo, elephants, panthers and tigers are commonly to be found.

And then, just in case I had any lingering ideas about tackling the terrain and the wildlife, it added:

A specially hazardous feature of the region for the unwary traveller is the prevalence of quicksand.

Quicksand. The whole thing was beginning to sound like *The Island of Doctor Moreau.*

I then went outside, thinking, yes, well, tigers, you'd have to be pretty unlucky to fall foul of a tiger, endangered species and all, and there on a news-stand outside the bookshop was a headline banner saying TEACHER EATEN BY TIGER IN NORTHERN LAOS.

Thinking dark thoughts, I mooched off to find a bar where they served beer and pangolin crackers. Bugger ecology.

And then, of course, God thought, 'Why not, after all? Let him have his fun,' and threw a ray of hope in my way. Over a bowl of ginger soup in a café across from my little guesthouse, I met two German students. Pit and Ulli were from Stuttgart and accomplished travellers with broad grins and a lively intelligence. We got chatting about travel plans, and I ordered another dish of something random off the menu. As I waited for it to arrive, I told them all my wishful hopes while downing lemongrass tea. But when the new dish arrived and it turned out to be boiled fish-heads in brine, my enthusiasm died and I faced up to the decision I had made earlier that evening.

'It's all no good, you see. I mean, I think all the signs are there, don't you? God keeps dropping these enormous hints not to go and when I say, "Yes but ..." he goes and drops another one. Rebels. Tigers. Quicksand. Landmines,' I grumbled, morosely stabbing at the bobbing heads. 'And even if all those things could be dealt with, which I am sure they could be, I can't even get out of this bloody town onto the northern road in the first place. The Tourist Police watch every road. Who eats these things, for God's sake?' I finished, pushing the bowl away from me.

'But *nein!*' the two Germans exclaimed, and pounced on the remaining broth like a pair of famished otters. In between slurps and crunching and much lip-smacking, they proceeded to tell me something intriguing. It appeared that they had spoken to an English girl who only one week before had managed to catch a series of buses and boats and trucks right up the northern road to a village called Vang Vieng, halfway to the Chinese border. She was not blown up. The people of Vang Vieng were thrilled to see her. She was stopped by the police twice but just stuck out her jaw and looked as though she knew where she was going and was waved through!

A few days of planning, and I might just do this too. Of course, there would be a lot to organise. I could seek Doran's advice, perhaps. And stock up on food, and see if I could get a better map of the terrain. Some tiger repellent, perhaps.

I glanced out of the café window into the darkening street and stiffened. A second later, my two new German friends were surprised to see me drop to the floor under the table. Out the window, in the street! The vulture-headed chief of the Secret Tourist Police. He had just gone in the front door of the guesthouse where I was staying.

Pit and Ulli looked at each other in concern and then down at me under the table. 'Is it ze fish-heads?' they said in chorus. 'Is zere somezing wrong viz ze fish-heads?'

I shushed them quiet and peered over the table top. A minute later, I saw the commandant emerge again, this time with the *patronne* of the guesthouse in tow. He was gesticulating crossly and I saw the woman point up the street, in the direction I had gone earlier that evening. There seemed little doubt that he now knew where I was staying. There also seemed little doubt that he would be displeased to find that I had lied to him. If he found me, I knew, I would not get away again. I would most likely be deported immediately. If I was going to go, it would have to be first thing the next morning or not at all.

Once the Vulture had swooped off into the night, I turned to the Germans and asked them how the girl had done it, scribbling all the while their instructions on a paper napkin. By the time they had finished, I felt as though I was about to take part in a scenario from *The Great Escape*. The bread market at dawn. A certain Mr Veng who would put me on a local truck going north to a lake. A small fishing boat across the lake, thus avoiding the police roadblocks. Then a second truck heading northward to the village of Vang Vieng, some forty miles beyond the cordon outside which tourists are not permitted. The police would not be looking for escapees so far north. After that I was on my own, heading into rebel country and the long road to Luang Phrabang and the Chinese border.

No time to buy supplies, no time to find a map, or for farewells. There was only just time to scribble off a hasty letter to Chris, and to ask the Germans to post it for me on the morrow, before they both wished me luck and said goodnight. The letter, after outlining the general plan and some of the hazards involved, ended thus:

I have absolutely no idea if this decision is going to be suicidal or a non-event – probably the usual blend of high jinks and anti-climax. Anyway, here's what I'll do. I'll write the next paragraph (a) as though I'm going to die. Then the paragraph after that (b) will be written with the full knowledge that I will be writing to you again, probably from bloody Bangkok. So here goes.

a) Thanks for everything. Have a nice life. If there's an afterlife, I'll come back and let you know somehow. I know, I'll make that wedding-present clock of mine start working properly. Then you'll know. Gosh, we had some fun, didn't we? Keep up the good work in all those important things: Treasure Hunts and Long Walks and Letter-writing and Wildflowers and Music and Being-a-Splendid-Chap and Knowing-Poetry-To-Be-Recited-On-Sunny-Hillsides. And that sort of thing.

Love to everybody.
Your friend,
Sandy

b) Cheer up, laddie! It's not over yet! Goodbye once more. Do or die! Fortune favours the brave!
Geronimo!
Lots of love,
Sandy

P.S. DON'T TELL DAD.

Chapter 16

Above all, do not lose your desire to walk: every day I walk myself into a state of well-being and walk away from every illness: I have walked myself into my best thoughts, and I know of no thought so burdensome that one cannot walk away from it ... Thus if one just keeps on walking, everything will be all right.

—SØREN KIERKEGAARD

It was chilly when I rose the next morning before sunrise and made my way down to the bread market as per my scribbled instructions on the napkin. Even at that hour I was taking no chances and kept to the shadows, skulking around the stalls in case I bumped into the Vulture or his cronies. There were, in fact, a couple of uniformed officials chatting with some of the drivers, so I immediately went off to a stall that was just opening up and purchased from a sleepy woman a Laotian straw hat – one of those conical Chinaman's lampshades beloved of music-hall variety shows. The only thing missing was the pigtail. I pulled it down low over my eyes and surveyed the scene.

Vans were being loaded with bread and crates of what sounded like live ducks, there were clouds of blue exhaust in the cold morning air, and drivers and passengers milled around in no great hurry to leave. Many were squatting on their haunches, drinking coffee out of battered tin mugs and tearing great mouthfuls of fresh bread from long French breadsticks. Once the two policemen had sauntered off, I tentatively joined a group, asking in bad French where I might find the mysterious Mr Veng. I was immediately poured a coffee amid much chatter. When after a few polite sips I asked nervously again for Mr Veng, I was poured a top-up and laughed at a lot. After another hour of nerve-stretching waiting, my every sense tuned for the presence of the Vulture, it seemed that I would be there forever – and still no Mr Veng.

'Where you want to go?' asked one of my fellow coffee-drinkers.

'Well, Vang Vieng, but I need to—' I started, but before I could finish I was swept bodily to a waiting bus, my bag and hat were flung onboard and I found myself sitting at the very back between sacks of rice and a tetchy chicken while fifty other people crowded aboard. Two seconds later, before I could explain that, no, wait, I had to meet Mr Veng, the bus roared out of the bread market and we were off.

Sure enough, it was as I had feared. Before we had gone two miles, we found ourselves slowing to a halt. A glance ahead confirmed that we were at a police checkpoint. This was it: all my hopes and plans were about to come crashing down. However, as the police officer climbed onboard at the front of the bus, I noticed that somehow, unaccountably, the crowd of fellow passengers seemed to swell slightly, spilling out into the aisle, standing up to stretch their legs, sitting more upright in their seats – in fact, anything to make it difficult for the officer to see right down to the back of the bus where I was sitting. Surely they couldn't deliberately be trying to mask me, these complete strangers? Still, I edged my new straw hat down over my eyes and, as an afterthought, gently grabbed the chicken and held it on my lap. Would I look enough like a local?

The officer scanned the crowded bus idly, then turned and gave the driver a piece of paper. Then he disembarked and waved us through. It had worked – and when we were 300 yards up the road, every single passenger on the bus turned around and gave me a great conspiratorial grin. How I loved the Laotians then.

I don't know what happened to the plan involving Mr Veng, the lake and the truck, but three hours later we drove into the village of Vang Vieng and I had my first glimpse of the rural life of Laos, feeling once more the thrill that came from knowing I was seeing the deep-grained reality of the world, and thereby reaffirming the rightness of not flying. Vang Vieng was a sleepy village by a river with a million-dollar view to the mountains that rose 500 yards beyond the far bank. These were straight from a Chinese rice-paper print: sheer-sided steeples and pinnacles of rock clothed in forest greenery, but with grey stone fingers and petrified needles jutting up from every point, impossibly slender and precarious. The next morning, they looked even lovelier, shrouded in wreaths of white cloud, fresh and shining from the painter's brush. Steam was rising off the river, and out of it came three wallowing water buffalo, phlegmatic and mud-grey. All was perfect.

Despite my travels in the backwaters of Indonesia, everything was new. Sitting and eating at the little chop-house, for example, was a puzzling experience. The rickety table was spread with plates of bean-shoots and green beans and huge bunches of a fresh herb that looked a little like parsley, smelled a little like mint but had a wonderful peppery, gingery heat to it. Another plant looked alarmingly like the deadly dog's mercury of English woodlands, but for a purple tinge. It too had a kick like mint steeped in chilli. (Only years later would I recognise these as coriander and Vietnamese mint, when such exotics became a commonplace of the supermarket shelf.) Then an enormous bowl of soup arrived, with strange, smooth meat dumplings in it and rubbery white strips of something with hairy fringes, and masses of slippery noodles and red-hot chillies, and I set to. Everyone had a good laugh at my approach to eating.

'Look!' they whispered. 'He is eating the dumplings with a spoon! What? He is eating the green herb by itself! Ah, too many chillies! Ah, eee! He knows it now!' And the women and children dissolved in tears, as indeed did I, but for different reasons.

The next day, a truck came through the village, one of the orange and blue chicken-crate affairs that double as public transport in the wilds of Laos, and I spent five hours in the very middle of it, attempting to see the passing scenery through a haze of cigarette smoke and the two-inch slats in the sides. From what I could see, the same impossible mountains marched alongside the road like giants. It would be inaccurate to say that we were in a valley or gorge

because these pinnacles were so scattered. In fact, it was like driving across a vast chessboard, chequered in the silver and green of paddy fields but with all the chesspieces towering overhead, spread about the board in mid-game.

On two occasions we were stopped by locals. They had guns and I have no idea if they were rebels or soldiers, but each time I hid under my hat in the crowded truck as I had before and we were waved through. Their costume was extraordinary: long black bell-bottom trousers, black tunics with magenta woollen collars and on their heads little round Cossack hats trimmed with bright-pink bobbles. They looked far more like my idea of Mongolian tribesmen than anything one would expect to find in Indo-China.

We ended up at a place called Kasi, the end of the road for the passengers and, it seemed for a while, for me also. Would there be any vehicles going on to Luang Phrabang? Maybe, I was told. Maybe not. Wait and see.

So for two nights and two days I stayed in Kasi, in a tiny guest-house where my room was a bare wooden attic with a mattress on the floor, a mosquito net and a kerosene drum of water to wash from. On the second day, the rain came down in solid sheets of steel that turned the red clay road into a red lake and drove the goats and chickens and pigs indoors with us. Here I learnt to like sticky rice, the staple of Laotian cuisine. I had to: there was nothing else.

On the third day the weather cleared and a convoy of five transport lorries came through the village. After some discussion about money, I was squeezed into the cabin of one of them, along with the driver's entire family and livestock, and was off again. Luang Phrabang, the old royal capital halfway up the country, was, I gathered, about sixty miles further north. I guessed we would be there that afternoon. In fact, it took five days. What no-one had told me about the road to Luang Phrabang was that its representation as a dotted line on the map was not a cartographical convention but an actual picture of its condition; that is, distinctly intermittent. Every half-hour the convoy would come to a halt because the road had ceased to exist. A pot-hole the size of a swimming pool, a missing bridge, a landslide, a fallen tree, anything at all. Then out would come the drivers, their wives, their children, their cousins and their chickens, and a collection of picks and shovels, axes, planks and props, and we would spend a happy three hours rebuilding the road.

The road by now had left the chessboard pinnacles behind and started tackling the serious mountains, great rounded ridged bulks and deep, deep valleys. Progress was very, very slow. I reckon that the first day out of Kasi we only made about twenty miles before coming down to a tiny village, little more than a couple of thatched hovels by a fast-flowing stream. I slept with the truck drivers and their families that night, all tumbled together on a great mat by a smoking fire. In this medieval setting, the one hint of the modern world was a tangled bundle of unspooled cassette tape, hung up as a festoon from the ceiling. It was bitterly cold, but we finished the evening drinking several rounds of a filthy whitish liquor, which the drivers told me was called whisky-lao or lao-lao. This takes out the nasal passages pretty effectively, but certainly warms the bones. It was passed around from person to person in one small cracked glass, each man downing the glass and then refilling it for his neighbour. I joined in with gusto.

The next day saw more stops every half-hour to rebuild the road, and we also picked up a troop of young soldiers, heavily armed with machine guns, grenades and a bazooka or two. You could see that they were itching to remove a distant hillside, given half a chance. They rode shotgun on the cabin-tops of the trucks for about three hours, and I gathered that this was to repel rebels. I wondered cynically about the need for the display of military gung-ho but soon had to swallow my words. Too often we would pass a burnt-out jeep or a blackened hut and at every tight corner of the road the driver would look at me, say 'Bang! Bang!' and shake his head sadly.

Some hours later, the soldiers disembarked, and shortly we came to yet another pot-hole, bigger than any so far. All this time, I had been itching to get out of the truck and walk. In the cabin, there was constant smoking of clove cigarettes, the radio blared and everything jolted incessantly, while outside there was pristine jungle and oh! the butterflies! They rose in clouds around us, carpeted the road and were crushed heedlessly by our wheels. I asked the drivers if I could carry on walking along the road a little and be picked up further on. Yes, that was fine, they assured me, smiling.

'No rebels? No bang-bang?'

'No, no. No bang-bang!' they laughed.

So, leaving my hat sitting on top of my rucksack in the cabin, I walked off down the road, bare-headed and empty-pocketed, round the corner in the glorious mountain air, and never saw those truckies again.

Stupid, I know.

But wait. It has a happy ending. I set a cracking pace, hoping to get as much of the butterflies and mountain air as I could before the trucks came and picked me up. Soon the road began to climb and climb and I found myself coming to high windy saddles and bare hilltops with magnificent views over blue mountain ridges fading to dim, distant valleys in every direction. There were villages here too; they had a sort of sheep-nibbled look about them, with cropped grass and rough-pelted hill-ponies, and again the strange Cossack dress of the villagers. I might have wandered into a village waiting for Genghis Khan.

At one of them, three children raced out and came up to me, pointing at my fair hair, giggling shyly. One of them started stroking the golden hairs on my arm, her mouth an O of wonder. How must I have seemed to them, striding along the road across the hills, no pack, no goods, no sign of transport and the nearest town fifty miles away?

And hospitality I received in abundance. A venerable old man came, gently shooed away the children and led me silently to his hut, little more than a lean-to of banana palms and poles, with a king's vista over the blue hills of Laos. Here he wordlessly offered me a bowl of green tea and three bananas and then sat beaming at me, nodding. Eventually, as I was about to leave, he motioned for me to wait. He dug around under his sleeping mat and brought out a battered old exercise book. Tenderly he opened it and showed me what was inside. There were pages and pages of script, Laotian on the left-hand pages and English on the right, beautifully written even in the cheap biro that had been used. I could not read the Laotian, of course, but the English words were strangely familiar. 'Hey Jude'. 'All You Need Is Love'. 'Yellow Submarine'. Here in this

remote seventh-century setting they seemed out of place, though many would argue that they are timeless.

At the end of that long, glorious day, I was still walking and there was still no sign of the trucks. As the sun set and the mountain air chilled, I tried to feel apprehensive but could not. My pack, my passport, my wallet – everything I owned except the clothes I was standing in – was elsewhere. I was in a strange land and night was falling. I was as happy as I have ever been in my life. I had no idea how things were going to come right, but I was awash with a certainty that they would. It was free-falling. It was bloody irresponsible. It was marvellous.

Just before the sun dipped below the horizon, I came round a corner of the hillside and there was a village, surrounded by scarlet poinsettia trees, made more scarlet by the red sunset. As in all the other villages, out came the children and the inevitable old man, the head-man, who spoke a sort of French. A chair was brought out into the dusty square, a bowl of tea produced and in rusty French I explained my plight. In five minutes flat, it was settled. I must sleep the night here and tomorrow, I would accompany the old man on foot to Luang Phrabang. It was a twenty-mile walk along jungle paths, and we would be there by nightfall. As for the trucks, my rucksack, wallet, passport, sleeping bag – these were not important, it seemed. In the meantime, supper!

I was led to what seemed to be the village hall, and a bountiful meal of fish and chicken and papaya and rice was brought out – so much that I wondered if I had arrived in time for a communal feast. Certainly the entire populace of the village appeared to be there. When the repast was laid out on the floor, mostly in bowls of banana leaves, a few of the older women took me by the hand and pointed at the food.

Eat! they indicated, but I gestured back, sweeping my hand at the other people standing there. *After you!* I said. But no, further gestures indicated that this entire feast was for me. Helplessly, I began. The villagers, it seemed, were simply here to watch me eat. This they did with great delight, giggling when I dunked my rice in the wrong thing or found the chilli too hot. In all this, it soon became apparent that the chief player was a bashful maiden of nineteen who, I slowly gathered, was the head-man's granddaughter. She had long dark hair pinned back with a flower, and gentle almond eyes. She was the one who pointed out what I had not tried yet, or which sauce to eat with which dish and, towards the end, as I struggled to pick up a slippery morsel of papaya, she deftly caught it on a toothpick and popped it in my mouth. Laughing, I caught up a toothpick, speared another piece of papaya and popped it in *her* mouth. The reaction was surprising. There was a gasp of delight, a profound silence that stopped me chewing mid-bite ... and then a burst of excited laughter from the watching villagers. The girl blushed, giggled and looked away, and I swallowed my mouthful of papaya with relief. Goodness, I thought to myself, anyone would think I had just proposed to the girl.

After the meal, some of the men came and sat down on the floor with me and pulled out the now-familiar bottle of lao-lao. I tried to say no, but in the time-honoured custom followed wherever males and alcohol are brought together, they were having none of it. My manliness was about to be tested by the ancient ordeal of poisoning by alcohol. I braced myself but, as is usually the way, after several rounds it was beginning to be bearable and my head was spinning pleasantly. So comfortable had I become, in fact, that I loudly demanded a hanky from the assembly, folded it into a white mouse and made it jump up and down my arm as though alive –

Trick No. 2 in the *Easy-To-Do Magic Manual*. This may or may not
have impressed the gathering – less so perhaps after the fifth time
– but for whatever reason, I found the almond-eyed girl urging me
to put down the hanky mouse and have another glass of lao-lao.
'Certainly, beautiful miss,' I enthused, taking it and downing it in
one gulp. Then I clapped my hand to my lips, hiccupped slightly and
exclaimed owlishly, 'But where are my manners?! Allow me.' Then,
shaking slightly, I took the bottle from her, poured a shot and
offered the glass back to her, just as I had been doing for the men.
 This was possibly an error of judgment. There was a sudden
silence in the hall. The girl looked abashed and glanced at her
grandfather, who had stiffened like a mongoose spotting a cobra.
Only when he nodded his head very gravely – once, twice – did she
take the liquor and, smiling shyly, drink it.
 Ahhh! There was a great sigh from the villagers, and a sudden
burst of animated chatter from the women. The men were winking
at each other and nudging me roguishly. When she had drunk the
glassful in small gasping sips, she spluttered a little, tears of pure
lao-lao squeezing from her eyes. Encouraged by the watchful eyes of
the womenfolk, however, she poured me another glass and handed
it to me. By this time, I was well beyond the ability to pick up social
nuances in an unfamiliar culture, so, playfully making the hanky
mouse leap at her bosom, I called out a cheery 'Chin chin!' and
downed the lao-lao in one fiery gulp.
 And poured her another.
 By this stage, I might as well have presented her with a fifteen-
carat diamond ring and a copy of *Bride To Be* magazine. Grandfather now looked like a mongoose that has successfully caught the
cobra, sliced it into fillets and is frying it up in a cashew and beetle
sauce for his mongoose mates.
 Suddenly we were no longer on the floor. Despite the unaccount-
able unsteadiness of my legs, we were standing up and had formed a
circle. There was a bout of singing, in which I joined to the best of
my ability, though I must confess the timing was tricky, and then
some dancing, which is hardly my forte at the best of times, but
which I gave my best shot. After that, everything went very still and
quiet. Someone managed to dissuade me from performing a quick
solo of 'The Waves of Erin,' and I recall holding hands with someone, possibly the girl, yes, I'm almost sure it was the girl, while the
head-man asked me all sorts of questions. I beamed, nodded and

said 'Absholutely, why not?' to all of them and even remembered the Laotian affirmative, *Sabadee!*, which seemed to please everyone. Then more singing, more dancing, and lots of happy, happy faces.

Some time after this, I started crashing. I really needed to go to bed. I yawned loudly, mimed sleeping and was vaguely conscious of a dozen men nudging each other lewdly and making the Laotian equivalent of *ho-ho* noises. I couldn't think why. The next thing I knew I was surrounded by soft hands and being led out into the cold night air. I was shown into a hut with surely the largest bed in the village. Two young boys were pulling back the covers, lighting the lamp and helping me out of my clothes and under the sheets. Both were grinning broadly. Just as I was about to roll over and dive head-first into blurry slumber, the elder of the two shot a question at me. What? I don't understand? Sorry?

He pointed out the door and then back to me. He held his hands down by his sides like a choo-choo train, and thrust his hips backwards and forwards several times. Before I could protest, there at the door appeared the girl, smiling shyly in the soft glow of the lamplight.

The drinks. The dancing. All those questions cheerfully agreed to. I wondered just how easy it was in Laotian inadvertently to say the phrase 'I do.'

But no. It had been a long, long day and thanks, really, but no thanks. I hardly had to mime the next big yawn and the big, hopefully obvious, goodnight-and-roll-over-eyes-shut-tight charade. I heard a whisper, a giggle – and did I imagine a faint sigh of dashed hopes? – and all three tiptoed out again, while I pretended to fall fast asleep in three seconds flat.

In ten more seconds, there was no pretence about it.

*

I woke the next morning in the early dawn with mixed feelings and a throbbing headache. As I lay there listening to the incessant cock-crow beyond the doorway, I felt apprehensive about facing what might well now be my in-laws, especially my newly acquired grandfather-in-law. I was unfamiliar with Laotian law as regards breach of promise and I climbed into my trousers with some trepidation.

I needn't have worried. The grandfather came bustling into the bedchamber, glanced around and did not seem too perturbed to find the girl absent. Perhaps this had happened before. Whatever the case, he said nothing and we hurried off on our long trek in the chilly dawn before the village awoke. Mind you, the pace that Grandfather set through the jungle was punishing and I did wonder if he was working out his disappointment by walking me to death. This'll teach the bugger to lead impressionable young girls on, his ancient shoulderblades seemed to be saying as they vanished up the jungle path thirty feet ahead.

The main road wound and zig-zagged its way out of the hills to the Mekong plain in great loops and switchbacks, but we did not follow it. Instead, we took little paths that cut off the loops in the road in sheer descents – and ascents. I trotted along as fast as I could but there was no breath left for talking. We stopped for lunch – sticky rice wrapped in a palm leaf – on a bare ridge before one last great decline. The old man pointed into the haze and said, 'Luang Phrabang.' There, seemingly twenty miles away across the plain below us, was something shining gold in the noonday sun, like a fallen star. It lay by a broad sweep of silver ribbon, and I later knew this to be the great golden stupa of the temple on its hill by the Mekong River. It was a fine first sight of the ancient capital, the jewel of Lao, City of a Thousand Elephants. There were barely another five hours of jogging to get to it.

And so at last we came down out of the hills to Luang Phrabang, feeling pretty epic. Six days it had taken me from Vientiane across those wild hills, though it is a mere hundred miles as the crow flies. The next problem was what to do about the loss of my pack and my valuables. The old man had told me earlier that the trucks had been heard going through the village in the middle of the night and when we arrived in Luang Phrabang, he made his way to a tiny shop on the outskirts of town and made some enquiries for me. No, he told me, the trucks were not there. They had arrived early that morning, well before sunrise, but had gone on to another town far off to the east. But what of my backpack, I asked? What would I do? He shrugged, said something incomprehensible and then without further ado strode off and was lost in the crowd. I was left standing in the middle of the street in despair. What the blazes was I going to do without wallet, passport or clothes?

I say despair, but in fact it was more a feeling of giddiness, guilty delight, a secret glee, the same feeling I had had back there up in the hills at sunset when I realised I was at the mercy of ... of what? Of Mercy itself. I had always sat and nodded approvingly at Christ's exhortation to cast off worry about our daily bread and to live as the lilies of the field. But it is easy to nod from the rosewood pews, when one of the many lifelines of the modern age is always at hand: the phone call, the credit card, the car key. It felt strangely good, therefore, to be in a situation where my response to Christ's maxim would be fully tested.

Filled with a sense of liberty and fizzing delight, I set off to explore Luang Phrabang, leaving my problem to be worked on by angels, or however these things are organised. Very soon, my backpack and wallet and all my worldly goods and chattels were forgotten in the sheer wonder of being in this extraordinary place. Luang Phrabang lived up to its reputation as the true heart of Laos. I wandered up to the golden stupa'd temple on its hill by the wide Mekong, and looked down on the little junks and sampans plying the river below. I poked around the cool, cavernous, richly ornate chambers of the temple, watched by unconcerned monks in saffron robes who smiled serenely and bowed their heads in silent salutation. Perhaps my penniless state was a divine invitation to join the monks in their life of devotion. Did one have to provide one's own begging bowl, I wondered idly, or could I borrow one? Coming outside again, I surveyed my surroundings. There were forested mountains all around, but down below frangipani and poinsettia trees lined the grid of wide streets with cream and scarlet blossom. I could see a smallish square where people seemed to be congregating, so made my way down the flights of wide steps to the town. Here I discovered a market from a forgotten world, selling incense, woven cloths, fireworks and what I think were rough-cut sapphires, and gold and ivory measured out in little brass pans by the ounce. There were stalls selling raw indigo in great crumbly blocks. I had imagined indigo as a rich peacock hue, but it is a slightly disappointing shade of dull navy, the colour of Levi's jeans. Alongside these were blocks of something that looked like solidified lumps of treacle and which I suspect was raw opium. Animal pelts – mongoose, civet cats, ocelot – were distressingly common on the market stalls, as they had been in Vientiane. All I needed was a solar topee and an ivory-handled fly-whisk to complete the picture of Phineas Fogg abroad. And of course, a Gladstone bag full of pound notes or gold sovereigns. A valet would have been nice as well.

For the market had stalls of roasting meat and pots of scented rice for sale and the aroma of these impressed upon me my penniless

state. My wallet, my backpack, my passport – even my Chinese hat
– were now in all likelihood on their way to Burma with a cache of
washing-machine parts or soap powder or hand grenades or whatever it was the faithless truckies had been transporting. Even now,
my passport was probably being sold on the Laotian black market
for a ground-to-air missile launcher or a sack of ocelot pelts. And
my beautiful sleeping bag? And my telescope? And what's more, it
would soon be night. Perhaps there was a British consulate. Perhaps
I could trot the seven hours back to the village and borrow some
housekeeping money from my wife.

Meanwhile, the hot afternoon declined to an evening of blue and
gold. I had wandered down to the river and spent an idle hour
watching the busy wharf and the boys fishing in the turbid waters.
Then I had wandered back to the centre of town, where the lamps
were being lit and the smell of roasting meat was stronger than ever
on the evening air. Consider the lilies? Consider the kebabs ...
Consider a quick snatch-and-run-for-it?

No, absolutely not. And besides, it wouldn't do me any harm to
be hungry for a while. I resolutely turned my back on the markets
and started marching out of town. Fruit, I thought. In the forest.
There had been plenty of it growing on the trees, I'd noticed, big
pinkish things high up, and if I hurried, I might get there while
there was still light enough to see. And to climb. And to avoid landmines hidden on the forest floor.

I had gone just two streets when the angel who watches my steps
relented and said to his celestial colleagues, 'Okay, enough, joke's
over, let's get this miracle done with. He's gonna poison himself if
he tries those pink things.' Or rather, I heard a voice calling out
behind me, 'Sandee! Sandee! Mister Sandee!' My first foolish
thought was, 'Hmm, funny. San-dee must be a Laotian name as
well.' Then I turned to see a boy running towards me in the dusk.
He panted up, took me by the hand and led me down a dark side-
street into a low doorway. Cautiously I peered inside. There in a
room stacked with sacks of rice and sugar was a single lantern and,
by its light, a familiar shape. It was my rucksack and my lampshade
hat and, a quick check revealed, my passport and wallet, untouched
in the inner pocket. A closer look at the boy – surely no older than
ten – had me recognising him as one of the dozen or so children
who had accompanied the truck convoy.

'The trucks? They're still here?' I asked the boy.

'No, no,' he replied. 'Trucks go long time now. I wait you. Show you bag, nice hat. Now me catch trucks. Bye!'

He turned to go but I caught him by the shoulder. 'Sorry, do you mean to say that the trucks, along with your parents and everyone on them, left you here on the off-chance that I might one day walk past and be needing my bag?'

He nodded, glancing uneasily to either side. It was clear he didn't understand a word.

'And have driven off to another town? Without you?'

Another nod and a worried grin as he picked up my trembling distress.

'But that's so stupid,' I said. 'That's so … that's so … ridiculous. That's so … beautiful,' I sobbed and began to cry.

The boy paused, puzzled as to how to react. Then he handed me my hat, patted me gently on the hand and said again brightly, 'Nice hat.'

And with a wave of his hand, he sprinted off down the road into the darkened east to catch up with his long-departed convoy.

*

Over the next two days, although ensconced in relative comfort in a good hostel, I found myself banging my head against officialdom at every turn. I had assumed rather naively that up here, away from the capital, the rules and regulations would be more relaxed, so I had determined to be more up-front with the officials than I had been in Vientiane. Luang Phrabang was too small a town to be playing hide-and-seek with the Vulture's counterpart. To that end, I wandered down to the police station, a cool sleepy building of white-washed concrete, and made enquiries about further travel north. From my map, the rivers seemed the likeliest route up to the Chinese border, in particular the Nam Ou, which branched off the Mekong to the right a few miles up from Luang Phrabang. I shared these ideas with the nice young police officer behind the counter.

Then I rather wished I hadn't. Nice he might have been, but he was also a stickler for the rules. Having come unscathed through the rebel territory, it seemed that I was now not allowed to leave *this* town either. In fact, the officer went on, further up-country travel was expressly forbidden. My only route out, he explained helpfully, was to catch a tiny local plane back to Vientiane.

Here we go again. I nodded politely and resignedly and wandered down to the Mekong to watch the river-traffic ply up and down, crafts of every shape and size: canoes, sampans, little fishing vessels with single outboard motors on the back, even a medium-sized junk. Commonest of all were large ferries crowded with people, goats, pigs and goods in splitting sacks, some of them heading upstream, just the direction I wanted to go. There seemed to be a genial confusion of people coming and going and nobody much monitoring the boarding procedure. Perhaps I would have to be clandestine after all.

That very afternoon, I surreptitiously checked out of my hostel, went down to the river and joined the bustling throng boarding a ferry travelling up to Pak Beng, way up the Mekong. There were no officials in sight. Once on board, I pushed my way towards the crowded bows and immediately hunkered down among the rice-bags and goats, with my Chinese hat pulled down over my eyes, giggling maniacally.

I shouldn't have pushed my luck. Ten minutes later, from beneath the brim of my hat, I saw a pair of shiny black boots. There was a shrill voice coming from somewhere above me. I pretended to ignore it, but a hand grabbed me by the collar and pulled me sharply upwards. It was the very same policeman who had made the travel regulations so abundantly clear to me earlier that day, and I found myself blushing like a schoolboy as I was hauled off the boat, trying ineffectively to explain that yes, I had been a *bit* confused by some of the conversation earlier.

The next day, precisely the same thing happened, this time on a bus. I blushed even harder. Then I stomped back to my guesthouse and sat in the courtyard, watching the menagerie of caged animals, sympathising with them more than ever. Every little hotel prided itself on keeping a small zoo, a few tiny, filthy cages where skulked or trembled half-a-dozen or so animals. In this one were two nervous skinny foxes, a type of large raccoon, a stupefied and starving crocodile in three inches of water, three dejected monkeys and, worst of all, a large black jungle-bear crammed in a cage the size of a dog kennel. It had bluggy eyes and a snout twisted into an odd shape and it lay in the bottom of the cage and whimpered day and night. It did occur to me that I might try the ferry again, but this time release the animals from their cages before I left so as to occupy the police while I slipped away. Then I remembered all those crocodile dreams and thought better of it. The grim irony of being devoured by a ravenous crocodile just as I was setting it free would surely be too tempting for Fate to resist.

That night I found myself chatting to a local man who wished to try out his English over a glass of whisky-lao. While we were still both conscious, he told me that if I was planning to go further upcountry, the most valuable thing I could take with me was ... packets of monosodium glutamate. Apparently it was much prized by the locals in remote areas, all that chilli and coriander so dulling the palate, I suppose, that even the spiciest morsels of wild moose bleeding come to seem as bland as tapioca. The man had a dozen or so sachets on him, and told me that I'd be doing myself and the villagers a big favour if I would take these along and hand them out in return for hospitality. The only thing, he warned, was that I'd be advised to do this surreptitiously; apparently the government took a dim view of monosodium glutamate, eating away as it was at the cultural fibre of the place. I was reminded of Patrick Leigh Fermor's classic account of his journey by foot from Holland to Istanbul, where he found himself travelling with a saccharine smuggler, carrying loads of illicit sweeteners across the Danube into pre-war Czechoslovakia.

By the time we'd drunk another few shots of lao-lao and had a long and blurry conversation about the bloody government, bloody commies, ay? ay? bloody interfering police, we'll show 'em, ay?, we'd rather lost the thread of things and I staggered back to the guest-house without any packets of food-enhancer. Later I was to realise just how complicated my life could have become had I taken up his offer.

I had been feeling extremely guilty about the fact that I had taken off from Vientiane without contacting Doran Butts to let him know that I would be missing from dinner the following night. I therefore sat down to write a long letter of explanation and apology. I detailed all the adventures of the road north: the police check, the road-building, rebel territory, my accidental marriage to the high-land princess. I hoped he and his wife might enjoy these escapades and forgive me. I had got on so well with them, in fact, that I rather hoped they might keep in touch, so I added that if they were interested in writing, they could send any letters via my father, whose address I would write carefully on the back of the envelope. I then added in a jocular fashion that, speaking of my father, it was a jolly good thing he didn't know what I had been up to, ha ha, what with the quicksand and tigers and rebels and all, as he was inclined to worry unduly, you know what parents are like. Then I signed the letter, sealed the envelope and trotted off to the local post office.

Here I encountered the oddity of the Laotian postal system. When I went to stick the stamps onto the envelope, the girl behind the counter stopped me and turned the envelope over, and then proceeded to stick them all over the *back*. There were so many that I worried they might have covered up my father's address, but no, the girl firmly indicated, that's where the stamps *always* go here in Laos. I hadn't quite worked out the currency, but I guessed it was about seven million kip to one dollar or something ridiculous like that. The price of the stamps was something astronomical like twenty-three billion kip just for a letter to Vientiane, so no wonder there were so many of them.

None of this rang any alarm bells whatsoever.

By this time, I had become so frustrated by the prohibition on travelling further northward that I decided I'd simply start walking. *Solvitur ambulando*: it is solved by walking. Nobody takes seriously a man out for a stroll. He's clearly not going very far.

And it worked! I sauntered down the road, past the bus depot, past the police station, past the last straggling houses, looking as though I were perambulating in search of wildflowers, and soon found myself far enough out of town to stop sauntering and start marching. Ten minutes later I heard a jeep coming and, fearing it was the police coming for a third recapture, I turned down a side lane into the paddy fields. For the next two hours I was lost, wandering in a maze of flooded fields and bamboo brakes and buffalo wallows, desperately trying to find my way back to the main road.

Eventually I stumbled out onto the banks of the Mekong itself and did a spontaneous, audacious thing. I waved and shouted across the water at a small sampan going upstream and, to my astonishment, the fisherman and his wife came over to the bank, picked me up and continued on their way. Four hours later, I was bedding down for the night in a remote jungle village twenty miles north of Luang Phrabang, without a policeman in sight.

This village was at the confluence of the Nam Ou River and the Mekong, and for the next few days I continued travelling in the same style, winding deeper and deeper into the hills of northern Laos. I journeyed up the Nam Ou aboard one of the boats that

ferried people to and fro through this trackless wilderness. These
were like very long, low canoes and could seat about ten people,
their goats and chickens and, in one case, the biggest sow I'd ever
seen. There was a fish-tail of wood at prow and stern and a sort of
outboard motor with the propeller on a long shaft. This allowed
the boatman to navigate up the rapids and over the rocky shallows,
a task he did with remarkable skill and tenacity. Every now and
then, water would sluice over the sides and we would rock dangerously as he wriggled us up another rapid like a spawning salmon,
barely making headway even with the throttle fully open.

The scenery, if you could ignore these perils and the stench of
pig and exhaust, was breathtaking. The whole way we were over-
shadowed by pinnacles of limestone mountains. At times the walls
would close in and we would be roaring along in a gorge between
sheer cliffs, the sky a narrow ribbon overhead. On two occasions we
passed by gaping caverns in the cliffs that were clearly Buddhist
shrines: steps had been carved up to them and one could catch
glimpses of carved golden Buddhas and, beyond the stalactites and
swallows' nests, candles glowing their devotions.

Wallowing buffalo, palm-thatch villages, forested banks and
reedy islands, mountains cutting off the sun and sky, brown foam-
ing water racing by the gunwales an inch from my nose – these were
the treasures of those days!

And later, when the river ran out and I took to jungle roads once
more, the butterflies! Down in the valleys where the air grows
sleepy and the road is tiger-striped with sunlight, the butterflies
cluster.

I saw, just for the record, a pair of Laotian scarlet razorwings, the
famous fighting butterflies of Indo-China *and* the rare carnivorous
Siamese emperor, which can, in flocks, strip a dead horse to the
bone in five minutes. Or rather I didn't, but I did amuse myself each
night by describing such things in a long and knowledgeable-

sounding letter to Chris. Normally an unflappable chap, Chris can nevertheless be stirred to a righteous passion by my tendency to claim an expertise in any field I have touched upon for more than ten minutes. 'Ah, the call of the wicket bird, I think you'll find, Chris – that distinctive double note. William Morris in his earlier phase, of course, indicated by the *unfurled* acanthus leaves. The giant Burmese sabre-wing, old chap, source of the golden dye reserved solely for the Imperial Guard. Did you not know ...?'

Readers may be wondering what I was doing for food and accommodation during this time. Each night I arrived in a village, often no more than a cluster of huts in the jungle, and I was treated like a visiting god. There was gentle wrangling among the families as to who got to have me sleep under their roof, and meal times were invariably a spectator sport, the whole village gathering to watch the long-nose tackle his food.

The food was – to borrow Huck Finn's description of *Pilgrim's Progress* – 'tough but interestin'.' The staple was sticky rice: soft white rice that is compressed into a lump and eaten much as we eat bread, by tearing off morsels from the main 'loaf.' Then it is dipped in various sauces, which came as tiny, oily smears wrapped in palm-leaves. The first time I tried dipping my sticky rice, I barely stained it, so I scraped away until I had got a good wodge of flavouring before munching into it. Three seconds later, my head nearly came off. So intense, so concentrated, so chilli-bitingly hot was the sauce that the merest dab would have sufficed to flavour the whole thing.

Another favourite condiment was dried fish crumbled up into brown flakes, like anchovy-flavoured confetti, and I could never get used to it. Soup was common. In the bigger villages it might be chicken soup, made from the entire chicken minus the feathers – head, feet, bones and all. Before cooking, the chicken was evidently put through a crushing mill whole, as I was forever spitting out little bits of splintered skull or vertebrae or toenails and trying to look polite about it. In the poorer villages, the soup was made from fish, and it was a murky brown liquid in which floated the eyes and scales and shredded flesh of a river-carp. There were always huge bunches of coriander to anaesthetise the tongue against anything too outlandish. I tended to stick with the rice, and found myself becoming wonderfully lissom.

After four days of travelling, I guessed from my very rough map that I must be drawing near the Chinese border; I might possibly even reach it the next day. There was a lot to consider. Things might begin to get interesting, for the very good reason that I didn't have an entry visa.

Even I recognised this as a drawback. I had a few ideas, however – most of them stupid. First, I thought that if Southern China was anywhere as remote and peaceful and primitive as Laos, then perhaps I wouldn't need a visa for the first few weeks … and then I'd be in Beijing and boarding the Trans-Siberian Express and on my way out anyway.

But, just in case they *did* want to see something official at the border, I had a cunning plan. I was going to wave at them … wait for it … my reference from Mr Murray, my old headmaster from Westminster School, which I had carried in the bottom of my rucksack all the way from Australia. It was printed on the official school paper, with the school crest at the top. It was the most official-looking piece of paper I had with me, and I planned to tell them that it was from the Queen of England, personally requesting passage for her faithful servant through these dominions. I had even managed to forge a very realistic Laotian stamp, using a trick taught to me by the two Germans, Pit and Ulli, as we had sat plotting in the Vientiane café. I took a potato, cut it in half, heated it slightly and pressed it down over the real Laotian entry stamp in my passport. It picked up the red and blue ink and I stamped the Westminster reference with it.

Clever, eh?

Illegal, eh?

Bloody stupid thing to do if I'm caught, eh?

This plan assumed that they wouldn't speak English, of course. If by chance they did, and came back with the subtle counter-argument that the Queen's name is not Murray and nor does she sign herself 'Mister,' I planned to back-pedal like mad and claim that I was merely showing them the reference *as* a reference, of good character you see, and that 'the Queen' was merely a term of affection, a nickname if you like, for our dear old headmaster.

Have I mentioned that I had a bag full of fireworks in case I met any tigers? I bought them off a boy in Vientiane down a back alley. I'd been dying to use them, but thought I might need them in case I was attacked by Shere Khan or, if holed up somewhere and under fire from rebel troops, I had to give the impression that I had a platoon of armed soldiers with me. I was planning to let them all off in one big display as a celebration for making it into China. I also had a secret phial of flash-powder tucked away, almost full. That, I thought, should keep any tigers at bay.

With these thoughts whirling in my head, I lay down to get a good night's sleep, possibly my last in Laos. I was sleeping under a mosquito net that night. The moonlight fell on it, making strange ghostly patches of white, and I was reminded of mad Bertha Mason slashing up the wedding veil. No knives here, I hoped. These were my darling Laotians. China tomorrow. China and the rest of the world.

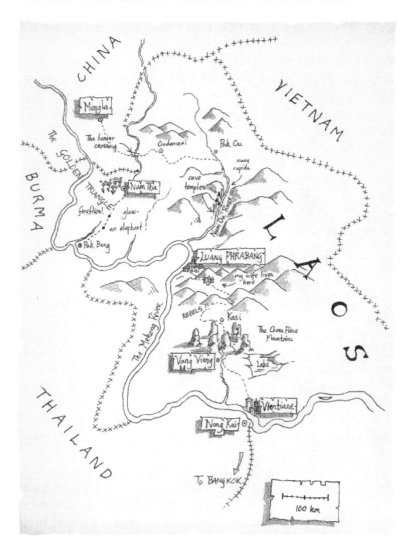

Chapter 17

When constabulary duty's to be done (to be done)
A policeman's lot is not a happy one.
      —W.S. GILBERT, *The Pirates of Penzance*

From Oudomxai, the last village I slept in, I set out walking very early, through a white mist that made the spiderwebs along the way look like great jewelled cartwheels. I was hoping for a lift from a passing truck, goodness knows why, as for the last three days the nearest thing to a truck I'd seen was a water buffalo towing a stack of bamboo, so I just walked.

In the afternoon I came to a long, winding green valley, mild and flowery and soft-curved. At the head of this dale was the road into China. A man at a tiny checkpoint looked at my passport, wordlessly stamped it and handed it back. After the worries and tension of the last three weeks, I could scarcely believe it.

As I turned to go, the man stopped me with a sharp word. Ah. This is it. This is the axe-blade falling.

'*Loi kip!*' he snapped out.

Relief flooded me. The exit fee was *loi* kip, 100 kip, about twelve cents. I paid up and skipped off down the road into China.

Two miles on I came to another checkpoint. Here there was a concrete bunker tangled in razor wire. A jeep stood outside it and five soldiers leant over a red-and-white striped barrier pole. I may have left Laos, but here was the entry into China. The last two miles had been a no-man's-land, a fool's paradise. The soldiers were dressed in crisp khaki green with red stars on their shoulders and caps. They looked more thoroughly businesslike than their Laotian counterparts by several light-years.

I was ordered in Chinese to halt, and my passport was demanded. They pored over it for a while, scratched their heads, said no. I sat down on my rucksack, smiling, nodding and pointing, and then flourished my Westminster reference. More head-scratching, and just a hint of admiration for the Westminster crest. (Mr Murray *would* be pleased.) But still a stalemate. Then I produced my magic tricks. The little red hanky vanished and reappeared again, the three ropes did their stuff and the soldiers' faces lit up. A big bowl of hot green tea was produced and I sat on my rucksack in the middle of the road and drank it down thirstily. After a while, there was some shrugging of shoulders and the barrier was lifted. My passport was returned and, trying not to look too incredulous, I thanked them, hoisted my pack and sauntered into China.

Yes! Yes! I had done it! I had crossed one of the world's most fiercely guarded international borders. All that tedious business of visas and embassies and entry permits applied only to those fool enough to let it. And I had done it with Shank's pony and a pocket-ful of magic tricks. Once I was out of sight round the bend, I gave one high-kicking leap for joy and then marched towards Beijing, borne on a cloud of smug euphoria.

Two miles later, I thought I must have walked in a big circle. There was an identical scene – jeep, bunker, pole, five soldiers. Pre-cisely the same routine was enacted. *Click* went the guns, *flip-rustle* went my passport and the Westminster reference, *scritch-scritch* went the heads, *flicker-flicker* went the little red hanky and out came another bowl of green tea. The only variation was that, no longer being thirsty but feeling dishevelled, I saw an opportunity. Here was steaming hot liquid in a bowl. Like Doctor Dolittle in time of crisis, I pulled out my razor and soap and, to the soldiers' initial con-sternation, and then high amusement, sat in the middle of the road and had a shave.

And again, baffled by such eccentricity, they waved me through.

It was five miles before I allowed myself another leap of jubilation. Now, surely, I had made it. I had crossed into China and I would be letting off fireworks that very night. Mind you, I was disheartened by the change in scenery. Gone was the scented bird-ringing forest, replaced by bare brown terraced hillsides. Gone were the butterflies, replaced by the odd watchful crow. The few buildings I had passed, instead of being the pretty bamboo-thatch huts of Laos, were squat, ugly bunkers of grey brick. Ahead, the air was smoky and the few trees were clipped and cut and half dead.

It was beginning to get dark and I was almost deliriously tired. I had walked solidly since dawn on just a handful of rice and a bowl of tea and I was faint with hunger. A long way ahead I could see the lights of a village on the other side of a wooded valley but lo! there below me, 500 yards ahead, was a large house, its lights blazing out onto a lawn cut out of the jungle. In my dizziness and desire for something wonderful, it seemed Georgian in its elegance: three storeys, an ornate portico, a gracious hall glimpsed through the open door. For a fleeting second I had the idea that it might be the home of some retired British colonel left over from the Opium Wars, living here as a last outpost of the Empire, alone except for a mute Mongolian manservant and waiting to welcome me and hear news from dear old Blighty.

Heedlessly I rushed across an old stone bridge that spanned a wide river, which gurgled in the darkness; heedlessly I raced across the lawn; heedlessly I ran straight into the arms of a startled Asiatic figure coming out of the house. The mute servant, perhaps? Only then did I see that there were in fact two of them, and they were neither Mongolian nor mute. They were in military dress and were carrying pistols. Furthermore, this was no gracious manor. The walls were rotting, bare bulbs hung from flaking ceilings, the rooms were unfurnished and bare. It was a mere shell, but it was here for a reason. *This* was the real border crossing into China.

These two soldiers were infinitely more serious than the others. Bristling with red stars and gold buttons, they searched my bag from top to bottom, checked and recorded my passport details, and told me very firmly that I could not pass the barrier. I had no visa. Go back to Bangkok and get one. The magic tricks cut no ice whatsoever. I didn't dare try the letter from Her Majesty the Queen, Principal of Westminster. They would have shot me. When they found the fireworks, they practically did.

I pleaded, I mimed hunger and cold, I mimed the whole overland trip from Invercargill in New Zealand, dolphins, bus crashes and all – but to no avail. Returning all my goods and chattels, even the fireworks, they pointed sternly Laos-wards.

I must go back. Steamingly, blindingly furious, I stomped back across the bridge and up the road back towards Laos. Then, when I had gone a hundred yards, I thought 'Bugger this' and crept back. I sat down a little way off in the trees and got out my telescope, the beautiful little brass and leather telescope that had sat uselessly in my rucksack for ten months. I put it to my eye and spent the next thirty minutes spying on the border guards. In the creaking silence of the forest, the blood thumping in my ears played the *Hogan's Heroes* march thirty-eight times through without a pause.

First the two soldiers paced watchfully up and down, but after a while they went and turned on a radio. Good!

Then they went and fetched a pack of cards.

Relaxing their guard, were they?

Then they got out a card table.

Excellent!

No, wait ...

Blast! They were setting it up on the bridge itself. The radio was turned up and I could hear it blaring into the night. Cigarettes were lit, cards dealt and soon they were engrossed in the game. Nevertheless, positioned right where they were, it was patently impossible for me to sneak back across the bridge that night. There was only one thing for it. I would have to swim into China.

And that I did. After an hour of plucking up courage and praying there weren't landmines around, I sneaked my way into the jungle and down to the river's edge a hundred yards below the bridge. The river looked very black and deep in the starlight. I stripped right off except for my boots, and waded in. Have you ever gone skinny-dipping in a lake at night and experienced the slow wade into black, possibly eel-bedizened, depths? And the particularly squirmy part when the water, night-chilled, comes up to the dangly bits? Now imagine all that with the added piquancy of fear at the thought of giant Laotian leeches, Chinese river crocodiles and a bullet in the spine any minute – not normally hazards of night-swimming back home. And the water was freezing. As is often the case in moments of high stress, my brain coped with the situation by focusing on a matter of complete irrelevancy. In this case, it was that crocodiles weren't called crocodiles hereabouts but something starting with 'g'. Gualins? Guavas? No. Guano? Nup ...

I felt my way across to the other bank, relieved to find that though wide, the river was only up to my neck at its deepest point. (*Garganeys? Type of duck, I think.*) Then back I glided once more to the Laotian bank, clambered out as silently as I could and balanced my pack on my head. Back I went to the other side (*geckos? gulags?*) and deposited my pack in the long grass of China. One more wade back to Laos, (*ginkos? gung-hos? gurrels?*) and then with my bundled clothes on my head, I made the final trip back to China. Got out. Dried myself off with my singlet, which is why you should *always* wear a singlet, and climbed into my clothes again.

Ten minutes of scrambling through the jungle and I was back on the road, my wet boots going *squelch-squeak-squilch-splish* with every step I took, loud enough it seemed to bring all the troops of China down on my head. But no. Half an hour later, I was waltzing soggily down the starry road on my way to Beijing.

Later that night I came to the village I had seen from the hillside above the border-post. I was suddenly very cold, very hungry and a little light-headed, and looking for a little of the hospitality that I had come to expect from the people of Laos. But here things were very different. On the outskirts of the darkened village, a crowd of people went by within arm's length in the faint starlight, but they were as silent as ghosts, behaving as though I weren't there. I couldn't see their faces, for they all wore anoraks with hoods pulled down low. I wandered into the main street, a sorry place of concrete and an open sewer and mean little houses heavily shuttered and barred. Getting desperate, I approached a house where lamplight showed through the shutters and where I could hear the murmur of voices and the odd laugh. I called out a soft hello and the reaction was astonishing. There was a quick shuffle, a fearful shooshing and the lamp was extinguished. Then silence.

The same thing happened again at two more houses and I was left wondering what it was these people were so scared of. By now I was beginning seriously to flag. The twenty-mile walk, the lack of food, the elation and the disappointment of the checkpoints, the freezing night-time swim in a welter of apprehension, the inability to remember that bloody word starting with 'g', and now the disorientation and the late hour had left me shaky and prickling with fear. I rather thought I had made a big mistake. And then a drunken man came rollicking along the road, stinking of cheap whisky, and I made one more effort to communicate. I stood plumb in his path, tried to look winsome and, in the absence of any Mandarin, said the one thing that might indicate that I was a long, long way from home and in need of help.

I said, 'Kangaroo?'

The figure stopped weaving about and swayed in front of me, peering at me with wild surmise. *Surely*, his eyes seemed to say, *kangaroos are furrier.*

Then, without a word, the drunkard took me by the paw and shuffled me off down the road. We came shortly to what may have been his house or may have been the local public conveniences; it was hard to tell. There were a few mattresses around and a tiny sink and primus stove, but the rest of the space was tiled in cracked blue tiles from floor to ceiling. There was what appeared to be a urinal trough along two walls and the floor was awash with foetid water. Unbelievably, he spoke English and wanted to practise. He also wanted to sing me a song he had made up, and dance a little, and tell me a long and incomprehensible story about his left ear. I just wanted to fall over and lie still for several days. I was beginning to think that it was all a dream when some of his friends arrived, and we ended up in a little chop-house nearby eating the hottest curry I have ever encountered. But it was wonderful, and I don't care if it was pangolin *foie gras* in a unicorn sauce; it saved my life. The rest is blurry and I think involved more lao-lao. The last thing I remember is being taken back to his house and falling asleep on a damp mattress while his friends sat around till dawn smoking what I think might have been opium or might have been the little yellow disinfectant cubes that they put in public urinals. They shouted at each other the whole time. I began that night to learn to hate China.

The next morning, my bleary host took my Laotian kip and exchanged it for Chinese yuan, at goodness knows what exchange rate, and put me on a local bus for Mengla, the nearest big town, about five hours away. Once on the bus, I tried smiling at my fellow passengers, hoping to elicit the same friendly unspoken conspiracy I had enjoyed in Laos, but as one they studiously avoided my eye. It came as no surprise three hours later, when we were stopped at a checkpoint and a soldier climbed aboard for a perfunctory look, that every single man, woman and child pointed straight at me and said, 'That's who you're looking for, officer, the greasy foreign spy in the corner.'

I was hauled ignominiously off the bus and handed over to a couple of village policemen. There followed a lot of shouting and a lot of spitting, which for all I knew could have been a gentle inquiry into my health and an invitation to high tea, had it not been for the gun pointed in my direction throughout the interview. The policemen discovered my fireworks and confiscated them. Having done so, they sat eyeing them and each other sideways like naughty children eyeing a bag of forbidden lemon sherbets, and then finally decided that the safest thing to do with such dangerous goods would be to let them off one by one in a controlled manner.

The interrogation had taken place in an open-air chop-house under a pink flowering silk tree. Now, as the whole village gathered round, the senior policeman handed out the rockets and crackers one by one, first to himself, then to his partner, then to me, just like an old-time TV gangster dividing up the spoils. We spent a happy few hours igniting them in dangerous and amusing ways. The officer's favourite trick was to hold a rocket upright by the stem, light the fuse and then, just before the rocket ignited, allow the whole thing to droop to the horizontal, pointing straight at the crowd.

Whooosh! The rocket would shoot off, the crowd would hit the dust and the thing would explode in a shower of pink stars over some rival chop-house across the square. But when I or the junior officer tried this, we were sternly reprimanded with a wagging finger and limited to a couple of sparklers each.

I gathered that we were waiting for senior policemen to come down from Mengla to deal with my case. In the late afternoon, they

turned up in a jeep and a cloud of dust. So started my acquaintance with the Laurel and Hardy of the Chinese constabulary.

One of the first things that struck me was their grasp of the English language. I thought it astonishingly well-educated of them to speak English at all in as remote a place as this, and these two actually spoke it quite well. It was just that their pronunciation seemed to have come from somewhere beyond Mars. They emphasised certain syllables with great strength, but invariably the wrong ones, and they were quite insistent that certain English vowel sounds were pronounced in certain ways.

The first thing they said to me when they climbed out of their car was, quite emphatically and crossly, 'This is a budging jip!'

'Er, how do you do.'

They interrupted me with some urgency. '*This* ... is a ... budging *jip!*'

'Sorry?'

'A budging jip! A budging jip!' they both danced in frustration.

'Um?'

'A *jip*,' pointing at the car, 'all the way from *Bud-ging!*'

'Ah, a Beijing jeep!'

And we climbed into the Budging Jip and drove the fifty miles to Mengla, where I was immediately thrown into prison.

Or was it prison? I was put in a bare cell with a barred window on the second storey. The only light was a naked bulb hanging from a lead so long that it dangled just an inch off the floor. If it was left on too long, the floorboards directly beneath it would start to smoulder. In one corner was a mattress on a wooden pallet. The ablutions block down the corridor was the foulest thing I have ever come across. It was a large concrete room with cold uncubicled showers along one wall, which wasn't so bad – standard English boarding school, really – but just six feet away, along the opposite wall, was what passed for a toilet in the fair metropolis of Mengla. It was a cement trough piled high with human ordure and a billion blowflies, over which one was meant to squat and deposit. When the showers were being used, the wash from the shower spread across to this overflowing trough and washed back, bringing raw sewage with it. The cement floor was littered with black razorblades, swabs of bloodied cottonwool, clipped toenails and gobs of spit. I spent the next three days showering in my boots, resolving to bury them in quicklime once I got away from there.

On the other hand, there was no lock on my door; I was taken to a chop-house for meals each day by Laurel and Hardy; there was only one grim, enormous woman at the entrance to the building to prevent me leaving – and so I rather think that this might have been the Mengla Novotel. Whatever the case, I was looking forward to checking out.

After a night in the cell, my two policemen came to fetch me off to headquarters and spent the next three days interrogating me. This didn't exactly involve being beaten with bamboo rods but at times it was frightening, more because of their unpredictability and strange hopelessness than anything else. I spent much of the time wondering if I had wandered into a surreal sketch penned as a co-operative effort by Kafka and the man who wrote *Dad's Army*. Inevitably, the duo were in sharp physical contrast. The chief was a diminutive man with a strutting air and beady black eyes as sharp as a mongoose's, and a way of smiling superciliously to himself and stroking an imaginary moustache. His junior officer, on the other hand, resembled an amiable dugong, glistening with oil and sweat and with droopy eyes and a lumbering manner. Together, their comic timing was exquisite. When we arrived outside the police station, for example, they ordered me sternly to follow them. Then they spent five minutes wrestling with the keys, trying to get the door open. I could see at once that they were attempting to put a Yale key in an older keyhole below the new brass Yale plate. Realising we might be here for some time, I leant forward to help, but they clearly considered this to be a ploy to disarm them. The chief snapped, 'White plus!' and kept fumbling away. While I worked out that *white plus* meant *wait please*, they each had a go, arguing over which key it could be, trying every other key in the bunch, until they eventually noticed the brass plate. Then, incredibly, they tried to insert one of the *older* keys into the Yale slit. As they became increasingly exasperated with each other, I watched them with the dumb patience that mules display when they know perfectly well you're trying to put the saddle on the wrong way round. Finally, after they had come to a baffled standstill, I gently took the keys from them, found the correct key, inserted it into the correct lock and let them into their office.

Once inside, the chief ordered me to stay standing – *Sty stunned!* – produced a wad of paper, an inkwell and a pen, fixed me with a steely gaze from behind his desk, and said 'Gnome!'

I looked around for one.

'Gnome!' he snapped again. 'You! Gnome?'

'Ah, name,' I translated. 'Mackinnon,' I said. 'M-a-c-k—'

'White plus!' The ink had dried up and the pen, a dipping pen from the last century, wouldn't work. A short tetchy exchange occurred, presumably concerning whose job it was to keep up the stationery supplies, and I had to butt in again, this time to offer my fountain pen. The chief took it gingerly, as though it might be some sort of rigid leech, and examined it minutely. When he went to dip it in the inkwell, however, I hastily explained that it didn't need dipping, it had ink inside it, and he examined it again with increased wonder. Who is this James Bond, I could see them thinking, who carries such devices with him? We must watch this man ...

And on we went. Having asked where I was from and been told Australia, their faces lit up like nine-year-olds.

'Ah, Australia? Have you pet kang-a-woo?'

'No,' I laughed, 'no, I don't have a pet kangaroo.'

Bang! A hand slammed down on the desk!

'*Why you no have pet kang-a-woo?!*' he screamed. '*Tell me!*'

It was this sort of thing that was so unnerving.

They seemed to think that they could catch me out in some deep cunning. On the first day, they went through my bag and found a photocopy of the title page of my passport, something useful to have in case you lose your travel documents.

'Hah! What is thus?' they asked, convinced that they'd found the top-secret documents I was smuggling.

'Oh that,' I said airily. 'That's just a photocopy of my passport.'

Again the hand came down and the voice shot up to a triumphant screech.

'No! You lie! We no stupid! We know what photo look like. This is no photo!'

And I had to explain what a photocopy was as opposed to a

photo, leaving them wondering again where one could obtain this super-spy technology.

'Where is this *pho-to-cop-i-er*, hey? You show us!' they demanded slyly, as though they expected to find it concealed in my wristwatch. They were equally at sea with my one remaining American Express traveller's cheque, demanding to know what express train it was I was aiming to catch.

Mind you, they did ask some shrewd questions about how I came to be in China without a visa, and I had to fudge the details. The story that seemed to hold, for the first day at least, was that I had gone walking in northern Laos looking for butterflies and didn't know that I had stumbled into China. When they expressed some doubt, I smugly showed them the bit in my letter to Chris where I had pretended to know so much about lepidoptery – the spurious Laotian razorwings and so on – and they seemed satisfied. But then a new thought struck them. They pointed out that I couldn't have stumbled into China without crossing a river, so I suddenly remembered how, in hot pursuit of the nocturnal sablewing damselfly, I had tumbled into a creek at night, thrashed about a bit and climbed out somewhere downstream, possibly the other side, who knows?

There was an alarming moment when they confiscated my papers and discovered the twelve pointless blank pages at the back of Newton's letter that had so mystified me some months before. As these were carefully numbered, they wanted to know why exactly they were there. Much of the first day was spent trying to explain Newton's eccentricities to them. Newton is difficult enough for his friends and family to comprehend, let alone Chinese policemen investigating potential espionage. Halfway through the interview it struck me that perhaps these pages were covered in invisible writing – lemon-juice or something like that – and if the police discovered that, then I was done for. Bloody Newton, I thought savagely, he's going to be the death of me one day. Probably this very afternoon, in fact.

*

Over the next two days there was less of the desk-slamming and more of the koala-bear jokes, but when I was hauled into the office on the fourth morning, we were back to steely gazes and standing to attention. The chief policeman looked at me steadily, a small smile curling around his lips, and then said quietly, 'Perhaps you can explain this!' For a few horrified seconds I wondered what he had found. A bag of heroin stitched into the lining of my rucksack? A stray page of Newton's invisible writing threatening the overthrow of world communism? I went cold. At this he brought out a great wad of papers from a drawer and slapped them triumphantly on his desk.

'Hah!'

It was my Trading Game, a project I had been working on over the last months, twenty-five pages of rules, designs and coloured diagrams.

Huge relief broke over me. 'Oh, that,' I sighed. 'This is just a game,' and I stepped forward to gather up the papers.

'NO! Is not a game!' he shouted. 'You may think is game, this smuggling, these guns, but we take very seriously. No games!'

I stopped dead.

'No, no, let me explain,' I gabbled. 'It's a game I'm making up, see, a trading game, a board game like Monopoly, only better, you see, because it's all so arbitrary, isn't it, Pass Go, Collect Two Hundred Pounds, er, do you know Monopoly?' I asked faintly, thinking the chances pretty slim in a place where fountain pens and photocopiers were things of the future. And they were communists, for God's sake. Could you be shot for playing Monopoly in a communist country?

He stopped me. 'You write here, *'Black equals guns. Red equals money.'* Where are these guns? Black-market guns?! Red money? Communist money? *Where?'*

'No, look, it's all just little chips, see—'

'And these maps?' he continued. 'Many maps. Where are these maps of? Where ...' – he peered closer at my rough diagrams – '... is Greentown?'

I explained what these were about and he listened sceptically. Finally he said with deep cunning, 'Okay. Okay. You say this is game. We play this game. You, me, him. We play so-called game.'

'Oh no, really, you don't want to play this—'

'WE PLAY GAME! NOW!'

The fact is that the one thing all game inventors want most is someone on whom to try out their newest ideas. And no-one could say that my captors weren't eager to play. They'd even loosened their pistols in their holsters. My heart wasn't in it, but I knew I had no choice. I pulled up a few chairs and started setting up a makeshift board.

'Right, we don't have any counters so you can be, er, paper-clips, and I'll trade with – what's in this drawer? – drawing pins, okay, and *you* – sit down, sit down – will be rubber bands. Fine, now we really need a fourth player, but I'll do that. Okay. Here we go.'

Well, I never thought we'd even get to third round, but we did – and I was winning by the way, having made a killing on the paper-clip market – when finally the chief said, with undisguised boredom, 'Okay, okay. Is game. Pack away.'

After that things moved swiftly. I was acquitted of being an international terrorist or gun-runner and although they probably weren't fooled by the lepidopterist story, they gave me the benefit of the doubt. The next morning they were going to deport me to the border. They counted up all the Chinese money I had, which was sixty-five yuan, and then informed me that by coincidence the fine for illegally entering the country was precisely sixty-five yuan. This left me with not a cent to get me all the way back to Vientiane. And even there I wouldn't be able to cash my fifty-dollar traveller's cheque; I had tried before and had been told the nearest office was in Bangkok.

I was foot-stampingly furious, of course. I did get out my map of the world and showed them both exactly where I had come from without flying, and pointed out how close Beijing was and how much sense it made to expel me the other way, but they became adamant and started playing with their pistols, so I didn't push it.

Didn't Philip Larkin say something like, 'I'd like to go to China, but only for the day'? Well, I agree, and that's nearly what I did. I suppose I can say that I did get there after all, and I did let off those fireworks, and it's a very interesting place, I'm sure. But you wouldn't want to linger. I'd been clenching my bowels for three days to avoid having to use those toilets, and my gastric system was looking forward to leaving the country.

*

The police didn't arrive to pick me up until mid-morning, and then we went shopping and picked up the chief's wife and daughter; if we were going to deport the mad foreigner all the way to the border, then we may as well make a picnic of it.

On the way I saw many military vehicles, masses of barbed wire and, in the distance, some huge factories churning out yellow smoke. The area showed all the signs of being a restricted zone, and the police now told me that no Westerners were allowed in this region, even if they had entered properly and had visas.

During the trip, the chief, who was in a beaming good mood, asked me if I danced. 'No, I don't dance very well,' I replied. 'Ah,' said he, 'I dance very well,' and squeezed his wife's hand.

'Do you sing?' he enquired next, although he pronounced it 'song'.

'Yes, I like to song,' I replied.

'Good. Song us a sung!' he commanded.

'Well, no, really, you don't want to hear me—'

'SONG US A SUNG!' he shouted and I skipped straight into a rather squeaky version of 'Waltzing Matilda.'

'Very goat sung!' he beamed when I was halfway through the first verse. 'I song too. I song very whale! You lesson!'

He then burst into an operatic version of 'Twinkle Twinkle Little Star' that had his wife, daughter, second-in-command – and, after a few startled seconds, me – bursting into rapturous applause.

'Plus. Plus. This is nodding. White plus!'

He cleared his throat, did a few vocal warm-ups and began, not to sing as I was expecting, but rather to speak.

'Stoat,' he said. 'Stoat at the fairy bee gong. Hiss a fairy goat plus to stoat.'

In his measured cadence, the words were strangely familiar.

'When you rot, you begin wee Ah Bay Say;

'When you song, you begin wee Door, Ray, May;

'Door, Ray, May ...'

Door, Ray, May ... ?

By George, I had it!

'Doh Re Mi So Fa La TE DOH!' the chief crescendoed in a rushing scale.

'You sing too!' he bellowed, and launched head-on into a soaring rendition of 'Doe, a Deer, a Female Deer!' from *The Sound of Music*. Well, I dared not refuse. And so it was that we all went rollicking back to the Laotian border in the Budging Jip singing numbers from Rodgers and Hammerstein. At the bridge I was relieved to see that the guards on duty were not the same as those who had sent me packing four days earlier. We climbed out of the jeep and while Mrs Chief and daughter unpacked the picnic, the chief and his offsider became formal once more. They opened a little maroon book and started reading from it very solemnly.

'According to the Low of the Pupple's Democratic Republic of China' – *flip flip flip of pages* – 'you have anted.'

He stopped with an air of finality. I must have looked puzzled.

'You have *anted*,' he said again.

Still puzzled …

They both bent over the book consulting. Ah!

'Solly! According to the low of – *flip flip flip* – the Pupple's Democratic Republic of China – *flip flip flip back again* – you have anted – *flip flip flip back once more* – the Pupple's Democratic Republic of China – *flip* – ully-gully.'

'Sorry?' I really was trying to understand.

The Chief gave an exasperated sigh. 'Ully-gully!'

'Um?'

'You have *anted ully-gully*! Against the low!' he pleaded desperately.

'Oh, I see! *Illegally?* I have entered illegally? Yes, I know. Sorry.'

'Yes! Anted ully-gully!' He beamed with relief. 'Still, you have copulated with the police …'

'Sorry? Never mind, carry on.'

'… and we must now deport you from – *flip flip flip* – the Pupple's Democratic Republic of China – to wince you comb. Is this claw?'

'Yes, reasonably claw, I suppose.'

'So now, Mackinnon Mister Sandee' – here he pointed across the bridge to Laos in a dramatic gesture – 'you must leave and never return!' Then he took me warmly by the hand, shook it and said expansively, 'Welcome to China!'

*

Thirty minutes later, back in Laos, I was picked up by a southbound truck, was dropped by the roadside two hours later, walked till the stars came out and there were fireflies in the trees all around me, was picked up by a second truck, nearly hit an elephant, and ended up twelve hours later at Nam Tha, the largest settlement in northern Laos. Which is not that big actually. It has about the population of a two-star caravan park. In winter.

There I was taken under the tender care of Mr Vong, a neat little Laotian man with good French, who runs the friendliest little hotel in all Laos. Hotel is slightly too grandiose a word; I slept in something resembling a stable, but I didn't care one bit. I was back among Laotians and therefore in paradise.

Shortly after I arrived, Mr Vong clapped his hands like an Eastern potentate in a fairytale and three daughters appeared. One was dispatched to cook me a meal, one to fetch hot water from a copper and pour it into a tin hip-bath for me, and the third to take away my clothes and spend the next day washing them.

Next day, in robes borrowed from Mr Vong himself, I was taken on a tour of the little village of Nam Tha. Here there was a market where we could buy crocodile kebabs, bats and large fried rats. I could, had I wished, have tried such delicacies as toads, eels, tortoises and silkworms, these last fried. There was also a beautiful grouse-like bird in soft mouse-browns but with iridescent 'eyes' in its plumage like those of a peacock except in violets and sky-blues. After a morning of gentle ambling, Mr Vong sat me down at a wooden table on a gentle hillside near the inn. From here, I could see poppy fields spreading to the horizon under a blue, cloud-scattered sky.

'Very pretty,' I enthused to Mr Vong. 'Is there a big market for cut flowers here?' I asked with mild surprise. 'Daffodils? Tulips? That sort of thing?'

Mr Vong beamed, shook his head and went through a little pantomime involving a lot of sniffing and eye-rolling.

The truth slowly dawned. The poppies were not there for their aesthetic qualities; they were a multi-million-dollar crop of death waiting to be harvested. We were in the heart of the Golden Triangle, and I began to understand the paranoia of the police about outsiders reaching the area, which contained the richest opium fields in the world. It also dawned on me that I had been incredibly stupid.

The man in Luang Phrabang who had encouraged me to smuggle sachets of monosodium glutamate might not have been absolutely frank with me. (I wonder if even now Mr Leigh Fermor is sitting some fifty-five years on with the slowly dawning suspicion that the saccharine powder he was smuggling across the Danube under gunfire was not exactly what it was claimed to be.)

While I was being treated like royalty by the dapper Mr Vong, I kept trying to explain that I had no money to pay for any of this. He would wave such sordid details aside and send his daughter scampering off to fetch more rice or candles for the gentleman. But on the day I was due to leave, he took me to the village bank. This wasn't a building, but rather a trestle table in the market where an old man sat surrounded by shoeboxes stuffed with Laotian currency. Here Mr Vong urged me to produce my traveller's cheque, which I had shown him the night before. I did so without the faintest hope of it being recognised for what it was.

I was right. The old man, who had a long, three-stranded beard such as you see in old movies about mysterious Chinamen, asked what it was. 'It's American Express, you may have heard of them? Didn't think so, thank you so much, I'll stop wasting your time now.'

But Mr Vong stopped me. 'He wants to know how much it is worth.'

'Well, fifty US dollars, really. But here, to him, nothing.'

'What is US dollars in kip?' he asked.

'Oh look, let me see, seven thousand, um, times fifty, no, that's Australian dollars, um ... about thirteen million kip ... but really, unless I sign it and you can find an agent to ...' I tailed off as Mr Vong and Fu Manchu exchanged words.

There was much shaking of the head from the ancient banker. Mr Vong explained that monsieur was not happy about me signing the cheque. It would spoil the look of it. Such a beautiful thing, all that purple ink and those curly lines.

'Ah well, never mind,' said I, preparing to take back my useless cheque and walk away. But no. I had misunderstood. Tucking the unsigned cheque into his robes, Fu Manchu stood up, beaming.

'Okay, here are your kip. Thirteen million, you say? Let me help you.' And the old banker and Mr Vong began piling me up with eight shoeboxes overflowing with kip notes.

Part II

'No, really,' I said as half the Nam Tha bank was thrust into my protesting arms. 'It's no good without my signature!'

I managed to slow down proceedings enough to grab the cheque back and countersign it, to a resigned shrug from the banker. Then I staggered away, leaving the old man to show the cheque to his neighbouring stall-holders. I suspect it has remained unredeemed to this day and has simply been passed around the region, exchanged for sacks of opium or forest elephants, its value in the eyes of the local populace fixed eternally at thirteen million kip.

To sum up, my clothes were clean, I was well fed, I was washed and bathed and I had a substantial portion of the Laotian economy in my wallet to see me back to Vientiane. Oh, and my bowels were empty. Things were looking up once more.

How the hell was I going to get back to Vientiane? I'd think about that tomorrow.

*

In the end it was easy, a non-stop glide from Nam Tha to Bangkok, as smooth as that sinister glide down the chequered serpent's back on a Snakes-and-Ladders board. A truck to Pak Beng, a ferry in stages down the Mekong to Vientiane, a sighting of a hoopoe (I know, not quite up there with marrying a Laotian princess and swimming into China, but I'd always wanted to see one), only to end up in trouble with the border-guards at Nong Kai because I had outstayed my fifteen-day visa. I was in the middle of explaining that I hadn't actually outstayed my visa because, no listen, I'd actually left the country by swimming and then re-entered it after three days in China and ... but from the look on the guard's face, I realised that this was cutting no ice whatsoever. He was about to fine me trillions of kip (five shoeboxes' worth) when who should turn up but Khamtoune Butts, the Laotian wife of Doran the UN worker. She was surprised to see me, as they had never got that wretched letter I had sent from Luang Phrabang, but I briefly filled her in about everything I had done. When I told her of my problem, she marched up to the guard, slipped 30,000 kip (four dollars) into his breast pocket, and said, 'Buy yourself a drink, handsome.' I was immediately waved through. God bless corruption.

Then a train back to Bangkok. These last three weeks had been the best so far, but within two days of leaving Laos the fumes of Bangkok were clouding them out and their sharp-edged gold was

219

rubbing thin. They *were* good. They *were*. I must keep remembering that. Someone blows cigarette smoke in your face, a tuk-tuk snarls by, another person slops tea all over the café table at which you're trying to write and it becomes so easy to forget.

Chapter 18

'You will have to go away then, to be his squire in the wide
world, and I shall go elsewhere. Do you think you have
learned anything?'

'I have learned and been happy.'

'That's right then,' said Merlyn. 'Try to remember what you
learned.'

—T.H. WHITE, *The Sword in the Stone*

In Bangkok, of course, I rang home to my parents. After I had hung
up, a casual observer might have noticed me looking a tad thoughtful. There was also a quite definite set to my jaw as I sat down to
dash off a postcard to Chris. There was not the customary fond salutation. I launched straight in.

You went and told them, didn't you, Chris? My parents. After
I specifically asked you not to. I have just rung home and Dad
immediately said, 'How was Laos?' when the last thing I told
him was that I'd be pottering around in the safer suburbs of
Bangkok before flying to England.

Lucky guess? The old antennae?

Well, he certainly seems to have sensitive ones. How were
the rebels, he asked. Luang Phrabang fine, was it? Still counting twenty toes, are we, or has a landmine blown them off, he
quipped. Silly old us, he bantered. When you said Heathrow,
your mother and I assumed you were talking about the inter-
nationally known airport of that name, when all along you
were actually referring, of course, to Hi Phro, the lesser-
known lost lotus temple of Pak Beng.

Then the coins ran out before he could blow me sky high
for keeping him in the dark.

You certainly did spill the beans, didn't you?

So how did it happen? Did he ring and wheedle it out of

you, or did you get my last letter and think, 'God, he's going to die, get his father onto it before he does something stupid'? I'm not sure that we needed to go into quite so much detail, old chum, old chap, old stool-pigeon.

Last time I let you into any little secrets.

I guess you've worked it out already. It took me another four weeks.

In the meantime, I was stuck in the Malay Peninsula and no closer to England than I had been two months ago. But I remained intent on not flying, so it was time to check out a rumour I had heard that ferries still went from Penang to Madras. I doubted it somehow. I think that last happened in an E.M. Forster novel. Nevertheless I doggedly travelled to Penang on a series of trains, watching Thailand and Malaysia pass by in a tropical blur of mango plantations and sugarcane beyond the steamy window.

As I was making the ferry crossing from the mainland to Penang Island, I sat up with renewed alertness. The harbour was full of yachts, rattling and rustling like a flock of egrets in the brisk wind. These could be the very yachts with which I had sailed for ten weeks through Indonesia, and which I thought I had farewelled forever. At that distance it was hard to make out details, but I whipped out the little brass telescope – it was certainly paying its way – and, glancing around to make sure Maggie wasn't watching, scanned the distant fleet. Yes. Surely that was *Sitisi III* with her distinctive mustard hull, and the slim lines of *Winsome* as graceful as a gull on the water ... and yes, at last I had it in the enchanted disc of the telescope's lens: a green-blue hull and two masts. Without a doubt, it was my beloved *Flying Dolphin*. Laughing, I leaped ashore from the ferry. Laughing, I went to book into the nearest hotel. Laughing, I skipped back down to the harbour twenty minutes later, and laughing, I stopped dead in my tracks at the sight of an entirely yachtless harbour. A different harbour perhaps? I then spent an increasingly mirthless hour sprinting round the island before collapsing sobbing on the docks.

'Lost anything?' an old salt enquired.

'Yes. A hundred and thirty yachts.'

'Oh, them? They've just left. It's the Rajah Mudah race up to Langkawi in Thailand. You won't see them again.'

Deciding that I may as well cap off this disaster with another letdown, I stomped into the nearest shipping office to enquire about ferries or freighters heading west. It was a ramshackle place above a warehouse last refurbished in the 1870s. In the greenish light that permeated the rattan blinds, I could see mahogany cabinets, yellowing invoices stuck on spikes, out-of-date shipping schedules and a Dickensian system of bells on overhead wires for a purpose I could not fathom. All the chairs were made of wickerwork and the phone was an old-fashioned bakelite model with a trumpet-shaped mouthpiece. It was manned by a plump Malaysian lady in a sarong who looked up enquiringly when I entered.

I'd done this so many times now, in Auckland, Darwin, Singapore and Bangkok, in offices steelier, more soulless and more efficient than this place, that my enthusiasm had waned almost to nothing. My spiel had dwindled from a motivational lecture about the aesthetic and spiritual virtues of flightless travel to a markedly briefer version.

'Look,' I sighed. 'I want to get out of here by sea, don't ask why, stupid idea, I know, and yes, I realise there's a perfectly serviceable airport in Penang. Can you suggest anything?'

To which she replied, 'Oh yes, I think we can arrange something for you. There's a freighter leaving for India on the sixteenth of December. Shall I make a booking?'

And that was that. I wandered out into the sunshine again, unsure whether to be cast down with despondency after missing my Dolphins or elated to have found a sea-passage. Four weeks was an awfully long time to be hanging around in Penang, I thought to myself as I wandered into a noodle shop and ordered a plate of red-curry duck.

Two minutes later I had flung the duck into a bin and was racing for the pier. A casual conversation with the noodle chef had elicited the information that Langkawi, where the yachts had gone, wasn't in Thailand after all; it was only two hours up the coast and a hydrofoil was leaving in ten minutes. There was no time to return to the hotel and fetch my rucksack. There was no time to think about toothbrushes or spare underwear. Fifteen minutes later I was zooming up the coast in a welter of hydrofoil spray with only a wallet and a hat, on my way to catch the Dolphins.

The next afternoon I glowed with pleasure to hear Mason's welcoming drawl as I stood on the blinding beach at Langkawi, hailing him across the glassy waters.

'Well, howdy do!' he called. 'It's been too long.' A few minutes later, I was clambering onboard and being handed an iced tea by Catherine and a sheaf of drawings of dwarf-armour by Peter. Heath gave me a shy kiss and Mason a bone-cracking handshake and I felt that I had come home. And in a way I had. Once I had told them of my plans with the freighter, Mason didn't hesitate. 'Now, we offered once before and you had other commitments, but I'd like to extend that offer again. We'd be mighty pleased if you could see your way to joinin' us all aboard for the next lil' bit. These young ones need some tutorin' and keepin' in line, and it'd suit us fine if you could fill that post.'

And so it was official. Until the sixteenth December, when my freighter would leave, I was to be one of the Flying Dolphins.

The next few days were a tedious muddle of phone-calls to the shipping office to confirm the freighter booking, a race back down to Penang by train to recover my rucksack, and a hundred other of those things that take up ninety per cent of one's time when one is travelling.

Langkawi, where we were moored, is the site of Malaysia's top resort, a luxury complex with pools and palms and a white beach. There is a swimming pool with a waterfall and underwater barstools, so that you don't even have to get out of the water to order a drink. All the facilities were at our disposal as competitors – or in my case as a gatecrasher – in the Rajah Mudah race.

One warm tropic night, the Rajah Mudah himself, also known as the Sultan of Selangor, hosted a feast for the yachtsmen on the resort lawns. As we wandered up and down the buffet tables, helping ourselves to lobster claws, green curries, pink slices of tenderloin and chickens stuffed with pineapple, the balmy air and the floodlights overhead attracted swarms of white moths, which whirled and sizzled around the dignitaries on the platform, just like they had in the outdoor speech-days of my youth. In fact, what with all the speeches and trophies and awards, it was exactly like a school prize-giving. During one particularly tedious speech, Peter and I slipped away from the festivities and disappeared down the moonlit beach for a chat about the Fisher King or something and so stumbled across something few people witness: a giant green turtle coming up the beach, ready to lay her eggs.

This only happens on certain nights of the year when the moon is full and the tide is very high, and what's more, so the wildlife documentaries say, only in remote and inaccessible places. Obviously this turtle had not seen any of these documentaries but had read the glossy brochures about Langkawi.

Peter and I sat and watched entranced as she painfully heaved herself up into position and started to shovel sand out with her hind flippers. It was a slow process – turtles are not naturally excavating animals, as Tigger would put it – and it was very tempting to say, 'Look, love, you save your strength for the long haul back, and let us have a go at that,' and do in five seconds what she so laboriously strived to achieve. While we waited, I quoted Ogden Nash:

The turtle lives 'twixt plated decks
Which practically conceal its sex.
I think it clever of the turtle
In such a fix to be so fertile.

After a while, and perhaps to avoid more poetry, Peter ran back to fetch Catherine, and we sat and watched the process through to the end in hushed silence: the laying of the eggs, like soft, squashy ping-pong balls; the slow filling up of the hole; and then the last painful haul down to the water's edge. Ah, the relief to see the first wavelet come hissing up the sand to wash the grit from her gummy eyes! Then a last heave into the dark milk-warm water, a lift of a flipper and she was gone, as fluid in her own element as she was cumbersome on land.

From Langkawi we sailed up the coast to Phi-Phi, the pearl of the Andaman Sea. There we anchored in a bay, not large but ringed with sheer cliffs of white limestone that rose to grey pinnacles seamed with forest greenery. They were very like the mountains I had seen in Laos, but these giants stood knee-deep in water as green as emerald. They over-towered the bay on two sides; on the third side was a long white beach fringed with palm trees where the water paled to delicate glass green. My main role aboard *Flying Dolphin* was to tutor the two children. Heath and Peter were doing a correspondence course, which I took them through daily, but there was also the opportunity to teach them things beyond the rather dry syllabus.

On one particularly fine day, we sat on a strip of smooth white sand under a few reclining palm trees. We started with mathematics, getting Heath to see how many seashells it took to make up a perfect square with three along each side ... and then four ... and then came the exciting discovery that all those seashells combined, nine and sixteen, could make a perfect five-by-five square. Would this always happen? Well, you keep experimenting to see what happens with other numbers, Heath, while Peter and I do some geography.

With a makeshift spade fashioned from a palm branch, we scooped out a winding channel down to the sea's edge. Then, filling a bucket with seawater and pouring it into the top end, we watched the effect the running water had on the curves of our miniature river. Outer bends turned to steep cliffy banks, inner bends silted up. Why? Theories were offered, considered, tested, rejected. Loopy bends became even loopier until, after the twentieth bucketful of water, the neck of a bend was broken through and the river ran straight through the shortcut, leaving an oxbow lake to one side. Pebbles were fetched to dam certain sections of the river, deeper and shallower sections were compared, experiments were conducted with artificial canal cuts, and meanwhile, Heath was discovering another set of Pythagorean triads in seashells. All this under an azure sky on a desert island, with Catherine making iced tea and peanut-butter-and-jelly sandwiches for lunch on the yacht moored out in the bay.

Even when the official hours of tutoring were over, it was difficult to stop the flow, such was Peter and Heath's curious interest in every aspect of life. In the evenings I taught them how to make a hexahexaflexagon from a strip of paper, or showed them mathematical tricks with cards, and one afternoon we made a tiny galleon out of a cork and matchsticks, equipped with tiny paper sails held by cotton thread. Years later, when I visited them in their home in North Carolina, I was almost moved to tears to see that in their great glass cabinet, filled with all the treasures of four years' cruising, the little galleon was there, intact and perfect in every pin and spar.

And best of all, before bedtimes, I was called upon to tell stories to put them to sleep. I recounted all those I had heard long ago: the Norse myths of Loki and Thor and the great wolf Fenrir who was bound by the magical Nothing; the Hebrew story of the merchant's wife and the great jewel; the tales of King Arthur and the treachery of Mordred and the adder's bite. In particular, I told Peter about Merlin in all his representations: T.H. White's eccentric and passionate genius, Lewis's shaggy druid and, best of all, Mary Stewart's canny and compassionate narrator, steering the Matter of Britain with a careful hand. I tried explaining how Mary Stewart sought to show how legend grows out of bare reality; that what seems miraculous and improbable – swords in stones, flying dragons, giant-killers, plotting witches – arises from seeds of historical truth, worked upon by time and the imagination of a people. I tried to explain how subtly Merlin's magic was presented in these books – a smattering of second sight, yes, but, more significantly, a deep understanding of people and the world, a love of learning and a taste for solitude. Here was true magic for the mind, and within anyone's grasp.

All in all, this was a very effective way of getting the children off to sleep.

*

One evening, while sitting around the cabin, the Flying Dolphins helped me to sort out a confusion of mind that had been with me for some time. I had been asked to recount my adventures in Laos and China and had taken great relish in telling the story in rich detail. Finally, in response to a query from Catherine about what my parents would think of all this, I finished on a note of tetchiness.

'Ha! Dad and Mum know all about it already, can you believe it!' I snorted. 'My old friend Chris, the one I've told you about – ex-friend, actually – went and told Dad about it even when I'd sworn him to secrecy. He was worried, I suppose, but even so … he needn't have snitched quite so fulsomely. When I rang home from Bangkok, Dad knew everything! Names, details, everything!'

'Well, that seems mighty strange,' said Mason thoughtfully, sipping his coffee. 'I wonder now ...'

Catherine was looking thoughtful too, with a faint, worried smile on her lips.

'You don't think perhaps ...' she began.

'Think what? Perhaps what?' I asked.

'Well,' said Mason, 'That ol' letter now, the one you posted from Loo-ang Pra-bang? I guess that was pretty full of details an' such, for the benefit of that UN feller?'

'Doran Butts?' I said.

'That's the feller,' said Mason.

'And you said he never received that letter, honey?' asked Catherine, handing me another cup of tea.

'That's right,' I said. Cogs whirred. My mind reached back to that little post office and the quite extraordinary number of stamps it had seemed were necessary to get a letter just eighty kilometres down the river – several million kips' worth, I seemed to remember. And all of them clustered on the back, almost obscuring my father's address. So easy to confuse the back and front of an envelope, especially when there is an address on each side ...

They watched me rise, put down my cup of tea and climb up onto deck into the cool night air. Peter rose to follow me, but his father called him back, and I heard him mutter something about needing some thinking time. Out on deck I went to the bows and stood for a long while gazing out over the starry sea. I was remembering with shame the letter I had sent Chris, reprimanding him. My face burned hot under the accusing stars.

And then I laughed out loud. It seemed that my father did have some sort of magical antennae, at least where his family was concerned, some quirky way of finding out where we were and what we were doing, like some latter-day Odin sending out his two ravens Hugin and Munin, Spirit and Mind, flying through the world to report all that goes on. It was a wonderful irony, that the thick and detailed letter of my secret journey, which was to be kept from Dad at all costs, had ended up winging its way directly to his breakfast tray, as swiftly as any magical raven to his master's shoulder.

When I went down again, the others had gone to bed but someone had thoughtfully left out a glass of whisky, some writing paper and a pen. Whoever it was had read my mind. 'Dear Chris,' I began, and it was a long hour before I finished, signed off and climbed into my bunk to sleep.

Not long later, after blissful weeks of sailing aboard the *Flying Dolphin*, it was time to say goodbye, for good this time, and catch a train for Penang. Mason had offered me passage all the way to the Mediterranean and beyond, but I had this freighter passage lined up for Madras, God willing, and was looking forward to seeing if Newton was still waiting at the Kathmandu post office.

Chapter 19

Ignoranti, quem portum petat, nullus suus ventus est.*
—SENECA THE YOUNGER

Crossing the Thai–Malay border on my way back to Penang, I was nearly shot. The train had stopped, when into my carriage burst three huge Thai women, carrying big baskets of mangoes, durians and bread and giggling hysterically as they churned up the aisle like sweaty galleons. Close behind them came a posse of police, narrow-eyed, slick haired and – alarmingly – gun-toting.

'Halt!' barked one of the police, or the equivalent in Malaysian.

The three women froze for a second, shot each other furtive glances and in one great tsunami of bosom, surged on their way, pursued by the police. While one massive woman barred the aisle with a wall of shaking flesh and remonstrated shrilly with the police, her companions grabbed her baskets and bags and escaped out the far end. Once the police had squeezed past the first woman and hurried off after them, the other two women reappeared at the window next to my head, threw the baskets and bags back into the train and showed empty hands to the police, who had galloped back. Meanwhile, I was juggling half-a-dozen mangoes and a split durian, which had landed in my lap.

A few seconds later, I had the first woman trying to hide under my legs while the two outside the window tried to convince the police that she had got off the train and gone that-a-way. This was as absurd as trying to hide a sea-lion under a stick of celery, but when the police went to climb aboard once more, the other two women pretended to faint into their arms, collapsing in a heap of flesh and sarongs and waving pistols.

The incident would have been highly amusing were it not for the

---

* If one does not know to which port one is sailing, there is no such thing as a favourable wind.

fact that beneath the breathless horseplay, there was real terror in the women's eyes. I don't know what they were trying to smuggle into Malaysia, but the mandatory penalty for drug-smuggling in both countries was death. Finally they were hauled off the train and ushered firmly out of the station and I saw them no more. A minute later, one of the policemen returned, shot me a suspicious glance, peremptorily relieved me of the mangoes and squashed durian, and stalked off after his comrades. A bizarre incident indeed, and one that haunted my dreams for the next few nights.

As did the durian. These are a large green fruit, the size of a watermelon but covered in spikes. They look like the vegetable equivalent of a puffer-fish. I have never tried one for the simple reason that they smell like one of those Chinese lavatories. I assume that this is a bizarre adaptation to assist their pollination by blow-flies or dung beetles or sewer-rats or something – David Attenborough would know – but I marvelled that anyone had ever discovered that they were good to eat. So noisome are they that there are signs put up in Malaysian train stations and shopping plazas depicting a durian with a bar through it. For the next day and a half, until I could change my clothes, I stank like a sewer from head to toe.

*

In Penang I had a financial crisis. I had been relying on my thoroughly modern and unromantic cash card to withdraw funds whenever I was in places that had bank machines. Penang was one such place. I sauntered up to a hole-in-the-wall machine, inserted my card and immediately forgot my pin number. Now this was ridiculous. I knew my pin number like the back of my hand, had used it a thousand times, had worked out all sorts of mathematical and alphabetical mnemonics for it – and couldn't for the life of me remember what it was.

I punched in 3062, watched in agony as the machine thought about it, and then winced when that number was rejected. I tried another combination – 2063 – and again, *whiz, brrrr, click, ponder,* and a green sign popped up on the screen saying *Care to try again, Mr Mackinnon?*

I suspected that if I was wrong a third time, the machine would swallow my card. It being a Saturday the banks were closed, and my freighter was due to leave at dawn on Monday. If the card was swallowed, there would be no chance of recovering it. I didn't dare risk it. Yet I was penniless and smelt like an open cesspit. What to do? It seemed odd to be as helpless in the middle of a great modern city as I had been in the wilds of Laos but there it was: I had no money and no prospect of a good night's sleep and a feed unless a miracle occurred.

For want of anything better to do, I walked to a park and pulled out my tin-whistle to cheer myself up. I was about three bars into 'Cockles and Mussels' when a Malaysian family threw five dollars at my feet and hurried off. After three seconds' thought, I'd grabbed my bag, my hat and my whistle and headed to the nearest shopping mall to try my luck busking.

An hour later I had $283 in loose change jingling in my straw hat. I was all set to carry on for another couple of hours and retire for life when a smart young Malaysian woman came up and enquired what my ailment was. When I seemed puzzled, she pointed out what I hadn't noticed before: three or four beggars crouching further along the mall. One was blind, several were missing hands or feet, and all were extremely needy. Again she asked what my problem was that I needed to suck funds away from these poor wretches. Before I could stammer out 'Just a bit bored, really,' she had stalked off down the mall. In a fit of confused conscience, I went and deposited half my savings into the outstretched hands of the astonished beggars and with the other half treated myself to a night at the Eastern & Oriental Hotel. This is said to be the poshest hotel in Malaysia, though I did see a large rat scuttle across the foyer floor just as I was checking in. Possibly it had been stalking me since the train station, tracking me by my pungent scent. I was going to point it out to the reception clerk but he was too busy fishing my payment for the room, in two- and five-cent pieces, out of my lampshade hat.

The following day, I embarked on a Polish freighter for India, as organised a month earlier in Penang. I had just two Malaysian dollars in my pocket, but my bag was stuffed with every bottle of complimentary shampoo, perfume and aftershave the hotel could provide. The legacy of the durian was proving hard to dislodge ...

*

The staple diet aboard a Polish freighter is beetroot, a vegetable I had up until now vigorously eschewed on the perfectly reasonable grounds that it tastes like earth soaked in vinegar. Here there was no escape. Apart from that, life aboard the *Boleslaw Ruminski* – for that was the freighter's name – held few challenges except for finding ways of coping with the protracted and mind-numbing tedium. It was very comfortable, very restful, but very, very quiet. As a paying passenger, there was no question of me being expected to peel potatoes or swab decks, but after four days of enforced in-activity, I would have cheerfully licked out the engine-room if I had been allowed. I had barely spoken a word to anyone in eight days. The Polish crew spoke no English and even among them-selves seemed strangely uncommunicative. In the officers' mess at meal-times, there was no sound but the clinking of cutlery and the gentle slurping of beetroot soup. It was as if they had all been told that there was a man aboard who, suffering from a nervous breakdown, had taken passage in order to have complete rest and quiet and who must on no account be subjected to noise or excite-ment. So the steward would tiptoe into my cabin making sooth-ing shooshing noises while he apologetically cleaned up around me. The captain would whisper a demure 'Goot mornink' to me at breakfast and leave me to tackle my beetroot omelette in silence. Wherever I went, people would smile gently, slow their movements and lower their voices to protect my ravaged nerves from the slightest harm.

All this coddling could not, however, protect me from the shock I received when I noticed three days into the trip that my urine had turned bright pink. At first I wondered if I had picked up a ghastly infection in the Pat Pong district – you can't get things just from looking, surely? – but I soon realised that it was all the beetroot.

A further shock came four days into the trip when I was leaning on the starboard rail, wondering when Madras and the eastern coast of India were due to appear. There was a distant lump of land vanishing astern and I was idly considering which one of the Andaman Islands it could be. One of the crew, Tomi, the only one who had a smattering of English, came and joined me at the rail. After a soothing period of silence, he pointed out the vanishing blue lump.

'Sri Lanka,' he said. 'Old Ceylon. Bye bye!'

'Sri Lanka?' I puzzled. I tried drawing a map in my head. 'But aren't we going the wrong way for Madras?'

'Madras?' queried Tomi.

'India?' prompted I.

'Ah,' sighed Tomi. 'This ship no ees goink India.'

'Not India?' I yelped. 'Where then?'

'Africa.'

So there we were. I strolled up to the bridge, looked at a map and the captain told me we were indeed on our way to Mombasa, Kenya. We were due to dock there in three days. I was rather pleased, actually. Okapi hide drums! Blackbird trading out of Zanzibar! Ivory poachers! King Solomon's mines! The Dark Continent itself.

*

Yes, well, forget Africa. Four days later, I had an experience identical to the one just described, except replace the word starboard with port, the words Sri Lanka with the word Somalia and the word Mombasa with the word Egypt. I was somewhat bewildered. Tomi explained that we weren't going to Kenya, never had been, no, we were off to Egypt and the Suez Canal. This was getting ridiculous.

Again, I didn't actually mind so very much because Egypt sounded like a good place to visit, but I did wish these Poles would make up their minds. We'd be in Warsaw soon at this rate.

*

Three days later, it was Christmas Eve and I was going out of my mind. At ten minutes to midnight, I was sitting in my cabin wide awake and unable to sleep, having already had three longish naps that day. I was feeling particularly friendless and nostalgic. In all the letters I had been writing, I had complained that the Polish crew were dour, unsmiling individuals who had not said a single word to me in eight days. But, I added jocularly, I was secretly confident that come Christmas Eve, they would shyly troop into my cabin, set up a Christmas tree, bring out a bottle of vodka, present me with a host of crudely home-made but touching gifts – a set of nativity figures carved from clothes pegs, a model ship, a badly embroidered hand-kerchief inscribed with MERY CRISTMASS ON BOLESLAW RUMINSKI 1990 GOD BLES YOU, a jar of Polish preserved plums, et cetera – sing a moving Russian carol or two and leave me in a haze of tears and vodka. It would turn out to be the happiest Christmas of my life, full of the true spirit of Bethlehem, and so on and so on.

Well, it was now one minute to midnight and not a carved king-and-camel set anywhere in sight. It was as quiet as the grave, as ster-ile as a hospital and I was as maudlin as it is possible to be without the aid of lickerous spirits. All this despite the fact that earlier that evening, we had all partaken in a special Christmas Eve dinner, incidentally the main celebratory feast in Polish tradition. Can you guess what this jolly feast consisted of?

Cold fish and beetroot. Lots of it.

Facts about a Polish Christmas:

- Christmas Eve is the main day of celebration and yet is also – get this – officially a day of fasting. Consequently the tradi-tional Christmas Eve dinner, although consisting of thirteen separate courses, is nevertheless Spartan in content. Beetroot predominates in various forms – borscht, boiled beets, mashed beets and cold pickled beets – but there are also such bucolic delights as red cabbage, cold boiled fish, jellied peas, rollmop herrings and bean paste. Not one of the dishes is hot and there are no desserts, wines or red meats. It is a long way from boar's heads, plum duff and exploding brandy snaps. In fact, it's a bit bloody cheerless.
- Christmas Eve is sacred not only to Christ's birthday but also to Adam and Eve; it is their 'saint's day', as it were. It is a last

reminder of the awfulness of Original Sin, hence all the beet-root and herrings in vinegar.

* The liquid that looks promisingly like claret is just beetroot tea, the traditional drink of the celebrations.
* No-one talks very much.
* Bedtime.

It was now about one minute to midnight and I had decided to pack it in. One couldn't expect a Christmas so far from home and family to be quite the cheery occasion it normally is. But then – and this stretches credulity a little, I realise – as I was drifting off, there came a tap at the door. On opening it I found six members of the Polish crew, including Tomi, of course, bottle of vodka in hand, inviting me to the engine-room for a midnight drink. No haunting carols, or peg-nativity figures, but they *had* set up a Christmas tree twinkling with lights and the vodka flowed freely and all in all, I think it was the nicest Christmas I've ever had, filled as it was with the true spirit of … well, vodka mainly.

*

Another few days found us in the Gulf of Suez, where dim smoky plains closed in on either side and the odd stony jagged Mount Sinai-ish shape rose out of the desert. There were pillars of fire by night and pillars of cloud by day: the great oil-rig funnels lit like giant torches dotted along the Gulf. We were apparently due to arrive in Suez at midnight. It was now eleven days since I had had a proper conversation with anybody. I had written 200 pages of a novel and worked out the most amazing things about Fibonacci's Series, which I had tried to explain to Tomi in pidgin-Polish but not terribly successfully, I think.

'Only connect.' Did E.M. Forster write that? Was he on a freighter at the time? I think he must have been.

*

It was now twenty-four hours later and I was still on the good ship *Boleslaw Ruminski*, a name that hardly compares in euphony with such names as *Roundelay*, *Arietta*, *Cloud of Islands* and *Wind Shadow*, to name a few.

We hadn't stopped at Suez. I was getting seriously worried.

We were churning up the Suez Canal at full speed when I went to see the captain, who solemnly promised that I really would be able to disembark at Port Said at the northern end. Apparently, to get me off at Suez would have cost me 250 American dollars in cash, so they had decided that Port Said would be better. I sincerely hoped so, because apparently the next port of call was Rotterdam and I didn't want to have spent my grand year of intrepid travel going from Penang to Rotterdam in one fell swoop. I might as well have flown. I still felt as though I were on a giant Snakes-and-Ladders game. I had shaken a dice and landed on Mengla in China and a huge slippery snake had taken me all the way back to Malaysia. Now I'd moved one more square onto Penang and appeared to be on a fast-track ladder to the very top of the board, a mere two squares away from England.

As we ploughed up the canal, my fit of the fidgets reached its height. I could not wait to be heading somewhere purposefully once more. As soon as I was on land again, I planned to ring Newton and get him to fly out to Cairo and join me for the last leg across Europe as we had planned. That would be fun, I thought – somebody to whom to explain Fibonacci and the rules of my board game.

*

Right, this was it. It was about two o'clock in the morning and we were due to reach Port Said in about an hour, according to Tomi, my only friend in the whole world. I had just been up on deck in the freezing winter air and seen the lights approaching from the north, the horrible sodium-orange glare of modern lights. I had packed my things and once the ship had docked, I'd be off like a greased rat. Egypt! I went below out of the cold and waited to be called.

*

Bugger, bugger, bugger. An hour later, I went up on deck again, just in time to see the lights of Port Said disappearing off to the south. I could not believe this. The ship appeared not to be stopping and we were heading out into the Mediterranean. Tomi was nowhere in sight. What was the Polish for 'Stop! Stop! I want to get off!'

Storming the bridge, I found the captain standing bathed in the glow of green radar screens and said something along the lines of, 'Excuse me, remember me? The one who paid for a passage to India, if I may borrow from the classics. We appear to have gone several thousand miles past my stop and it's a long walk back. What, may I ask, happened to docking at Port Said?'

'Ah, *ja*,' he murmured, stroking his beard. '*Ja*, ze passenger. Port Said. I am forgettink. I must radio ze port people, *ja*?'

'Yes, well, could you hurry, please? We'll be past Italy in a moment.'

Half an hour later I was told to fetch my rucksack and come up to the top deck, where Tomi would be waiting to see me off. I stepped out into a blast of freezing midnight air in time to see the lights of Port Said twinkling in the distance some three miles behind us. The freighter was forging out into the Mediterranean at full speed on a black midwinter night, merrily on its way to Rotterdam. Before I could protest, Tomi pointed over the side and I saw the arrangements that had been made for my disembarkation. At that point I very nearly decided to stay aboard. About a hundred feet directly below, skidding over the waves to keep pace with the freighter, was a motorboat the size of a coffee table in which sat five Arabs clinging on for dear life. Between me and my rescuers, a thin rope ladder plummeted vertically down the freighter's mighty flank. It was about as wide as a packet of Minties and its bottom end was being regularly doused by ocean waves capped with pale icy foam.

'This is how I get off, is it?' I asked with some asperity.

'*Ja!*' said Tomi brightly. 'Nice to meet you. Bye bye!'

'You do know that I am not a trained acrobat, don't you?' I asked, just to be sure.

'Ha ha. You are very funny man. Bye bye!'

There was nothing else for it. Saying a final shaky goodbye and a wan thankyou to Tomi, I climbed over the railings with my rucksack on my back and started to descend the swaying ladder. By the time I was ten rungs down, my hands were chilled to the bone. After some time I reached a rung just yards above the water. Now the Egyptian motorboat moved in closer to the iron cliff of the freighter's side, bringing it into the full wash of the bow-wave. I realised that I was expected to leap horizontally off the ladder like some freak spider, launch myself across a three-metre gap of black turbulence and hit the minuscule decking of the motorboat, now bucking and veering like a surfboard on the freighter's wash. I also realised that if I didn't do it soon, I would either be washed off by an ocean breaker or freeze solid to the ladder; the good ship *Boleslaw Ruminski* would be using me as a fender all the way to Rotterdam.

Accompanied by the enthusiastic but bloody irritating cries of the five Arabs aboard calling, 'Come, Mister! Jump, Mister! We catch, Mister!' I took a deep breath and leapt.

There was a horrid moment when I hit the greasy deck with such speed that I skidded right across the boat and nearly toppled over the far side, but an Arab did indeed catch me, pick me up, dust me down and, in doing so, deftly remove my wallet from my trouser pocket. I didn't care. I was safe. I was off the freighter. And he was welcome to the two and a half Malaysian dollars held therein.

*

There followed a long and tedious time spent sitting in a large, dimly lit office with yellow walls in Port Said, inhaling the smell of clove cigarettes while various people of differing degrees of officialdom tried to extort money from me. Some of them may have had a right to do so; I was happy to see that the owner of the boat got a hefty sum and I'm pretty sure there was a customs official or two who probably had a right to know why I had entered Egypt without a visa. But I drew the line at the thin droopy man who kept bringing in silty coffee or the ragged street boy in what looked like pyjama bottoms who tried to suggest that I owed them large sums of cash.

I was kept awake by a cocktail of cloves, coffee and sharp questioning until the morning, and was then marched down to a bank and watched like a hawk while I extracted large wads of cash. (The memory of my pin number had been mercifully restored by twelve days of enforced silence aboard the freighter. It was a multiple of two Fibonacci numbers, I had remembered.) After distributing sums to anybody with a bit of gold braid about their person, I headed off to a guesthouse and spent the next few hours catching up on sleep. I was pleased to note that already my urine was returning to its normal colour, now only the faintest shade of rose-gold.

Chapter 20

Despina can be reached in two ways: by ship or by camel. The
city displays one face to the traveller arriving overland and a
different one to him who arrives by sea. In the coastline's haze,
the sailor discerns the form of a camel's withers … He knows
it is a city but he thinks of it as a camel from whose pack hang
wineskins and bags of candied fruit, date wine, tobacco leaves,
and already he sees himself at the head of a long caravan taking
him away from the desert of the sea towards oases of fresh
water in the palm tree's jagged shade.
—ITALO CALVINO, *Invisible Cities*

Newton arrived three days later. He is tall, gangly, moves like a
giraffe on roller-skates and looks a little like a stone curlew after a
sleepless night. As I sat waiting in the airport for his arrival, I meditated on the journey so far. I had been right to shun air travel, I
thought. Airports are ghastly at the best of times but Cairo's took
the cake. Had the terms ill-lit, clamorous, jarring and grubby been
the key words in the architects' design brief, then Cairo airport
would have won several major awards.

I meditated further. My plan to travel by any means except flying
had, surprisingly, worked so far, generating just the right amount of
adventure and now depositing me here beyond all major geographi-
cal and political barriers. The route from Egypt to the shores of
England would be straightforward enough; the challenge was now
likely to be whether I could survive the rest of the journey with my
sanity intact. My acquaintance with Newton had taught me that he
tends to progress through the world like Wile E. Coyote at large in
an Acme warehouse. His mind is fertile and razor-sharp but things
tend to go *twang!* or *whoosh!* a lot in his vicinity. Ropes snap at his
touch, reels unspool, and overhead electric circuitry starts sparking
as he passes. If Newton's approach to travelling was anything like
his approach to other spheres of life – driving, cooking, social banter

– then I feared the worst. Eccentric was one way of putting it; suicidally accident-prone was closer to the truth.

My fears were confirmed within two minutes of his arrival. He emerged through the barrier with his customary staccato stride looking about him in slight alarm like Wile E. Coyote who has just realised that the fizzing stick of TNT is now stuck to his hand. He strode up to me, punched me hard on the arm and said, 'That's for Kathmandu post office. It was awful,' and then we got down to the business of greeting each other properly. God it was good to speak to someone familiar, even if my arm was smarting. I started looking around for the baggage carousel. 'No, no,' Newton explained proudly. 'I'm travelling light. Just this one bag and the coat, see!' and he proudly patted the light haversack over his shoulder.

'Good-o!' I said. 'Well done, you! Er – what coat?'

Newton stopped, glanced down, patted his shirt and pockets and gave a great snort and a roll of his eyes. 'Bugger! Wait here!' he cried and flung himself back against the tide of emerging passengers, his limbs flailing like windmills. I watched him vanish through the gate. Some time later, he emerged again, flanked by two irate airport personnel.

'My coat will not be joining us,' he said. 'It is taking a holiday flight to Libya.'

He stalked onwards, patting his pockets.

Ten seconds later he turned and added, 'As is my Visa card, in fact. How are we for cash between us?'

When we reached the Cairo hotel room, I watched him unpack and my fascination grew. There was no sleeping bag, no footwear more sturdy than a pair of light canvas beach-shoes, and no jumper. He did, however, proudly produce the following items:

- a brand-new camera, which he soon discovered didn't work;
- a plastic bag full of new hypodermic syringes;
- a water purifier the size of a medium-sized tea-urn; and
- a mosquito net.

We were, it seemed, in every way fully equipped to tackle the disease-ridden tropics, but the frozen wastes of Europe in January might prove a challenge. I knew then that Newton's arrival was like drawing some odd Chance Card in the final stages of a complex game. After the tedium of the *Boleslaw Ruminski*, life had suddenly ceased to be dull.

We both took some adjusting to Egyptian notions of friendliness. Stepping outside our Cairo hotel, we were greeted by a host of amiable young men saying, 'Where you from, mis-tah? Australia? Ah, my brother, he is in Australia! From Sydney, yes? No? Ah, Adelaide! So too my brother! Adelaide is a very fine city, yes, very fine. And your name, mis-tah? Ah, San-dee! My brother, he too is called San-dee! He is an astrophysicist! Please, we are friends! Come to my shop and drink tea!'

Three out of five such invitations will surely lead straight to a carpet or perfume shop, where you will be badgered into buying wares at a very special low price, as is fitting between friends. But the other two are likely to lead to a long, gentle afternoon drinking mint tea in some tiny home, being shown the family albums, meeting the wife and five kids and, sure enough, being shown a photo of the improbable brother, San-dee, standing outside Adelaide University and waving a degree in astrophysics at the camera.

Both Newton and I were taken off-guard by the cleverer of the peddlers and it was only thanks to my Scottish parsimony that I didn't end up buying five brass lamps, a remarkably cheap 2000-year-old papyrus and a stuffed purple camel in the first day. Newton was less fortunate. We staggered back to the hotel with nine bottles of perfume – genuine Nile Lily, Lotus Flower, Sahara Rose, the very essence that Cleopatra herself wore, sir, would I lie to a friend? – and Newton firmly defending his purchases on the grounds that there were several young ladies back in England who would be expecting gifts. Yes, but nine, Newton? I asked.

Cairo is busy, hectic, crowded and charming, despite most of it being a uniform dust grey, the colour of the contents of a Hoover bag. There are still enough grand old buildings from the nineteenth century for an air of faded splendour to persist, and our hotel room was high-ceilinged and tiger-striped with gold through the varnished Venetian blinds as we siesta'd in the long, hot afternoons. For several days, we trailed around the usual sights, including the Egyptian Museum, a gloomy, dusty place where one fully expects the mummies to come to life, scattering moths and winding sheets. Here too was the fabulous gold and lapis mask of Tutankhamen, displayed somewhat carelessly, propped up on what looked like an old shoebox.

So excited were we at the thought of adventure that we decided to hire horses and ride down to the less-visited pyramids at Saqquara. In this venture, we were accompanied by an Arab boy called Rashid. We rode through a portion of genuine desert, real Lawrence of Arabia stuff with sandhills and not a green leaf in sight, trotting at first and then boldly breaking into a canter on occasion. Then we came down to a stretch of green oasis with palm groves and orange trees and the Nile somewhere off to our left. The sky was blue and the day fine; at one point, we saw a hoopoe flashing out of the undergrowth, its salmon plumage contrasting with the black and white zig-zag of its wings. Riding along behind Newton, I was amused to see him start his usual clowning stunts, clearly bored with the slowness of the journey. He swayed from side to side with ever-exaggerated moves, his limbs moving like beanpoles strung together with elastic – perfect comic exaggeration as usual, a priceless parody of the lank, loose riding of Lucky Luke or some other cartoon cowboy. As I watched, chuckling, from behind, his moves got even more daring. I was about to call out and warn him not to overdo it when he executed a perfect Buster Keaton stunt. He slipped right around, his legs still clamping the horse's body in a closed loop but his body hanging vertically straight down from the horse's belly, his hair brushing the ground. For another few paces the horse plodded on and Newton's body swayed like an old stocking full of spaghetti. Then – I knew he couldn't keep this up – his legs unclamped, and he dropped lifeless onto the sand between the horse's legs. The horse plodded to one side and took the opportunity for a quick graze, and Rashid and I took the opportunity for a quick panic attack.

There he lay on the ground, the colour of fetta cheese and quite lifeless. *Oh, God, I've killed him,* I thought. *He's dead.* Rashid loyally burst into tears and then went and gave the horse a furious kicking. I emptied my water-bottle over Newton's face and hoped for the best. After thirty seconds, he revived and I breathed a huge sigh of relief. Thirty seconds may not seem very long, but you try counting it out aloud now, dear reader, and you will see how very long it is; long enough, for example, to compose a detailed letter to Mr and Mrs Harris back in Australia explaining that their son had just passed away in the Sahara Desert, how awfully sorry I was, and would they prefer burial, cremation or perhaps mummification since here we were in Egypt and it seemed a pity to waste 5000 years of expertise?

Once Newton had recovered enough to sit up and his colour had returned somewhat, we hopped back on the horses and terminated the expedition. We hobbled home, I put him to bed, told him in time-honoured Mackinnon fashion to snap out of it soon, reminded him gently how much money we'd wasted on our abortive horse-trip and kindly left him in peace for the next two days in a darkened room.

While Newton was recovering from what turned out to be a severe bout of gastro, I went off exploring Cairo's markets and bazaars. In the famous Khan-el-Khalili bazaar, I found a large, stately pharmacist's shop lined with shelves of beautiful jars and painted boxes and drawers, labelled with names straight out of a sixteenth-century apothecary's den: cardamom, ginger pods, lotus roots and cinnabar, amaryllis, saltpetre, linctus, molasses, tartary lamb and adder's tongue, St John's wort and facience. There was also a whole range of more sinister products, straight out of *Macbeth*: lizards' eyes, tigers' claws, corkindrills and pipistrelles, ibis bills, foxes' tongues and powdered iguana.

Looking for something for Newton's stomach, I found that one section of the pharmacy resembled a modern-day chemist's shop, stocked with band-aids, aspirins, shampoo, cough mixture and cotton buds. But at another counter, I noticed the shopkeeper, while serving a middle-aged woman, reach up behind him, take down what looked like a dried jackal's leg and turn on a little blender. There was a whirring noise as he inserted about two inches of the leg into the spinning blade before turning the machine off again and returning the leg to its place next to a dozen other dried animals or parts thereof. Then he poured the grey powdered remains into a white paper bag, labelled it as neatly as any modern-day pharmacist with a sticky label, and off she went with that and a packet of tampons in her shopping bag.

When the pharmacist served his next customer, I noticed him write something on a piece of thin, yellowish parchment, using what appeared to be soot and gum. I presumed this was some form of prescription, but no. After the woman had paid for her goods, she took the thin paper and a small phial over to a little shrine in a corner of the shop, just beyond the shampoo shelves. There she read the writing on the paper aloud, poured the contents of the phial into a tiny font and then folded up and *ate the paper*, soot and all. It was, I realised, not so much a prescription as a spell.

(I got some medicine for Newton, by the way, which worked a treat. Dried donkey's pizzle in aqua mirabilis, steeped in fresh bat lard. He's not complained of sickness since.)

*

With Newton now recovered, we were keen to travel back two thousand years to Old Testament times. With a faint memory of a little plastic pen and a gliding camel and date-palms from when I was eight, I suggested a destination off the usual tourist route. A back-breaking eight-hour bus trip took us to the remote oasis of Bahariya, and a village that was all mud-cube houses and dusty lanes. Here old yellow-toothed Bedouins sat grinning in the sun and donkeys laden with panniers of brushwood staggered by. Young Arabs in white robes and burnouses thrashed chestnut stallions across the crest of a distant sand dune. There were hairy black goats, as hairy as Esau, and baskets of oranges and melons, and at the village well, women covered from head to toe in sweeping black came to fetch water in jars and pails. There were also, somewhat disturbingly, piles of dead cats, dry and stiff and stinking in the sun, and mud beehive tombs and mosque-chanters chanting and rudely painted walls and squat archways with thick doors where, peering through the square grille, we could look into little courtyards with dried-out fishponds in the middle.

The loveliest part, though, was wandering down into the oasis itself, as we did that first afternoon. Here there were groves and groves of date palms and rustling papyrus, and cool sweet green grass beneath orange trees. These were hung with huge globed fruit, which glowed like lanterns against the dark polish of their leaves, the veritable golden fruit of the Hesperides. Here there were persimmons and tamarinds, sandalwood trees and pomegranate trees, vines and olives and bulrushes, and always the feathering and whispering of the desert breeze in a million leaves, and the *tsu-crooing* of turtledoves in the cedar trees. It was like some silken tapestry out of Old Persia or one of Oscar Wilde's Eastern fairytales.

Wilde would have appreciated our self-appointed guide, a twelve-year-old boy called Husuf who was dressed in a Joseph's coat of striped linen that fell to his ankles. He kept shinnying up various trees like a monkey to pluck us dates and oranges. I don't care for dates much – they are what I imagine candied cockroaches to be like – but the oranges were divine. Lying in the sun-dappled shade in the heart of such an oasis, lazily playing marbles in the grass with an Arab faun, came pretty close to Paradise. No wonder the oldest literature of the region talks of a garden filled with all good things, where the Lord comes walking in the cool of the evening. Perhaps this was in fact Eden.

It certainly had its serpent. On our arrival at Bahariya, the bus had been met by a pushy young man called Mustafa, who hustled us off to what he insisted was his four-star hotel on the edge of the village. This, he assured us, was the only accommodation in the area and he may well have been right. It consisted of a row of tents and an unfinished ablutions block with no plumbing. The lack of water had not prevented someone from making use of the toilets, all of which were full to the brim. The tents, however, we rather liked: it seemed a very Arabian thing to do, to sleep under canvas beneath huge hairy camelious blankets, so heavy that we were scarcely able to roll over in our sleep. It was like sleeping under a carpet.

That first night, Newton and I and a girl called Jane who was also staying at the camp went into the village to see what we could see, and to escape the stench of the ablutions block. Bahariya was even more Bethlehemish at night: dark archways in mud walls, empty crooked streets, pools of honey-yellow lamplight and soft black shadows where scabbed cats slunk. As we wandered, we were picked up by three young men who invited us into a tiny shop, stacked from earth floor to mud roof with tins of dates and anchovies and yellow soap in brown paper and bags of chickpeas and flour. We sat and grinned at each other in silence for a while until I broke the ice with a magic trick, ignoring Newton's heavy eye-rolling sighs. Despite his misgivings, it brought the usual response; twenty other people were fetched from around the village and I was urged to do more and more tricks to their ever-growing delight in an ever-more crowded space.

Having got the party going, they began clapping in rhythm, beating on cans of sunflower oil and chanting in that peculiar Arab wail that becomes more blood-throbbing and frenzied as it goes. Newton and Jane were prodded to their feet and expected to dance. They did a few rock-around-the-clock swirls and wiggles, prompting tumultuous applause and much *oohing* and *aahing* at their racy display of Western decadence. Then there was some animated discussion and a decision seemed to be reached. Cries of 'Mister Shu-Shu! Mister Shu-Shu!' rang out above the wailing, and somebody was dispatched to fetch this mysterious person.

Soon there appeared a sleepy twelve-year-old boy, who was pushed to the centre of the room. Space cleared around him. Going by the smiles and pointing of the village elders, this was Mister Shu-Shu, and boy, must he be good! But at what?

Then, to the accompaniment of a much slower beat and a gradually rising wail, Mister Shu-Shu smiled shyly and started his act.

A dance. A belly-dance, in fact. To be even more precise, a belly-dance of the seven veils, although in this case, the veils to be removed were three rather grubby jumpers and several layers of pyjama flannel.

Newton, Jane and I sat transfixed, darting glances of alarm at each other and wondering what on earth we were being offered, and how to refuse politely without offending our hosts; most of whom, we now noticed, were sporting large curved daggers. Meanwhile, Mister Shu-Shu had removed most of his clothing, flung it coyly into our laps and was now suggestively waggling his twelve-year-old bottom an inch from our noses, while all twenty-eight watching

Arab men were smiling paternally and waggling their eyebrows as if to say, 'Well? What do you think? Good, isn't he?'

Suddenly it was rather hot and stuffy.

At this point, the sack of chickpeas I was sitting on split with a soft pop and I tumbled sideways onto the floor. It was enough of a diversion to bring the belly dance to a mercifully premature end. We took the opportunity to applaud loudly, make our thanks, restore the lad's garments to him and depart hastily into the night, before we could be offered any more Bedouin hospitality. We walked back to our accommodation in a thoughtful silence, punctuated only by odd snippets of dialogue.

'Um, that was interesting.'

'Hmph.'

'Do you think …?'

'No.'

'We weren't being offered … were we?'

'What?'

'Never mind.'

'Was that what I think …?'

'Shut up.'

*

The next day we were joined by an exceptionally likeable trio of German tourists. Along with them we were persuaded by Mustafa to hand over a substantial sum to be driven five hours in the back of a pick-up to see the White Desert, the most spectacular but least-known site in the whole of Egypt, according to our guide. Here we found a lunar landscape, limestone stacks, petrified mushrooms polished white by millennia of sandblasting. At sunset, the shadows lengthened into impossibly long strips of cool blue and the glaring white of the rock turned to palest gold, the colour of cool glasses of sauvignon blanc. Newton and I and the Germans responded to all this delicate splendour by playing commando raids in and out and over the rock stacks, lobbing stones at each other – small, jet-black stones covered in perfectly formed cubic crystals of iron, an oddity in such a white landscape. Then there was the little matter of the five-hour drive back to the oasis in the back of the pick-up under the freezing stars.

'Shall we move on from Egypt?' asked Newton after an hour's jolting in numbed, contemplative silence.

'Yes,' said I.

But that night, we sat around a brazier out under the stars, very bright and clear in the desert air, and Egypt seemed once more a good place to be. The Germans were a musical bunch, able to harmonise with anything, even my tin-whistle. Using a battered guitar and an old wooden chair as a drum they produced the most wonderful music under the trembling stars.

The only fly in the ointment was Mustafa. He was the only Egyptian I really hadn't been able to like. Over the past three days, his manner had veered erratically from unctuous fawning to aggressive pestering and it had bugged the hell out of all of us. The tension came to a head on the last night. The brazier was glowing like a small dragon in a black-barred cage, and Franz, one of our fellow campers, was playing a haunting cavatina on his guitar. Several times, Mustafa reached over mid-chord, grabbed the guitar from Franz and bashed wildly at the strings, asking us if he was not indeed the very picture of some famous British rock-legend. We would all nod and laugh politely, then Franz would gently take back his guitar and try to pick up where he had left off. After two or three repetitions of this, Franz pointedly put the guitar away and suggested we try something else. Another of the Germans pulled out a length of soft rope and started doing a few magic tricks. He was superb, and very modest along with it. This elegant display spurred Mustafa to new heights of excitement and, like a spoilt child, he kept trying to grab the rope out of the patient German's hands. In order to deflect his attention, and never one to lose an opportunity to steal the limelight, I pulled out one of my favourite tricks.

'Ladies and gentlemen, I have here a red silk hanky,' I began. 'I push it like thus into my fist, add a little magical dust, call upon the djinn spirits of the desert to aid me and ... lo! The hanky has vanished!'

Sure enough, the hanky was gone. There was an impressed silence; even Mustafa was watching with open mouth and widened eyes, his braggadocio gone for the time being. Emboldened by this success, I carried on. 'But if our friend Mustafa would care to look in his silk burnous, perhaps he will find it rematerialised there?'

Puzzled, Mustafa unwrapped his white headdress and searched it carefully, a suspicious frown on his face.

'No?' I asked. 'But surely? Sometimes these things are very hard to see, once they have been made invisible. Allow me.'

And taking his burnous in both hands, I unfurled it with a flourish, showed my audience that it was blank on both sides, made a small well in its folds, and delicately removed from this well the red silk handkerchief.

The magic seemed to be working. The Germans applauded, ill-temper forgotten, and Mustafa watched in gawping silence, cigarette dangling from his bottom lip. This was going rather well. The trick, of course, is knowing when to stop.

'And finally,' I exclaimed, 'I take this lit cigarette' – here I plucked the cigarette from Mustafa's lips – 'invoke the fire-spirits of the desert once more' – a quick mystical pass in the air – 'and push it straight into the silk burnous, still burning, where ... it vanishes away, leaving not a trace! Da-daaa!' On my final flourish, there was a tiny flash and a gentle puff of smoke from somewhere near my raised fist. A second later, I flicked open the glimmering white silk to show it unblemished on both sides. There was no sign of the glowing cigarette.

In the seconds of silence that followed, I mused smugly to myself what a good investment it had been, not only to learn a few simple tricks but also to carry with me that secret cache of flash powder. It was a mixture of gunpowder and magnesium concocted long ago in a school laboratory, and it lived in a little ornamental brass tube that seemed made for smuggling illicit substances across international borders. The merest pinch of it had been enough to give a magical sparkle and smoky puff to the old vanishing ciggy trick.

But far from being overawed by this last trick, Mustafa was enraged. Perhaps it had been the stealing away of his cigarette, or the unauthorised use of his burnous, but his agitation and fury were obvious. He leapt to his feet and cried out shrilly, 'Hah! You call yourself Mister Magic! Hah! Ees not real magic! Ees simple, what you do. You show us real magic, mister! Yah!'

I froze, embarrassed. The Germans tried laughing it off and Franz reached for his guitar again, but Mustafa was not to be so easily placated.

'Noh! Noh! You ees imposter! You show us real magic! No tricks! Real magic!'

And with contempt, he flicked me hard with his burnous.

Well, I didn't mean to drop the whole phial of flash powder straight into the brazier, of course. One wouldn't, not the whole lot at once. Not unless you wanted to crack open a six-inch steel bank-vault. I don't think anybody else noticed the little tube fly from my hands and land in the red-hot coals and sit there for a few seconds – but I did. I had the briefest moment to wonder just how big the explosion would be – even a pinch was enough to give a hefty flash – before taking a quick step back from the fire. Mustafa was still glaring at me like an enraged weasel, his lips quivering.

'Er ... abracadabra,' I said weakly, and the world exploded.

There was a fizzle and a flash, and white lightning seemed to blaze upward from the fire in a great column of silver flame. A rush of sparks shot skywards, mingling with the red sparks of the brazier, and a perfect ring of thick white smoke, as big as an inner tube and expanding all the time, billowed to the stars above. A second ring of burning embers spat out of the fire on all sides, and half-a-dozen people feverishly brushed glowing fragments of charcoal from their laps. It was damned impressive. But we never got to ask Mustafa what he thought for, as our eyes adjusted after the silver explosion, we saw him disappearing over a distant sandhill into the dark, leaving us to enjoy the gentler magic of Franz's cavatina and the desert starlight in peace.

Gandalf is alive and well, and living in Bahariya.

*

On returning to Cairo, Newton and I sat in the luxurious lobby of the Nile Hilton, drinking good tea over the morning papers and discussing our onward journey. Newton, it emerged, had ideas about popping overland down to Kenya for a few days, possibly taking in Victoria Falls and some gorilla-spotting in the Congo and putting the mosquito nets to good use. But when I showed him the map, he revised his somewhat shaky grasp of geography and agreed to let me plan the next stage. Look, I said, as we pored over the map together. We could cross the Sinai Desert, dining on manna and miraculous quails, and then wiggle our way up into the Holy Land to Jerusalem, where Maggie was now working – yes, she gets around a bit, does Maggie. Think of it! The Dead Sea, Jerusalem, the Sea of Galilee and then up into the High Lebanon, where Mary Stewart, I explained, had set one of her novels, *The Gabriel Hounds*. A brilliant book, I gabbled, set in a crumbling palace in a remote valley, the feisty young heroine encounters – but I was cut off mid-flow.

'Who?' said Newton.

'Mary Stewart,' I enthused, 'the writer, you know. Lady Stewart now, actually, I think. I wrote to her once, did you know? Years ago. A 28-page letter.'

'Lucky old her,' said Newton. There was a certain dryness in his tone.

'Well, she did write back,' I pointed out. 'A lovely letter, in fact.'

'Really? How long?' asked Newton.

'Well, more a note really.'

'How long?' he asked again.

'Five lines.'

'Goodness me,' he said at last, 'best of friends, clearly,' and turned to pick up his newspaper. Two minutes later, he asked casually, 'Is there another route we could take, Sandy, avoiding the Holy Land and Lebanon?'

'Look,' I said tersely over the rim of my teacup, 'I won't even mention Mary Stewart and *The Gabriel Hounds*, if that's what's bugging you. We'll just see these places and avoid the literary references, okay?'

'No, that's not what's worrying me. I'm more anxious to avoid the gas attacks,' he replied and pointed out the headlines of the day's paper.

Saddam Hussein had chosen just that moment to follow up his invasion of Kuwait by threatening to bombard Jerusalem with chemical warfare. A quick call from the hotel lobby to Maggie in Jerusalem confirmed the news. In fact, she had been issued a gas mask that morning. The Middle East was closed.

'Bloody Newton!' I thought instinctively. In typical fashion, he only had to approach the Middle East for it to blow up. Wandering back to where Newton sat in a deep armchair between tall jars of pampas grass, I considered an alternative route. Although heartily sick of seafaring and longing to wear out some shoe-leather, I would have to resort to ships once more, it seemed.

'Here's what we'll do, Newton. A ferry to Crete. Crete, Newton, birthplace of the Minoan civilisation, the Minotaur, the Labyrinth of Knossos and all that! It will be wonderful. And besides, Mary Stewart set *The Moonspinners* there, one of her best, I think. Set in a remote coastal village, the plucky young heroine stumbles across ...'

But Newton was buried deep in his newspaper once more, groaning slightly. A return of the gastro, no doubt. I'd better dose him up with another shot of bat lard.

Travelling with a companion after nearly a year of solo voyaging had added a dimension to the trip. For a start, there was Newton's alarming habit of discovering a new allergy each week – cacti, horsehair, sand, for starters. When he inadvertently smashed three of the nine perfume bottles in his rucksack, he added three new and interesting substances to the list of things he should avoid. I never have any sympathy for this sort of thing and my unvarying recommendation that he go for a quick jog to work it out of his system was met with exasperated scorn.

What's more, there was now an eye-witness to all the improbability, all the magic, all the adventure of the trip. And a Gorgon eye at that. An eye that, falling on the airy spinnings of these pages, on the cloud-capped towers and gorgeous palaces of my web-weaving, would wither them to dry dust and hard fact. Someone, in short, who could say in five years' time, 'Yes, well. Now let me tell you how it *really* happened.'

I was going to have to kill him.

Chapter 21

Thence we turned and coasted up the Adriatic, its shores
swimming in an atmosphere of amber, rose and aquamarine:
we lay in wide land-locked harbours, we roamed through
ancient and noble cities, until at last one morning, as the sun
rose royally behind us, we rode into Venice down a path of
gold. O, Venice is a fine city, wherein a rat can wander at his
ease and take his pleasure!

—KENNETH GRAHAME, *The Wind in the Willows*

The White Mountains of Crete lie like a great jagged spine down
the length of the island, their silver flanks seamed with gullies and
ravines that peter out in the lower slopes to pockets of farmland:
olive groves, rough pasture for grazing and tiny whitewashed villages. Legend tells us that these wild mountains were the birthplace
of Zeus, Zeus the Sky-Father, the Thunderer, and I think that during our stay he must have been revisiting the place for sentimental
reasons, as it poured icy rain and hail non-stop for the three days we
were there.

The Cretans, though, were wonderfully welcoming. Each time
we passed through a village, we would be ushered into a tiny front
room, sat down before a brazier and plied with black, black coffee,
nuts, raisins, baklava, oranges and eye-watering slugs of ouzo.
Then would follow long periods of friendly silence, during which
we nodded and smiled and steamed gently as our clothes dried off:
the black-shawled mama, the moustachioed, nicotine-stained
papa, the plump daughter (often luxuriantly moustachioed as well)
and her fawn-eyed little brother. Old photos of Papa in his war uniform and medals might be handed round, and then the ticking,
hissing, settling quiet of the rain and brazier would steal over the
scene again.

These houses were tiny, whitewashed and square. Remnants of
ragged red vine leaves trailed over the outer walls and fig trees

dripped their silver mercury drops onto the thick windows. Inside they were rather bare, but some had bright woollen hangings on the walls and there was inevitably a crucifix or icon and a tiny red oil-lamp set in an alcove. It felt as though we still hadn't quite made it to the modern world.

On the first of these occasions, we became thoroughly alarmed. When we indicated that we were from Australia, the father immediately said, 'Ah! Australia! Bang-bang!' As the last thing we had heard before sailing from Alexandria was that Australia might join the war in the Gulf, we were alarmed to hear that this seemed to have happened. We tried to find out more.

'Australia? Bang-bang? War?' we gesticulated.

'Australia, war, ne, ne!' grinned our host.

'Ah,' we sighed in relief, sinking back in our chairs. Two seconds later we both remembered that '*ne*' in Greek means 'yes.' We sat up again.

'Really? War? Australia? When? How?'

'Australia. Ka-boom!' mimed our host, and we both had visions of the Sydney Harbour Bridge vanishing under an Iraqi nuclear missile. Our Cretan papa, on the other hand, seemed positively exhilarated at the thought.

Finally the mystery was solved. Off he trotted and pulled out an old set of photos, which he showed to us with tears of pride. There he was as a younger man in uniform, standing amid a group of Diggers from the Second World War. The Australians were instrumental in stemming the German invasion of Crete in 1943, and the older folk still greet any Australian visitor with great warmth and pride. The guns and bombs the old man was miming were, to our considerable relief, about sixty years out-of-date.

In Crete, I also made the discovery that Newton was a sort of idiot savant. We sat one night in a freezing bedroom in a little mountain guesthouse, unable to sleep because of the cold, and whiled away the time in increasingly mindless pursuits. Eventually, I pulled out my map of the world and found on the back a list of the countries of the world and their current populations. Idly I asked Newton what he thought the population of Croatia was. *Four and a half million.* Bang. Correct.

Ghana? *Fifteen point four million.* Correct.

Uruguay? *Three point one million.* Correct.

Right. Right. Hang on. Okay. Guadeloupe? *Four hundred*

thousand, just under, about the same population as Suriname. Oh, and Luxembourg.

Correct, correct, and … correct.

I went through another thirty countries. Newton knew the population of each and every one. When I expressed surprise, he looked a little puzzled and said, 'Doesn't everyone know this sort of thing?'

*

In Athens, I lost Newton. Four hours previously, we had been walking through a city park on our way to the Acropolis and had come to a place where the path went two ways around a sort of bushy island no bigger than a bus shelter. With a playful skip, he went one way and I the other, ready to resume our conversation on the other side of the laurels. That was the last I saw of him.

After some fruitless searching in the park, I assumed he was playing a game, so I wandered up to the Acropolis to join him there. Four hours later – four hours of ducking around crumbling marble columns and climbing steps, of failing to properly appreciate friezes and goddesses and statues, four hours of asking tour-guides if they had seen a tall chap, beaky nose, looks like a hawk who's just lost a fight with a cheese-grater – I gave up. We were booked on a ferry for Italy that night. The train to Patras left in an hour's time, I was carrying the tickets, and if he didn't turn up in the next twenty minutes, I didn't know what I was going to do. In a mixture of panic and rage, I positioned myself at a pavement café table on what I hoped was the only way up to the Acropolis and prayed that he would appear some time soon.

I wondered if I had upset him in some way. He had seemed perfectly cheerful just before he vanished. I did nearly kill him on that horse-ride, I thought to myself, and then set fire to his shirt with that gunpowder display, but he hadn't seemed too put out at the time. I thought we'd been having a good laugh, but perhaps I'd misread things.

Just then I spotted him meandering up the street, and all my good-humoured speculation dissolved. He thought he was on his way to visit the Acropolis, I could tell, but frankly, we had a train to catch in twelve minutes, so he'd have to see it some other time.

We made the train with one minute to spare. Soon we were on yet another ferry heading to Brindisi, Italy. Newton seemed a little miffed that we had done Greece in one day, but I patiently explained

that this was all Greece warranted in mid-January, and besides, it was entirely his own fault that he had missed the Acropolis.

'But I've *seen* the Acropolis,' he interrupted. 'I was waiting there for you half the bloody day. Where the hell were you?'

I paused, thought, and then pulled out a couple of postcards of the Acropolis. I handed them over the table to him.

'Oh. Is *that* the Acropolis?' he said. 'I may have been somewhere different then.'

We never did work out where, but I suspect it may have been the Olympic Stadium. 'I thought it looked a bit modern,' he said.

*

A few hours later, as our ferry continued towards its destination, I outlined my plan to Newton.

'Brindisi,' I explained, 'is not the sort of place we want to hang about. It's just a port town, nothing of interest there at all. We should try hitching straight to Rome the moment we arrive.'

'Just a port town?' said Newton. 'Like Athens, you mean? The bloody capital of Classical Western Civilisation? See-the-Acropolis-and-Die Athens? Aren't we doing this tour of Europe too quickly?'

'Nup. And anyway, you did see the Acropolis, so stop complaining.'

'From the outside, yes. The Acropolis visitor-centre café. Not the actual Acropolis, I didn't!'

'We're hitching to Rome,' I said, and closed the conversation. Outside the window, Corfu glided by in a haze of purple and gold, and I considered letting Newton know that this was the enchanted setting for *This Rough Magic*, in which a likeable heroine finds herself embroiled in – but no. I kept my peace and he kept his. The next two hours were spent in grumpy silence, but we couldn't keep the dudgeon up forever. The last leg of the trip saw us trying out a version of the Trading Game using a pad of paper and a pocketful of hypodermic syringes. Good old Newton. Perhaps we *would* slow down a tad ...

*

On our first night in Italy we almost died. Stupidly, stupidly, stupidly, we set off hitching from the perfectly acceptable – charming, some would even say – town of Brindisi at about five in the afternoon to see if we could make it to Rome. I am a fan of hitching: I like the fact that it is a mode of transport fuelled by the kindness of strangers and mutual trust. I like the Taoist nature of it: it teaches patience and a philosophical approach to life. All of this I explained to Newton as we stood on the roadside that frosty January evening. What I failed to add is that it can be a bugger at times.

We hadn't realised that:

Rome was about 300 miles away.

Once the sun set, the temperature would drop to about minus twenty-seven degrees.

Nor did we realise that in Italy, hitchhikers are regarded as carriers of the Black Death and are shunned at all costs.

By midnight, I was actually crying from the pain, the tears freezing into crackly films of ice on my cheeks. You know how sometimes your thumbs get so cold that it feels as though someone has just hit both thumbnails with a hammer? That was the feeling, except in *all* my fingers and my toes, and my knees and my elbows and my entire spine. After attempting to hitch for hours with no luck, we had decided to start walking along the motorway to try and keep warm. Beside me, Newton was muttering, 'See the Acropolis and die. It's not an *instruction*, Sandy.' For my part, I was beyond words.

Two hours later, we were in the middle of a pitch-black frozen waste. The few cars travelling at that time of night were going so fast that they couldn't possibly have seen us. By now I thought we were both going to keel over. At about two in the morning, we staggered into a service station, where I embraced the knees of a man who was filling up his car and pleaded with him to take us somewhere, anywhere, and not to leave us here to die. He refused at first – but when he tried to drive off, his car conked out twenty metres up the motorway on the hard shoulder. Looking back at us, he indicated that if we managed to push the car and get it started, we could have a lift. This we did.

This driver turned out to be terrifically kind. A few miles up the motorway, he pulled into another service station and bought us both double espressos, which went through our numb systems like a shot of adrenaline. He then drove us all the way to the outskirts of Rome, pressed 10,000 lire into our hands and, before we could explain that we might be idiots but we weren't penniless, drove off.

That was at dawn. We finally got into the centre of Rome via the Colosseum, aided by two stunning Italian girls who fell for Newton's stringy charm. They put us on the right bus (we had bought tickets for the wrong one), and by mid-morning we were at the Vatican, lying on the white marble steps in glorious sunshine. From thereon, I decided, it would be trains all the way.

*

Somewhere in the depths of the Vatican there is an architectural wonder that left my heart singing for weeks afterwards but nearly killed Newton with grief. It is a large spiral staircase of broad marble that curves its way around the inner wall of a great chamber, and this Newton and I began to ascend, making our way to the upper galleries of the palace. As we trod up and around, we could not only look down over the balustrade at the dazzling tiled floor below, but also across the echoing space to the far curve of the chamber, where the sinuous spiral of the same staircase hugged the opposite wall. Here other visitors were descending, taking in the marmoreal splendour as we were.

Suddenly Newton caught his breath. 'Look,' he whispered fiercely, pointing across the gallery and upwards. 'It's our girls. It's them! Our girls of this morning!'

I peered up to see where he was pointing. Sure enough, two willowy figures were descending the spiral staircase several storeys above us. At that distance, I could not be certain they were the same two girls, but Newton was sure of it. He had been talking of nothing else all morning and now, here they were, clearly so taken by the charm of at least one of us that they had followed us into the city. Or so Newton explained to me in an exultant whisper as we carried on up the staircase. 'Oh God, oh God, thank you,' he was saying fervently. 'This way we can't miss them. They're coming down the stairs, we're going up, this is going to be so easy. Thank you, God!' Then he turned to me, jabbed me in the ribs with a bony finger and said with an earnest intensity I had not seen in him before, 'Sandy, you're not to muck this up for me, okay? I know they're Italian but they're just not interested in Fibonacci's Series, honestly, they're not. Please, please, just this once, leave this one to me.' And he strode on upwards, trying to slick down his unruly hair with a bit of well-applied spittle and trying out expressions of surprised delight.

But a minute later, Newton let out a groan of dismay and leant over the balustrade, pointing downwards. There were the two girls, chatting gaily as they descended, but now far below us, nearing the tiled ground floor. How could they have passed us on the staircase completely unseen?

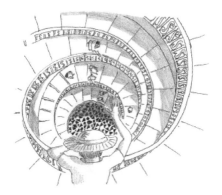

The answer was simple. This architectural marvel consisted not of *one* but of *two* staircases, forming a great double helix that spiralled in two separate threads up the walls of the gallery. Interweaving but never intersecting, one flight led the arriving crowd upwards and the other took the departing crowd down. By the time we had realised this, the girls had reached the tiled expanse at the bottom, clicked their way across it in staccato Gucci heels and disappeared through the doorway into the wide world. Newton would, I think, have flung himself straight over the balustrade were it not for the restraining presence of a uniformed guard, who motioned us onward and upward and explained that we still had another three miles of

Vatican corridors to traverse before we had finished the tour. Our girls of that morning – if indeed it were they – had vanished forever.

St Peter's Basilica is the most beautiful building in the world. There are mosaics which are so finely done that from ten feet away they resemble oil paintings. There are marble statues that writhe with life and power and seem more alive than the people standing there looking at them. The vast floors are tiled with endlessly different patterns in marbles of green and black and rose, white and purple and amber, all the natural colours of the stone itself. Best of all, shafts of light like solid columns of gold fall from high windows in domed vaults, bright and soft against the vasty darkness behind. It almost seems that the real building is built entirely of light – walls, columns, pillars, ceilings, floors of a living lambency – and that the darkness of stone all about is merely a heavy scaffolding, soon to be removed to reveal the real temple of Heaven in its finished state.

*

Newton wished to return to the Colosseum the next day. After a night of agitated thought, he was convinced that if we could retrace yesterday's bus-route to the outer suburb where we had originally been dropped off, we might be able to find our two Italian girls. He wanted to thank them with a bottle of Nile Lily perfume and a

3000-year-old papyrus painting each. I was all in favour of lightening his rucksack, but felt that somehow our chances were slim. I had a little trouble persuading him of this. Besides, we were due aboard a train to Venice that afternoon. I thought we'd seen enough of Rome.

*

If you have any plans to die, do try to see Venice first. One of the first charms of the city is that it is truly labyrinthine. A traveller arriving by train finds himself emerging from the ferrovia and decides, perhaps, as we did that first afternoon, to make his way to the great square of San Marco. This is made easy for him. There are bold yellow signs painted on walls or pinned to gondola posts saying SAN MARCO in thin black capitals. The way is clear, and he makes his way down a broad street under a Canaletto sky, running along the banks of the gondola-jostling Grand Canal. But after 300 yards, a puzzle is set the traveller. There is one of the yellow signs, but indicating with a crooked arrow that San Marco is down this lightless alley. Absurd! This is clearly a graffiti artist's little joke on unsuspecting tourists, and not a very subtle one.

But we have all the time in the world, so let us indulge the joker and see where he is leading us. The traveller ducks down the alley into the shadows. After fifty yards, he turns left, then right again. He finds himself crossing a tiny wooden bridge over an isolated stretch of canal, hemmed between blank walls of fading stucco. The joker is certainly persistent, for here there is another yellow sign, pointing down a tunnel away to the left. Now convinced that he is being led into some den of thieves, the visitor treads warily along the passageway, turns a sharp corner with his rapier drawn ... and is out once more into a bustling thoroughfare as broad and as safe as one could wish. And there is a faithful yellow sign, telling him that he is indeed still on his way to San Marco.

This experience is to be reprised another dozen or so times before he reaches his destination. Again and again he will thread his way through noisome, ill-lit streets, emerging from time to time in little piazzas where as many as three of the most beautiful churches he has ever seen will vie for his admiration, a whole chess-set of marble saints guarding each arched portico. And then for his faith, he will be returned via another maze to the broad ways once more, where he can walk with his elbows out wide and marvel at the city that is Venice.

It is like some old morality tale played out in brick and plaster and waterways, urging the pilgrim to beware of the easy and obvious paths, but to trust the signs most when they lead to the crookedest of ways. The first shall be last and the last shall be first, and my way is narrow and hard for those who seek it. And indeed, as Newton and I tramped along in the late-afternoon light on that first day, it was tempting to think that these yellow signs were jokes after all. But no. On trying to find our way to San Marco by what seemed more obvious routes, we found that each of these high streets curved slightly. What seemed to be a clear march to the north would imperceptibly bend away, so that without knowing it we were soon heading north-east and then fully east and would find ourselves coming to the edge of the city, looking out over the vastness of the lagoon to the lonely marshes beyond. Then we would turn and look back and the whole city would be standing silently behind us off in the distance, reproachfully wondering why we were so interested in the abandoned wharves.

We would turn, take our bearings, consult fiercely, and set off once more. Half an hour later, we would be standing yet again on a desolate bit of shoreline looking out over the pale sea. For all this, I love Venice. I am thrilled by it, terrified by it, entranced by it.

Here the merchant Antonio once rated Shylock upon the Rialto, here Vivaldi composed his fizzing glories, here Othello wooed his white ewe Desdemona with tales of the cannibalistic anthropophagi and men whose heads do grow beneath their shoulders. Here sickened Von Aschenbach for the pale sailor boy and here still the horrid-eyed green crabs swarmed upon the furry black walls of the canals.

In the days that followed, Newton and I assigned ourselves a thousand dollars each from an invisible purse and went out shopping, showing each other what we would spend our fortunes on. An ebony cane with a globe of pure glass set in the top, a little silver Viking ship with every pin and spar and line in place, a large vellum tome with a marbled cover and creamy parchment pages, and, best of all, a Fool's costume, quilted in heavy old satins and velvets – faded blues and brick reds, old golds and gamboges and worn, wintry greens – with a thousand pockets to hide a thousand tricks. I determined to go back and buy it one day when my currency was more tangible than those soap-bubble florins we played with then.

We caught a ferry one morning to the quiet little island of Burano, forging across a lagoon as pale in the thin winter sunshine as any glass blown by the city's craftsmen. Burano is as open and simple and homely as Venice is crowded, palatial and decaying. Its houses are painted in the simple bright colours of a child's paintbox, pink and azure, green and orange and lemon yellow. Here there are trees, bare and delicate in wintertime as a Japanese sketch, and there is a great silence under the dome of pale, cold sky. For the first time we were seeing Venice from a distance, with perspective; we could see it more clearly in the stripy reflection in the lagoon's mirror than in its insubstantial and incredible palaces.

On another evening Newton and I polished off an early dinner in some far-flung square over near the Arsenal, where seven giant lions of different styles and sizes guarded massive portals of black iron set in a red wall. After dinner we sat and chatted of this and that as the city came alive around us. This, it seemed, was the student quarter

and a number of bars spilt their bright lights out onto the pavement where we sat sipping white rums by the canal. It was an idyllic scene; the passing of the occasional boat sent the inky water slap-slapping along the steps and not far away there was a gondolier singing to an accordion a throbbing tenor solo. But Newton looked glum, so I thought I'd cheer him up with an explanation of something new I had figured out only that morning concerning Fibonacci's Series and a rather nifty new set of numbers I had dubbed Mackinnon Numbers.

I reached under the table to where my knapsack lay to fetch out a pen and my jottings – and it was gone. No! Perhaps it had been kicked sideways a little. No. Or was sitting on one of the other café chairs? No.

It had been stolen.

I cursed myself for my stupidity – we had been warned often enough about bag-snatchers in Italy – but was relieved that nothing too vital had gone missing. In fact, the only contents of my knapsack were my tin-whistle and a bundle of papers. There were about fifty pages of calculations concerning Fibonacci's Series, which had been keeping me occupied ever since I had made some rather startling breakthroughs on the Polish freighter. I had had to invent a whole new set of hieroglyphics to express mathematically what I was finding, and much of the document was covered in exclamation marks and arrows showing sudden links between random ideas. I wondered what the thief would make of his haul.

My tin-whistle had accompanied me from the beginning, had been trodden on in Auckland street markets, won me much-needed cash in half-a-dozen cities of the world, earned me rides on ocean-going yachts, been dropped – and dived for – in coral lagoons in the Spice Islands and comforted me in long solitary periods when the silence of solo travelling had become well-nigh unbearable. And now it was gone.

There was nothing to be done except sit and have another rum and gaze speculatively at Newton across the table. To be sure, he commiserated and offered to buy the next round, but I thought I could detect a certain relief in the set of his lips and eyes. As he went to get the drinks, I reflected on the number of times I had told him how carefully he should look after his stuff, ever since he had stepped off the plane in Cairo sans Visa card and overcoat. Since Rome, too, his interest in Fibonacci had waned and, to be frank, he had never been a great fan of the tin-whistle. I wondered whether Newton, in an effort to preserve his love-life and his sanity, might not have pushed both Fibonacci and the whistle into the canal when my back was turned.

'Ah well,' he beamed as he returned with two large rums, 'we can't always be lucky, can we, Sandy, old chum? Just a matter of being a little more careful, I suppose. So that's the last we'll see of Fibonacci, I expect, old fellow! Never mind, cheer up! Let's go and chat to those girls over there.'

But an hour later, just as we were thinking of heading back to the hotel, a woman came sidling up to the table.

'*Scusi*,' she said hesitantly. 'One of you lose ... how you say? ... a bag, *si?*'

I nodded and she continued. 'Ees very funny, I no understand, but a man, he come to me just now and he say, tell that man ... this is you ... that his bag is ... how you say? ... round the corner, hidden under a bridge.' I gaped at her. 'Eh, ees funny, no? Oh, and I forget. You are from the university, *si?*' she asked.

'No, no, I'm from Australia,' I stammered.

'Then I no understand, but this man' – she pointed into the shadows – 'he says to say you a message.'

'Which is?'

'Ah, it is this.' She stopped, cleared her throat and then declaimed carefully: "Thanks for nothing, professor!"

And sure enough, when I sidled round the corner into the shadows of a dark alley, there was my bag, complete with notes and whistle. I wondered what the thief had made of them. I sauntered back to show Newton, giving a quick fol-de-riddle on my trusty flageolet as I did so. His new-found cheerfulness evaporated as I took out my notes and commenced a lengthy explanation of those freshly minted Mackinnon Numbers.

*

As we approached England, I felt that things were growing tamer by the mile. In fact, as the landscape looked less exotic and less likely to kill me, I felt more and more as though I were no more than a backpacker taking a brief holiday in Europe like thousands do every year. It was difficult to hold in mind the romantic nature of my quest. I had almost forgotten Iona and the Well of Eternal Youth. I was desperate to get to England and start looking for a job. It was high time to return to real life. It had been nearly a year now, and Odysseus was pining, not for magical islands and the golden apples of the Hesperides, but for the work-a-day satisfactions of Ithaca. I had seen a robin in Athens, a real live English robin, and had felt that I could nearly reach out and touch England. As we travelled further west, little things kept slotting into place; first the robin, but the Greek alphabet still foreign and exotic; then in Italy the familiar alphabet but the words and Mediterranean faces still strange. As we crossed into Austria, even though I didn't understand a word, the people began to look like folk from Warwickshire or Herefordshire, and I felt just that bit closer to my goal – a respectable life in England.

We reached Salzburg safely, and gorged ourselves into a good temper on gugelhupfs and sachertortes, lavishly smothered in cream. Salzburg being the city of music, I wanted to whip out my tin-whistle and wow the crowds with *Danny Boy* as I had done in Malaysia. But Newton put his foot down. He led me silently around a corner into a busy shopping street, where a busker was playing a violin outside an open-fronted bakery. We stood and listened to him performing some virtuoso piece by Bach so brilliant, so piercing, so ravishing that the very pigeons were sitting around in tears of quiet joy and ignoring the crumbs dropped by passing shoppers. But that was all that was being dropped. Certainly no schillings were coming his way. Behind the counter of the bakery, a stout Austrian lady in a floury apron and a hairnet stood listening intently with a frown on her pink-white face. *Tsk*, she muttered. *Tsk, tsk.* When I turned to her with an enquiring smile, she exclaimed tetchily, 'Zis is very poor. It should not be permitted. His intonation in the lower registers is very clumsy, and as for his interpretation of the cadenza – pah! It is a travesty. Zis is Bach, not Buxtehude.' And she stomped off to get another tray of gugelhupfen out of the oven.

Newton turned to me and said, 'Perhaps she'd enjoy a little rendition of 'London's Burning,' Sandy. Or 'Three Blind Mice'? To make up for the incompetence of Paganini over there, perhaps?'

The tin-whistle stayed sheathed.

Our next stop was Stuttgart to see Pit and Ulli, the two German students I had met in Laos. The sheer kindness of Pit's family was overwhelming. For three days we were fed delicacies that made our Salzburg coffee-house treats seem like a couple of dry Ryvitas and a glass of water. One of Pit's many hobbies was model-making, and his parents' flat was dominated by several ships he had designed and constructed, every plank individually steam-bent, every rope, pin and sail perfect. One of these had taken him three years to complete. Newton nearly knocked it off the sideboard.

After three days of warm hospitality, our new friends drove us through the Black Forest, thick with snow and glittering ice-needles, to Strasbourg at the French border. And once over the Rhine into France, after standing for two long hours on a frozen verge, we resorted to rail travel. The train we found ourselves on was the cleanest, swiftest thing I had seen for a year. It was all gleaming silver metal and tinted glass and aircraft seats in deep blue plush, and such was its speed that France dissolved into a green rainy blur outside the window. We watched Strasbourg disappear behind us, got ourselves baguettes and cups of coffee, started a desultory conversation and were interrupted by an announcement that we were due to pull into Paris in twenty minutes.

Criminal, I know, but we did Paris in one day and then I persuaded Newton to move straight on to Brittany, luring him with the tempting thought of seeing the Bayeux Tapestry. 'Did Mary Stewart write a book about it?' he asked.

'Er, no,' I replied.

'Good, we'll go then.'

I was aware that I was rather pushing Newton along, but more and more I felt the need to get somewhere and stop. Even while being whisked along in my wake, he was excellent entertainment value. In Brittany that evening after supper, he washed his feet in the bidet in our room, under the impression that it was a foot-bath.

Once I had explained the purpose of the receptacle, and as he started furiously applying the French equivalents of Harpic and Dettol in liberal quantities to his feet, we discussed our plans for the next day. The guesthouse brochure failed to mention the Bayeux Tapestry – for the very good reason that it was actually in Normandy.

'Never mind,' I said brightly. 'There's a place called Mont St Michel nearby, it says. Some sort of abbey on an island, I believe. Terribly touristy, it looks, but less so in winter, perhaps. Let's do that instead.'

And the next morning we set off for the last day of the voyage and a final adventure that nearly did for us both.

Chapter 22

Childe Roland to the Dark Tower came ...

—SHAKESPEARE, *King Lear*

You should arrive in Mont St Michel at dawn, on a misty grey morning preferably, and by foot. You will find yourself walking along hedged laneways through flat fields, silvered with cobwebs, and after about an hour's walking you will smell a tang of salt in the air and hear the susurration of slow waves lapping on shingle somewhere to your left in the thick mist. Clearly you are walking close by the seashore. Fifteen minutes later, you will be astonished to hear that the sea-noise now seems to be coming from the right side of the road as well. A quick scramble down the right embankment will reveal the grey water lap-lapping on that side of the road; a further check down the left embankment will turn up a similar sight. You are, in fact, on a causeway heading straight out to sea.

Then through the mist will appear a single yellow lamp, a fuzzy nimbus of light in the blank grey. Then another, a little higher up ... and another, then a fourth, a fifth, rising in a ghostly pyramid before you. Finally, as the dawn breeze stiffens and sweeps away the mist, you see what you have come to: a steep conical island walled and turreted and ringed with battlements of grey stone spiralling up to the base of a massive rock. Upon this rock is perched the abbey itself, a vast sheer-sided edifice that soars to a forest of steeples and pinnacles vanishing into the pearly blue of the fast-clearing sky.

The best thing about arriving at dawn is that you have the place to yourself for a whole three hours before the shops open and the first tourist buses arrive. Through the massive sea-gates, up along narrow streets, ducking up stairways to the battlements, diving under arches to hidden courtyards, and all the while the surging of the sea on the outer walls and the cry of sea-gulls keening in the wind.

But then, at nine o'clock sharp, the houses throw wide their shutters, the shops spill their wares out onto the pavements and the whole

place becomes as tacky and horrid as one can imagine. Bright-pink plastic cockleshells are the main item of commerce, along with saucy postcards, plastic aprons, badly printed tea-towels and cheap bejewelled crucifixes. It took me straight back to Rotorua.

After half an hour, Newton and I felt that we had thoroughly explored every cranny the town had to offer. The abbey itself would not be open for another hour or so, but it was too chilly to sit still for long. There was indeed one feature of the island that we had not yet been able to visit. On the western side was a tiny chapel perched on a rocky eyot of its own, connected to the main island by a little arched bridge. There was no obvious route to this bridge – it seemed to open out into the private woodlands that clung to the cliffs below the great abbey buttresses. However, glancing over a sea-wall, we could see that the tide was out a way, leaving a narrow strip of sand fringing the island. Surely it would be possible to make our way along this to explore the chapel.

Our steps brought us very shortly to a courtyard, where an archway opened straight out onto the sandflats. There was a small fishing dinghy stranded on the cobbles, and drifts of black kelp in the square's corners. Even as we watched, a curl of seawater licked into the courtyard like an exploring green tongue and retired again. Down some steps we hurried and over the slippery paving stones onto the white sand beyond the archway.

Our progress along the sands was not as straightforward as we had hoped. There were soft patches where we would suddenly sink to our knees and find ourselves floundering to extricate ourselves. At other points rocky promontories jutted out into the water, forcing us to climb up their slippery black buttresses and slide down the other side. And – predictably, really, considering how Mont St Michel had resisted invaders for so many centuries – the tide was coming in and coming in fast. Before we had gone a hundred yards along the shore, the strip of beach we had traversed was already under water, swirling, sandy-coloured water full of strange spiralling currents and rips. A minute later, a rogue wave came chuckling in, gave our boots a playful kiss and retreated, but not before turning the sand beneath our feet into a sucking quicksand. As quickly as we could, we clambered up onto the steep boulders that fringed the shore. There we considered our options.

Getting to the little chapel was now out of the question. The tide had covered the sand between us and the eyot and was splashing hungrily at the rocks on which we now perched like a couple of stranded cormorants. As we sat there pondering our options, a large black head bobbed up out of the water just metres away, round and sleek as a bullet – a seal, revelling in the element that imprisoned us. Newton eyed it balefully as he emptied his boots of sludgy sand.

'Well, we can't go on and we can't go back,' he said. 'Any suggestions, Captain Nemo?'

'Yes,' I replied, 'I think we'll just have to try up.'

And so up we went.

At first it wasn't too bad, especially once we were above the slippery rocks of the shoreline. We soon found ourselves on a loose scree of shale that rose straight to the roots of the abbey walls 150 feet above. Parts of this scree were stable enough to hold our feet and hands, but as we climbed higher in the breezy sunshine, the precipice became near vertical and large lumps kept breaking away and toppling – oh so slowly – into the sea far below us. To make things worse, the pitch of the cliff kept forcing us further clockwise around the island … and higher as well. Whenever we tried to clamber back the way we had come towards the town, the rock face became sheer and impassable.

We scrambled and clung and balanced our way up until we had climbed so high that we had reached the very roots of the abbey walls. There we wedged ourselves into the angle of a buttress and stopped for a breather. Above us soared the unscaleable walls. Below us the cliff dropped sheer to the sea, where the seal still bobbed and basked.

From this precarious perch, we were within metres of safety. Just

on the other side of the massive buttress, we could see the level grass
and stunted yew-hedges of the abbey gardens, hanging as they did
between the cliff below and the soaring walls above. This then was
our only route out. The problem, however, was that to obtain the
safety of the garden we would have to scramble across the smooth
paved face of the buttress, which overhung the cliff – a climb to tax
the skill of a gibbon, let alone two inexperienced fools. But then
these things always looked scarier than they were, I reminded
myself. Even the smoothest-seeming surface is surprisingly grippa-
ble by the human hand, I told Newton casually. To show him how
jolly easy it was, I offered to go first and edged out across the buttress. Halfway across the sloping stonework, and in the middle of a
breezy remark about the view, I started to slip, my boots failing to
grip the minute crevices of the masonry. For five dreadful seconds I
slid inexorably towards the bottom of the buttress, desperately trying to clamp myself to the stone like an overweight gecko. The stone
slithered under my fingers. My boots flailed. I willed myself to
adhere to the lichened surface. Be lichen! Be moss! Be a limpet! At
the very last second, my feet already dangling over the edge of the
buttress, a protruding clump of some frail plant gave me the slight
purchase I needed to swing myself along to the safe nook beyond.
As I crouched there, identifying my rescuing plant, which I now
held in my scraped and trembling hand, as a rather pretty ivy-leaved
toadflax, I considered my close escape. Without that little flower, I
would have been a mashed dinner for the seal on the rocks far below.

I was just calling out to Newton that perhaps he had better not
attempt the climb after all and that I'd go and find a helicopter rescue service when, with a quick slither of boots and a rattle of small
stones, he joined me. I gaped. Newton, so giraffe-like in the confines of a drawing room, had proven remarkably agile on the cliff-
face. He had scuttled across the buttress like a leggy triantelope.

A short scramble later we found ourselves dropping, to our
delight, over a wall and emerging like two ragged Robin Hoods into
the abbey gardens. These occupied the western and more private
side of the abbey complex. To our considerable relief, we discovered
a massive set of doors, promising an escape route back to the town,
presumably via the abbey itself.

These doors were, of course, locked.

Going back the way we had come was out of the question. It
would have to be the doors, locked or not.

On closer examination, these proved to be enormous affairs of double-planked wood, iron studs and keyholes you could fit your fist through.

'For God's sake, why, I ask you?' asked Newton. 'What are they locked against, hmm? Marauding squirrels? Let's climb the cliffs, you said. Piece of cake, you said. What are we supposed to do now?'

'I don't know, to be honest. How are you at picking locks?'

'Oh for Christ's sake, Sandy, this isn't a two-dollar moneybox. It's a bloody medieval castle door! Got a battering ram, have you? A siege engine, hmm?'

We decided to knock as hard as we could. The rapping on the door was translated by the vast vaulted chambers beyond into great booming echoes that wound on and on into the stone heart of the building, as though ... *BOOM!* ... some mighty Doom ... *BOOM!* ... had come ... *BOOM!* ... to the abbey ...

BOOM! ...

None of which disturbed in the slightest the three workmen Newton could see through the keyhole at the far end of the hall. They seemed totally oblivious to the fact that the abbey was shaking to its foundations with our mighty summons. Eventually, in desperation, we went and looked over the high terrace walls. At one point, it was only about a twenty-foot drop to the woodland floor, which seemed to be composed of a steeply sloping bank of leaf-litter. So it was that with faint squeaks of 'Geronimo' we leapt into the wood below. As Newton's fall was broken by some helpful brambles and my fall was broken by Newton, we both counted ourselves fortunate and staggered on our way. We progressed clockwise through the strip of woodland, scrabbling along the steep bank of rich humus, and came finally to the foot of the wall that separated us from the town. Fifteen feet above us was a sort of window-slit, a crannied hole or chink, and this looked promising. Some awkward climbing on Newton's shoulders, some clambering up among old ivy, then I hauled Newton up and we tumbled through this window-slit into the sober streets of the town. We were grazed, scratched and bruised, still with the dampness and leaf-mould of the shadowed wood on our clothes and in our hair, and we were precisely where we had been two hours ago. But despite the intentions of its medieval architects, we had successfully circumambulated the island. Time, we thought, for breakfast.

*

Later in the day, we visited the abbey properly, paying our entry fee and pretending to be tame tourists instead of warrior-spies. Usually tourists are confined to certain passages, halls and chapels along a set route. One files tamely up the monks' way to the information centre and bookshop, thence to the high cloister, followed by the abbot's chapel, the refectory and then out again by the main gate, processed and filled with knowledge like so many milk-bottles on a factory conveyor belt. Arrows mark the way and only certain doors are open.

However, it seemed that this was a day for misadventure. We had followed our guide tamely enough and come to one of the most beautiful spots in the whole abbey. It was a small cloister, with a double row of pillars surrounding a square of green grass. The pillars were slender columns of daintily coloured marble, greens and salmon-pinks and soft alabaster greys, but the best thing of all was that two sides of the cloister were open to the sky, with nothing beyond the upright columns but space and light. Being halfway up the great precipice of the abbey walls, one peered between the bars of this delicate stone cage at gulfs of washed blue air and the silver-blue sea stretching all the way to the faded horizon.

And England. England, somewhere over there, and my long journey's end.

So absorbed was I in this view, this dream, that I woke from my reverie to find Newton tugging at my elbow. The guide and the rest of the party had moved on some minutes ago. Newton had followed them but had realised I was missing and come back to fetch me. 'Come on,' he urged, 'or we'll lose them. It's down here and to the left.'

Ten minutes later, we were lost. We had retraced our steps several times and had come each time to dead ends and locked doors. We now seemed to be down a dark alleyway between two high walls. There was a swathe of red and white workmen's tape and some old trestles lying in a bundle on the floor, and a single door with a black iron ring on it. It looked like the last place a guided tour would have vanished through. Still, we were out of options. Newton gave the door a tentative rattle and it swung open into the gloom. We stepped inside, and so entered the labyrinth of my dreams.

Inside that first door, we found ourselves in a hallway not on the tourist route. Here we faced three more doors, each of them open. Which should we explore first? We dived through one, and for the next two hours we had the run of the abbey, six storeys of stone maze, from the deepest cellar to the very tip of the highest steeple. This was exploring, and with the added frisson of trespass. We never knew if around the next corner we might not stumble upon a monk practising a spot of private flagellation, or the full chapter in session, and be asked to explain ourselves.

One of the first places we came to was a stone chamber with a vaulted ceiling, supported by so many massive round pillars that it was like standing in a forest of squat stone trees planted too close together. From the centre of the chamber, one could see neither the walls nor how many doors led from here to other places. We christened this the Hall of Stone Trees in a furtive, excited whisper and paused. At that moment, we realised that we had both inexplicably become eight years old again. We moved on.

Another chamber was a perfect octagon, with delicate fan-vaulting overhead. In each of the eight walls was a wooden door. Entering from the south, say, one had a choice of seven exits, this one leading to a long, dim corridor, that one to a spiral staircase winding up out of sight, a third opening onto an airy cloister full of wind and light – spend too long pondering, and you would forget which door you had entered by. The bare walls of this octagonal chamber threw back a pure and resonant echo, like stone angels singing in perfect antiphon to my brief burst of a Tallis motet.

Later, we came upon a tiny little door, which led into a black pit that smelt like brandy and sewage. We wished we had a means of lighting our way. I was all for converting Newton's vest into a make-shift torch by wrapping it around a stick; reeking as it still did of Nile Lily, I was quite sure it would burn merrily. Newton was inclined to disagree.

Finally, after a blissful two hours or so, the moment came when we both agreed that we had explored as much of the abbey as possible, tried every door, every stair, every passage. True, there was one central area that had defeated us with doors locked fast against our exploration, but we would have to leave it at that. Besides ... look at the time! ... the abbey was closing its gates for the night in fifteen minutes. With an unspoken 'Meet you at the gates,' we separated and went our own ways in a race through the labyrinth.

My route took me through a corridor perforated on the left-hand wall with slit windows, which faced northwards over the wide Atlantic. Over yonder, I thought with a sigh, was England and the end of the journey. I could almost fool myself that I could see it, a cloudy blue smudge on the horizon. I sighed with rueful contentment. Tomorrow I would be catching a ferry over that last stretch of sea and the adventures would be over. After all the hold-ups and delays, the near-misses and the alarums, I would make it after all. It was almost a pity it had been, on the whole, so easy.

As I was thinking these thoughts, I passed a door I recognised as one we'd earlier found locked, one of the few that had resisted us. I gave it a playful rattle as I trotted by, and this time it opened.

I paused and peered in. Beyond was complete darkness except for a glimpse of a low sloping ceiling such as one finds under stairs. It was just a storeroom. I hesitated to go in – the cobwebs were unpleasantly thick – but suddenly somebody was coming – I could hear footsteps and the rattle of keys beyond a bend in the passage. The sense of trespass suddenly overwhelmed me and I didn't think I could face an irate abbot. I nipped into the dark space and pulled the door gently to.

I waited as the steps drew nearer ... and nearer ... and stopped, right outside the door. Obviously the game was up. Trying to think of some apologetic phrases in French, I prepared to open the door and face the music. But before I could emerge, the door jumped under my hand. There was the clank and jingle of iron and the scrape of a key being inserted in the great lock. Then, with a clunk, the key was turned and the footsteps retreated down the corridor.

I was locked in.

Standing frozen there in the pitch darkness in an unknown space, I must confess to thinking only of the irony in the situation. Having travelled all this way and through so many obstacles, and with England a mere half-day across the sea, I would fail in my task by dint of being locked in a medieval closet. Perhaps the next thing to pass through that doorway would be my skeletal remains, rat-nibbled and cobwebbed, in ten years' time. In the darkness, I groped for the handle and rattled it. It stood firm.

I felt gingerly about me for a wall and shuffled blindly towards it, feeling safer with my back to something solid. I took a deep steadying breath and leant back against the wall in the darkness – and then leapt in panic as a light suddenly blazed on. Once I had recovered my wits, I found that I had leant against the light switch. What is more, this was no closet after all but the bottom of a spiral stairway, which led up and out of sight into the gloom. Forgetting

Newton, forgetting the need to escape, forgetting the late hour, I sprinted up the staircase.

A few turns up, the dimness of the stairwell was pierced by a beam of light. On investigating, I discovered that this came from a tiny window, a peephole no bigger than a matchbox. Peering through it, I found myself looking, at floor level, into one of the main chapels of the abbey. From my mouse's eye view over the geometric black and white tiles, I could see a pair of black boots striding across the chapel to a far door, and heard once more the ominous jangle of keys.

I sprinted further up the winding stairs, six or seven turns, to another little window; this time, I had a starling's view of the chapel from above, perched right up under the fan-vaulting. From here I could clearly see the key-jangler, a black-bearded figure dwarfed by perspective, locking the last of the chapel doors. Up I went again to find door after door, but all locked against me – and still the stairs wound upwards.

I whirled up the last flight and came to a tiny wooden door, only waist-high. I pushed it open and was nearly blinded by the blazing windy sunshine. I stepped out and gazed about me in a dream of exhilaration. A second later I nearly jumped out of my skin when an explosion of pigeons went flapping and clapping off in spiralling flight, sparked by my intrusion into their high dominion. I had emerged onto the leads of the roof, high above the island. A hundred feet below me was the main courtyard and the front gates where people crawled like beetles. Even from this height, I could see an abbey official shepherding people out the gates and a familiar gangly figure gesticulating and pointing back the way he'd come, wildly explaining in pidgin English, no doubt, about his idiotic friend still inside. Above me was the main steeple, where a gilded St Michael slew a golden dragon, toppling in an endless dream against the racing clouds.

No time to linger. I had not yet found an unlocked door out of the stairwell and the abbey would be closing for the night within minutes. This was clearly a dead-end, here up in the heights, and with every other way locked, I really would be here for the next ten years, or at least until the following morning. There was no way out.

Far below me in the courtyard, one lone figure was still waving with windmill arms, trying to explain to the man shutting the gates that somewhere in the abbey, his stupid, stupid friend was

wandering. I wondered how long Newton's non-existent French would hold out. Could I shout from up here? Drop a hanky? I didn't have one.

The pigeons had returned and were lining the flimsy rail along the guttering, cooing reproachfully. I shot them a baleful glare and thought hard. Perhaps I could capture one, very carefully tie a message to its leg and then, wringing its neck, drop it straight down onto the gesticulating figure 200 feet below. Glancing along the guttering to choose my victim, I saw what I had not noticed before. The flimsy rail where the pigeons sat was in fact a handrail, serving a narrow catwalk above the gutter-line to another turret some thirty yards away. This was my only hope. Ignoring the plummeting drop below me and the flap of irate pigeons about my ears, I balanced my way along the narrow planks to the other turret. There, as I had guessed, was a similar door and behind it, I presumed, would be an identical spiral staircase. I prayed that the door would be unlocked.

It wouldn't budge.

I tried again. Shut fast.

In desperation I shoved at it a third time and to my intense relief, something gave and I tumbled forward into the darkness of the stairwell. Leaving the roof door open to illuminate the steps, I gingerly made my way downwards into the dimness. A few turns down and it was almost pitch black, but I kept a firm grip of the curling handrail and crept onwards. Halfway down I came to a door. Light seeped from underneath it, but it was locked. The faint jingle of keys and the retreating tread of heavy boots indicated that I had just missed it being open. Blackbeard was moving fast. Heedless of the darkness and the steepness of the stairway, I flung myself down and around the spiral, half flying, four steps at a time. I found the door at the bottom by the painful but effective method of crashing into it at full tilt. I scrabbled in the dark to find the handle, located it, turned ... and, blessed relief, the door swung sweetly open and I stumbled out into a stone passageway. Familiar footsteps were coming from one direction, so I fled the other way. A turn to the right, a flight of shallow steps, an archway, and I was back in the octagonal chamber. One of the seven other doors, I knew, led shortly to the main courtyard. I closed my eyes, spun, dived through the nearest door – and a minute later was panting out into the bright afternoon sunlight of the main gates. Newton was just coming to the end of a vivid pantomime, and I could tell that his resources were nearly used up. The abbey official, meanwhile, looked ready to call the local gendarmerie.

'Ah, you won, I see,' I called. 'Well done! Ready to go, are we?' And grabbing him by the arm I cut short the flood of reproaches and marched us out the gates and down into the town.

*

And so to the port city of St Malo in Brittany, with its massive sea-walls and its moules marinière and its ferry. No sitting on sun-bleached wharves, trying to attract yachties with a deft hornpipe on the tin-whistle. No suspicious negotiations with paranoid skippers who may or may not be sailing to Africa. No tedious trots from shipping office to shipping office in skyscraper cities. No waiting around on desert beaches, wondering about the aquatic capabilities of Komodo dragons. No, just a quick saunter to the ticket office, a check of the timetable and an absolute certainty that we'll be docking in Portsmouth Harbour in ... let's see ... five hours and twenty minutes.

*

This was it. The final hop. I was standing on deck and had just caught a glimpse of England, which appeared at that distance as a single flash of a lighthouse in the windy darkness. Three seconds after, a shower of Atlantic spray caught me across the face and I hurried back to the saloon of the St Malo–Portsmouth ferry, to rejoin Newton amid the wreckage of polystyrene tea mugs and half-eaten bags of chips. In two hours' time, we would be in Portsmouth, there to be met by my Uncle Geoff and Auntie Wendy. As an eight-year-old I had been rather awed by them, and had spent the next decade convinced I was related to minor British royalty: I remembered Uncle Geoff as a jolly naval chappie in lots of braid, always with a Union Jack nearby. Auntie Wendy was the only person I knew apart from the Queen who said 'tiss-yoo' rather than 'tish-yoo,' as in 'Would you like a tiss-yoo to catch the crumbs, dear?' Over the years, that initial awe had been replaced by great fondness for their warmth and charm, but I still thought it wise to warn Newton not to tell any jokes involving flatulence or to use the sugar tongs inappropriately.

And on this safe note, the year's voyage would be over.

An hour later, Newton was being looked after by the ferry's paramedics. Uncle Geoff and Auntie Wendy would be waiting at the dock, it was ten o'clock at night and the very first thing that I'd need to ask them to do was drive straight to the casualty ward of Portsmouth General Hospital and sit up half the night with my dying friend.

Let me explain.

We had decided to treat ourselves to a celebratory slap-up dinner, so took ourselves off to the ferry's dining room. Here we ordered, with great relish, a steak each, a bottle of red wine and two choco-late mousses. We chatted merrily about the last month's adventures and how jolly pleased we were, frankly, that it was all over. Newton pointed out the bits we'd missed or raced through and I happily described them from my last travels through Europe back in '82, which seemed to quieten him down a bit. Then I cheered him up by agreeing with his suggestion that over the next few weeks we should hire a car together and do a really thorough tour of England, taking it nice and slowly and going wherever he wanted before he flew home to Australia at the end of the month. We finished our steaks, quaffed the wine and tucked into the mousse while we waited for coffee to be served. It was about three minutes after this, as we were sitting back, well-fed and satisfied, that Newton began to look uncomfortable. His eyes glazed and his brow was sweating. A minute later he was doing impressions of a catfish having its head sawn off, and about thirty seconds later he was a fascinating shade of plum and lying on the floor.

'*All-er-gy!*' he gasped. '*Can't … think … what.*'

Neither could I. We'd avoided onions, mushrooms, cucumber, shellfish, feathers, Egyptian perfumes …

'Any other allergies that you know of, Newton? Try to think!'

'Well, there's histamines,' he croaked. 'Not much good at them, sometimes.'

'Right,' I said, a note of acerbity creeping unbidden into my voice. 'So you've never realised before that red wine is actually known for its high histamine content?'

'Is it? Never … knew that. But I don't … *wheeze* … usually have … *wheeze* … this sort … *hggghgh* … of reaction. Must be … *gargle* … something … *garrgh* … else.'

'Newton, there must be. Surely.'

His eyes bulged as he thought and wheezed some more.

'Well, there's eggs, of course … *gngngnhg*. Highly … allergic … *hhhhhrgh* … to eggs.' He gasped soundlessly for air as I sat back, struck dumb. 'But I haven't … *gasp* … had an egg … *gasp* … for … years.'

I took him gently by the hand and took a deep, steadying breath.

'Newton, are you aware of the principal ingredient of chocolate mousse?' I asked patiently.

'*Urrgh* … Chocolate? Chocolate mice? … Mooses?'

'Guess again. Rhymes with legs,' I said, and went off to find the ship's doctor.

*

That night I could not sleep. It was very, very late. I was sitting up in bed in the cosy bedroom of Uncle Geoff's house. English rain was falling softly outside in the dark. An English apple tree was tapping at the pane, buds tightly furled against the cold. Somewhere out there, no doubt, was a proper robin ready to wake me with the morning light. There was a clean hand towel on the dressing table and a new box of tiss-yoos by the bed. Newton had fallen asleep in the next room and had been well on the way to recovery before he went to bed, so that was all right. The reason I could not sleep was that something was bothering me. I got out my passport to glance through it, flipping back to look at the stamps from different countries. The latest one was Portsmouth, of course, stamped 2 February 1991.

The second of the second?

The date had been niggling at me, holding sleep at bay. It rang a bell, but I couldn't think why. Tap, tap, tap went the apple tree and the rain drummed softly on the pane. The second of the second.

And then it struck me. Groundhog Day, no less. I hopped out of bed and dug out my little diary and yes, it was true. On the second of the second, 1990, I had left Invercargill at the southernmost tip of New Zealand. It had taken me exactly a year to reach England, a year to the day, plodding earthbound all the way.

And they sailed away for a year and a day ...

Edward Lear, wasn't it? The Owl and the Pussycat in their pea-green boat. I'd beaten them by just one day. I switched off the lamp and closed my eyes.

Outside the rain fell softly in the darkness and the apple tree waited for spring. There was only one more voyage that night and that to the land of Nod.

Epilogue

> We could say that in walking along the road of life we keep it
> with us, know it; that is, the road already travelled curls up
> behind us, rolls up like a film. So that when he comes to the
> end, man discovers that he carries, stuck there on his back,
> the entire roll of life he led.
>
> —ORTEGA Y GASSET, *Historical Reason*

And here I am at last. Under the breezy Easter sunshine, Iona is lit
like a jewel across the greeny-blue strait and my heart is thudding
with pleasure. Soon the propellers are churning the water to white
as the ferry backs into the tiny harbour pier and my fellow passengers gather to disembark. There are more of them this time than on
that stormy December night some ten years ago – Easter pilgrims
come to visit the abbey – and the sea is so tranquil that there is little
chance of anyone getting soaked to the skin by a rogue wave. I am a
seasoned and organised traveller now, a teacher at a respectable
English public school no less, and as such have booked a room at the
Argyll Hotel in advance. My tatty rucksack has made way for a
smart little suitcase on wheels.

I look around with a shiver of pure pleasure. It is too late in the
day now for what I have come to do. That will have to wait for
tomorrow. I follow the last of the visitors off the boat and stand in
the warm sunshine, my feet at last on Iona soil again. There is that
same peace, that same mildness of air, and the thrumming of my
heart-strings is stilled once more by the unseen hand.

I think back over the few months since I arrived at Portsmouth
Docks, Newton turning cyanic and gasping like a puffer-fish under a
hair-dryer. He had recovered, of course, once the allergic reaction to
the mousse had worn off, recovered enough in fact to come down to
breakfast the next morning and knock a cut-glass bowl of Auntie
Wendy's grapefruit marmalade all over Uncle Geoffrey's *Times* crossword by way of a proper introduction. Auntie Wendy, looking more

like the Queen than ever – and much as the Queen would look had a visiting dignitary stepped on one of the royal corgis – waved Newton's apologies away with a stiff tinkling laugh and went to fetch him a towel. When a minute later the cream-jug went over as well, it was suggested that Newton keep the towel with him as a convenience.

We didn't stay long. Newton reminded me of my promise that we would hire a car and tour the British Isles before he had to return to Australia. Stonehenge, Snowdonia, the Lake District, the Yorkshire Dales, Edinburgh Castle – the lot!

'Splendid idea!' I agreed, and then ruthlessly navigated our way around the Home Counties from major public school to major public school so that I could drop in on various headmasters' secretaries and ask if there happened to be a teaching job going. My first few attempts were in London and were met with frosty stares at my travel-stained boots and tatty shirt. I had presented my dog-eared reference from Mr Murray of Westminster, which still bore a badly forged Laotian stamp and smelt faintly of potato. Newton would stand like a dishevelled elk in the background, stabbing morosely at the photocopier, and I would be told over the top of half-moon spectacles that the headmaster was unavailable for casual appointments and likely to remain so indefinitely.

Getting the point, I purchased a rather natty sports coat, a tie and a pair of shiny new brogues, and decided to try further afield. Down in the West Country, there is the renowned Sherborne School, set in the honey-stoned market town of the same name and nestled up to the great eleventh-century abbey. We arrived during a heavy snowfall, and I suggested Newton wait in the car and try to get the defective heater to work while I enquired about a job. I wouldn't be long, I assured him, and trotted off to reception. Before I could ask the usual question, the headmaster's secretary looked up and asked, 'Ah, have you come about the English vacancy?'

'Is there an English vacancy?' I asked in some surprise.

'Yes. Mr Blenkinsopp fell terribly ill yesterday and we need a new chap.'

I didn't pause for a second. 'Yes, poor chap, so I heard. And that is why I have come about the English vacancy, yes.'

A deputy head appeared and suggested I come and have lunch in the dining hall with the whole school, after which he'd ask me to teach a class of fifth formers to see if I came up to scratch. 'By way of an interview, you understand,' he explained gruffly.

'Yes, look, I've got a friend out in the car in the snow. Could he come in and have a bite to eat as well?'

'Certainly, certainly,' barked the deputy head. 'See you in there.'

I slithered my way out into the snowy quadrangle and watched as the boys came pouring out on their way to lunch. Every one of them was dressed immaculately in a navy-blue overcoat with a gilded crest, and many had bright red scarves about their necks and woollen mittens. They were clean and scrubbed and rosy cheeked and could have posed for a Christmas card. In stark contrast, I found Newton shivering in the car, looking a little more manic than usual. His hands were covered in grease and he was clutching some wires from under the dashboard. I think he had just electrocuted himself.

He wound down the window. 'What?' he asked shortly. The single syllable had the quiet force of a weasel snapping a rabbit's spine.

'Nothing,' I replied. 'I'll be another few minutes. All right?'

In the dining hall, I tried not to enjoy my lashings of bubble and squeak and custard sponge too much and comforted myself with the thought that Newton would be happy to have some time to himself. Besides, the chance of him being allergic to something on the menu was pretty high, and I didn't think another anaphylactic reaction would help my chances of landing this job.

After lunch, the deputy head led me back across the snowy quadrangle. A guilty glance at the car confirmed that Newton was not yet dead of hypothermia or electrocution; how could he have made such hand signals if he were? I was escorted into a room of fifth-form boys. The lesson was to be on poetry, and the poem under discussion was one from the First World War by Isaac Rosenberg, a new one to me. In it, a young soldier caught in a bombardment in the trenches finds his mind blotting out the horrors of death around him by focusing on a single red poppy against the white chalk of the trench wall. He is utterly absorbed by it, and I couldn't help but be reminded of something.

I glanced around at the bored faces and the disengaged eyes and decided to go with my instinct.

'Now listen up. Let me tell you a story of something that happened to me earlier this year in the Australian desert. It involves a bus crash and a chicken sandwich' – twenty-five heads looked up in interest – 'and it goes like this ...'

After the lesson, the deputy head took me aside and said, 'I'm a chemistry chap myself. Don't understand poetry one little bit, but they seemed to enjoy that and that's the main thing. Jolly good yarn about the chicken sandwich, I must say. How you English chappies manage to make this sort of stuff up on the spot, I'll never know. Well done!' When I returned to Newton in the car some three hours after I had first left him, I was able to announce with a certain pride that I had just landed a job.

I like to think that his utter lack of response was inspired by sheer awe at my good fortune.

'So now we can get on and enjoy this driving holiday we're meant to be on?' he finally said as we pulled out onto the motorway and headed north.

'Oh yes,' I enthused. 'Absolutely! Except—'

'*What?*' Another spine snapped, this time of some larger animal – a tapir, perhaps.

'Except that I have to be back here tomorrow night. I start the following day.'

There was a long, long silence as we hurtled northwards through the gathering dark.

'Well,' said Newton at last, 'I hope you've kept up your hitch-hiking skills.'

And on we drove in silence for another three hours, to Manchester and beyond.

*

In the excitement of the new job, Iona faded from my mind. My quest to revisit the Well of Eternal Youth was forgotten as I plunged into the enchanting world of English public-school life. For a whirling couple of months, I played at being a young Mr Chips. I stood on sidelines under a frosty primrose sky and cheered the house hockey matches on. I sat in studies with old house-masters, venerable as badgers, drinking whisky and reminiscing about the good old days, when you could thrash the buggers for not handing in prep. I regularly hid from my colleagues the letters that arrived from Newton, now back in Australia, because each one of them was addressed, in embarrassingly large handwriting, to 'Mr A.J. Mackinnon, Snooty Hall.'

And as February turned to March and March to April, the snow melted away and the crocuses sprang, waxy as candles in purple and flame-yellow, from the fine grass of the college lawns. Spindly trees espaliered against garden walls, Lenten and bare, exploded into masses of white and pink blossoms and revealed themselves to be pear trees, apple trees, cherry trees, the loveliest of all Nature's works.

Like the blossom trees, the ill Mr Blenkinsopp revived and announced his intention to return to the job. I had lined up a place at another school for the summer term, but first there were the Easter holidays and two weeks of freedom! How would I spend it? When the last day of term rolled around, I was still unsure. The final poem in the syllabus set by Mr Blenkinsopp was one I had not encountered before. Cavafy. Never heard of him. I read it out to the class while the boys fidgeted in their chairs.

> As you set out for Ithaca
> hope your road is a long one,
> full of adventure, full of discovery.

My heart beat harder at the words.

> Hope your road is a long one.
> May there be many summer mornings when,
> with what pleasure, what joy,
> you enter harbours you're seeing for the first time;

The wharf at Opua, the bay of the nautilus shells and the sea-cave. Singapore. Venice. St Malo.

> May you stop at Phoenician trading stations
> to buy fine things,
> mother-of-pearl and coral, amber and ebony,
> sensual perfume of every kind –
> as many sensual perfumes as you can;

The 500-year-old timbers of the classroom dissolved away as I read on, students forgotten, syllabus forgotten, all forgotten.

> Keep Ithaca always in your mind.
> Arriving there is what you're destined for.
> But don't hurry the journey at all.

Better if it lasts for years,
so you're old by the time you reach the island,
wealthy with all you've gained on the way …

The names of new stars. A hundred tunes. A dancing Fool.
Dragons. Laos and a wife, possibly …

Ithaca gave you the marvellous journey.
Without her you wouldn't have set out.
She has nothing left to give you now.

But she did. She did have one more thing to give me because I
hadn't reached there yet. Only her name was not Ithaca.

By the time I had finished reading, the classroom was empty.
Evidently my capacity to hold a class spellbound had not improved.
The bell must have gone and it was too late anyway; the term was
over. No matter. I had a train ticket to buy and one more journey to
make.

*

As the train clattered its way on the last leg from Glasgow to Oban,
through the loch-filled glens and soaring peaks of the Highlands, I
was studying the rail map when a name caught my eye: Loch Awe.
We were due to pass through this tiny village sometime in the next
half hour. The name rang a bell but I couldn't place it until … ah
yes! That was it! I had last seen that name on nothing less than the
letter sent to me by Lady Mary Stewart all those years ago – The
House of Letterawe, Loch Awe, Argyllshire. As the train rattled
onward, I conceived a bold and impudent plan. If this was indeed
the same Loch Awe, then I was quite sure, I told myself firmly, that
nothing could delight Lady Stewart more than an unscheduled visit
from a fan. In fact, she'd probably write me into her next book.

When the train pulled into the tiny hamlet of Loch Awe, I
jumped out into the cool, pine-smelling air. After booking into a
B&B, I wandered into the village to find the post office just about
to close. Behind the counter was a woman with red hair, who told
me with some wariness that yes, Lady Stewart did live here, and I
should perhaps ring to see if she would welcome visitors. I did so
from the post office. Now that I came to do it, I blushed and stammered my way through a brief conversation with Lady Stewart

herself, the upshot of which was that I was welcome to come and share morning tea with her on the morrow. The red-haired lady eyed me sceptically. 'You're a lucky one then,' she said. 'It's not many people are so fortunate ... or so bold.' Then she shooed me out and closed up the shop behind her.

Dinner that night was, perforce, eaten in the only café in the village, and to my surprise I was served by the very same red-haired lady, who took my order for sausages and mash and then left me to eat it in solitude while she went off on some errand across the street. A little while later, she returned and took my money and cleared the plates. I commented idly on how few people there were around. 'Aye,' she said, 'it's a quiet night for sure. But then again,' she added candidly, 'it usually is.'

To my enquiry about whether there was a pub in the village, she answered somewhat curtly, 'Och, yes, doon the street, don't hurry me!' which left me wondering whether she had mistaken my enquiry for an invitation to buy her a drink. Not that I minded, of course, but still, it was odd. I thought briefly of Pixie and her attempts to flirt with me all those years ago.

The pub, too, was completely empty and I sat for a while waiting for anyone to appear behind the bar. A few tentative yoo-hoos elicited no response, so I sat and chatted to the large, mothy moose's head hanging on the wall who also looked like he'd been kept waiting for a drink for a decade or so. After a little while, the front door opened behind me and I turned to see who it was. I had guessed correctly. It was, of course, the red-haired lady, slightly breathless from her trot from the café, and here to take me up on my implied invitation to share a drink or two.

'Oh, hello,' I said, smiling gamely. 'Here you are then. Lovely. What can I get you to drink?'

It was her turn to look surprised. She said, eyeing me warily, 'No, what can I get YOU to drink?'

'Well, um, that's very kind,' I replied. 'Tell you what, I'll order the drinks and you can pay. So what'll it be?' I pulled up two stools to the bar. 'Mind you,' I said in a lowered voice, 'I don't mind telling you that the service around here isn't exactly snappy!' I turned back to the bar, flicked my eyebrows skywards in a playful imitation of an exasperated John Cleese and called out, 'Hello! Yoo-hoo! Anyone out there?'

The red-haired lady sighed between pursed lips. 'No, ye don't understand. I need to know what YOU want for a drink, and no, I'll not be paying for it if it's all the same to you.'

Only then did I notice with horror that she was putting on an apron, opening the hatch between the saloon and the bar and letting herself in. This was job number three.

'Besides, you're too young for me,' she said with a perfectly straight face and pulled me a pint of bitter.

When I had stopped blushing, I drained my pint and, uncharacteristically, didn't stop for another. I made my way back to the B&B in the moonlight, smacking my forehead hard with the flat of my hand all the way. There I resisted the temptation to check under my bed and behind the bathroom door in case the red-haired lady had dashed ahead of me and was moonlighting as a chambermaid, and went to sleep.

Next morning, I set off for the House of Letterawe. At the grand front door, I hesitated. Lady Stewart had sounded cool the night before on the phone and why not, after all? She could have no interest in a complete stranger. My only hope was to talk about her writing, which had at least a hope of keeping her amused.

I rang the doorbell. After a minute or so, a tall, gracious lady opened the door and smiled warmly. 'You must be Sandy, then. I'm Lady Stewart.'

I blurted out an apology for intruding, but she waved it graciously aside. 'Now you're here, you'd better come in. I must say, I've heard some very interesting reports about you.'

I followed her into her sitting room, puzzled. Reports? Had she, like her character Merlin, ways of knowing things closed to other mortals? Then she called out, 'Eileen? Eileen, bring in the tea, would you? Thank you,' and in through the door with a silver tray of pikelets and tea came the red-haired lady, who gave me a mock-coquettish bow. I was glad I had stuck to just the one pint the night before: I could only hope her reports had included a note on my sobriety.

After the ubiquitous Eileen had retired, presumably to race back to the post office, pull some pints, and perhaps switch the points for the 10.25 Glasgow express, Lady Stewart and I sat in a little pool of silence, punctuated by the nervous rattling of the Crown Derby teacup in my hand. She was the first to break it by saying, 'Well, Sandy, let's chat then. But I do hope you're not going to ask me about my books.'

'Oh?' I stammered. 'Well, I was, actually. I mean, I wasn't sure what else ...'

I tailed away into silence, and Lady Stewart explained. 'What you must realise is that some of these books I wrote over fifty years ago, and I've not re-read them in all that time. I simply can't remember them. I know that seems strange, but there you are.'

These were books I had read again and again. It seemed inconceivable that their creator could have forgotten them so lightly. But when I turned the topic tentatively to her Merlin trilogy, there was indeed something to talk about. These were her pride and joy and the conversation moved effortlessly into full flow, as easily as a dinghy sliding down a ramp into the water. An hour flew by and the pikelets disappeared one by one and when the last one was gone, I realised it was time to let Lady Stewart get back to her solitude.

'And where are you off to now?' she asked as we moved out into the garden.

'Iona,' I said. 'I'm revisiting it after ten years.'

'Ah, Iona,' she said, and a warmth came into her grey eyes. 'For all my writing of Merlin and his powers, I'm quite sure that there's no such thing as magic. It's wonderful stuff for stories, of course, but best left there, don't you think?' We were making our way down the little path between trickling rivulets and ferns. 'But whenever I visit Iona, I must say I have second thoughts. Be careful, won't you?'

And on that note, we said goodbye. Be careful, she had said. I was quite sure she was only referring to the uneven section of path by the front gate, slippery with moss after the night's rain – a hostess anxious for her guest's safety. But the words stayed in my head and rattled in the tracks – be careful, be careful – as the train took me through the great glens on the last leg of my long odyssey to Iona.

*

In the pearly pre-dawn light of the following morning, I woke to the hush of waves on the shingle beyond my window and crept downstairs. Nobody was about at this hour. After a few minutes, I was beyond the last houses of the village and standing on the low grassy saddle that runs from Dun I in the north to the wilder moorland of the south.

And here, at last, I was at my journey's true end. Not the clamorous ferry terminal of Portsmouth, nor the civilised breakfast table of welcoming relatives, nor yet the feeling of secure belonging as the organ swelled for chapel service in Sherborne Abbey. No, here was the World's End, the Bay at the Back of the Ocean, as I had remembered it all these years. White shell-sand; fine, springy turf as golden and dry as lion's fur; tiny furled irises like spears of deep blue; glass-green water deepening to peacock further out; the friendly huff and hoosh of the Spouting Cave along to the southern end of the bay; and the piping double note of an oystercatcher paddling at the sea's edge.

The sky lightened, pearl-grey turning to faintest duck-egg green. It was going to be a glorious day.

I fell into a reverie. I had voyaged from the young lands of New Zealand at the eastern edge of the wide world, so young that the earths are still bubbling up with primeval fire, to the very western edge of the world, where the knuckles of pink Iona granite are said to be the oldest stone in the world. I thought back over all that I had seen. Tree-ferns and tall sails, whales and waterfalls, the roar of cities and jungle shadows filled with the wings of butterflies. The Warlde's Room, and I had inherited it to the full. And I had done it properly: a true pilgrimage, by ship and foot, by keel and thumb, wheel, rail and hoof.

A solitary gull glided overhead and out to sea, off to fishing grounds far out to the west. From this point on, I mused, I really could go no further without leaving the ground, without taking wing like the gull and flying to the uttermost parts of the sea. I *could* fly, of course – Glasgow was the nearest airport. But those wings would be no white gull's wings, crisp and light as a well-laundered cravat, but swathed in fumes and throbbing with unendurable noise, and set about with all the trappings of air travel – tarmac, departure lounges, baggage carousels, tannoys, duty-free shops and delays.

That was no way to go. Besides, once you started flying you could go on forever. There was no reason ever to stop, to say 'Enough.' And it was good to have an end to things.

The sky grew brighter still.

There was one more task to do and time was slipping away. Just a mile from this spot was the object of my journey. I turned my back on the World's End and started the steep trudge up the flanks of Dun I to find the Well of Eternal Youth. This time I would do it properly. There would be no bathing this time, just a straight-forward drink and eternal youth would be mine. There would be no Pixie Peterson to distract me from my purpose.

As I negotiated the maze of hillocks and bogs that lay between me and Dun I, I wondered what had happened to Pixie. Had she gone back to Randy? She still owed me thirty-five pounds, I remembered, and the Argyll Hotel a night's tariff. She had been so passionate about the island, I reflected. For all her cockamamie beliefs, she really had seemed set on tasting of its magic.

I jumped over a wide patch of bog, missed my footing, nearly lost a shoe in the black peat and scrambled onto drier ground. The going was harder than I remembered – but then I had never been this way. Before, I had approached Dun I from the eastern side of the island, from the abbey. This was altogether wilder terrain. Blood chugged in my ears like the wild, maddening tune of a fairy pipe. Sometimes the way before me was barred by trenches cut into the peat; these were full of black bog-water, too wide to jump across and too sheer-sided to clamber out of should I tumble into one. I would drown like a fly in molasses and, like my venerable ancestor the Abbot John Mackinnon, lie preserved for centuries to come.

Be careful, a cool voice warned. *Be careful*. Shaking these grisly thoughts away, I clambered on up the steep flank of Dun I and resumed my train of thought. Yes, if only Pixie had put aside her New Age ideas about druids and read the guidebooks, there was plenty of magic to be had here. The Well of Eternal Youth, for one thing.

In my remembered indignation, I stamped heavily. A piece of turf gave way beneath me and I toppled sideways, then found myself lying on the damp ground, peering into darkness. I was staring into one of the peat-trenches that flanked the hill. There was a rock ledge overhead, casting the trench into deep shadow and spattering a cascade of cold drops onto my head. There must be a spring just above.

As I lay there, winded, I peered down into the trench. It was sheer-sided and dark and full of water, a trap for anyone unwary enough to tumble down this part of the hill. But no-one would be foolish enough to come down this side; it was madness enough for me to be coming up it. All the paths were away on the further side of Dun I.

My eyes grew accustomed to the darkness and I gazed down into the peat-black water. There was something white down there, a large stone or something like it, and a pale clump of bleached root like a white starfish. Along the bottom of the trench grew some thick, luxuriant sort of weed, deep brown, as fine as sable.

Fur. Like fur. And this thought sent my mind wheeling back to Pixie once more.

If only she had read about the Well, I thought. There'd be no stopping her. How had it gone?

Any pilgrim who travels to this holy place, over land and over sea, who wishes for the fairies to grant their gift of eternal youth and beauty, must climb the height of Dun I as the sun is rising in the East and then, when the first rays of the sun quicken the waters of the Well, must drink deeply of the draught therein. Thus may Eternal Youth be won.

And my heart jolted. All the fragments of my thinking whirled, lifted and settled into a new pattern, a pattern that told an all-too-plausible story.

Of course Pixie had read about the Well. She had taken the book back to her room to read later that night after I had fled. Judith had found it there the morning I left, face down by Pixie's bed, ready to fall open at that very page when I read it later on the ferry. And there in the midnight hotel, she had been entranced as I was. No more druids. No more ley-lines. Here was real magic at last and it came with instructions.

And we had wronged her, Judith and I, all those years ago. She hadn't done a flit, sneaking down to the six o'clock ferry in the dreary half-light to escape a bill she couldn't pay. She had got up before dawn, taken her shoulder-bag and set off determinedly for Dun I and the Well. Then as the sun rose and touched the purple-headed mountains of Mull, gilded the basalt organ-pipes of distant Staffa, lay a glittering gold ribbon across the green strait and finally quickened the bright mirror of the pool, she had stooped and drunk deeply of the enchanted waters.

And then? Ah, be careful! Be careful! For this is fairy magic we are dealing with, the tricksy fairies who know how to keep a promise and break it at the same time. Macbeth learnt it, to his cost, and somewhere down there in his unmarked grave is cursing the day he ever listened to the magical promises of the folk he met on the moor. Perhaps Pixie felt the magic taking effect immediately she had drunk. Perhaps she had felt the first promise of eternal youthfulness coursing through her veins, ten, twenty, a hundred times more powerful than I had felt it dancing sky-clad in the gale all those years ago. Perhaps she didn't stop to consider the technical distinction between eternal youth and eternal life ...

And then, too dazzled by the eastern sun to turn back down towards the abbey, she had come this way instead, her shadow huge before her. A slip, a slither in those silly heels, a bump on the head and a tumble down the hillside into this deep, water-flooded trough at my chin – and eternal youth was hers. For here she would lie, her beauty preserved forevermore in the clear peat tea of her final resting place.

I hauled myself to my feet and brushed myself down. Tiny damp petals clung to my skin like flakes of gold. The sweat was cooling on me and my heart was slowing. I took one last long look into the trough – the pale oval face, the star-like hand, the soft sable – and set my sights upward. A minute later, I had clambered the last few yards to the summit of Dun I and emerged just below where the Well spilt its waters in a spattering cascade down the cliff-face.

Had I had a lucky escape, those ten long years ago? I had blundered as usual, bathed and not drunk, but that perhaps had been for the best. And in fact, this seemed to have been the pattern of my travels over the last year. I had arrived in New Zealand four months too early for a yacht ride out, but had met the Batemans and the saintly Les McLeod. I had sailed for New Caledonia without a visa but had stumbled right out again on the cheerful *Morwennol*. A bus crash and a chicken sandwich had won me a job at Sherborne. A free-spirited saunter into Vientiane had kept me from the eyes of the Laotian police. Another stroll along a jungle road had brought me wedded bliss, albeit a short-lived sample.

The list unreeled in my head, example after example of good fortune. It was tempting to call myself lucky, to imagine that the gods smiled favourably upon me at every turn, but I knew the real reason. It is trite but true. The fact is that the world is packed to the seams with good people, with extraordinary people, with people who don't care if you have made a hundred blunders along the way, but who are just happy that you are here. These sweet-souled people are not to be met in large numbers in airports, admittedly, but that is perhaps why the voyage had been such a fortunate one.

And as for my original plan? Did I dare now drink from the Well of Eternal Youth? That is what I had set out to do, after all. And of course it was safe enough. The white oval had been a stone after all, the clenched hand a bleached root, and the fur-like weed … just weed. There was no malicious fairy magic at work here, and Pixie was no doubt safe somewhere in California, still on her quest for druids.

So to drink or not to drink? Here was the chance at last to do it right. I knelt and stooped over the still pool and gazed at the reflection that gazed back at me. I blinked a little with surprise. The face in the pool was lightly tanned by a year outdoors and the cheeks were rosy with the morning air. The hair, thickly curling, had returned to a light sandy gold. The green-grey eyes were dancing. A slow smile spread across the reflection's lips. Then the face shattered and rippled into rings of light as I dipped my hands and washed my face. I was careful not to let a drop of water pass my lips. After all, you never knew who'd been bathing in it.

Besides, it was too late. The sun was fully up and it was time to go down and find out if the Argyll Hotel still did the Full Scots Breakfast.

Lightning Source UK Ltd.
Milton Keynes UK
UKOW06f1000081013

218679UK00009B/206/P